# Afrofuturism 2.0

# Afrofuturism 2.0

## *The Rise of Astro-Blackness*

### Edited by Reynaldo Anderson and Charles E. Jones

LEXINGTON BOOKS
Lanham • Boulder • New York • London

Published by Lexington Books
An imprint of The Rowman & Littlefield Publishing Group, Inc.
4501 Forbes Boulevard, Suite 200, Lanham, Maryland 20706
www.rowman.com

Unit A, Whitacre Mews, 26-34 Stannary Street, London SE11 4AB

British Library Cataloguing in Publication Information Available

Library of Congress Cataloging-in-Publication Data Available

ISBN 9781498510509 (cloth: alk. paper)
ISBN 9781498510516 (ebook)

∞™ The paper used in this publication meets the minimum requirements of American
National Standard for Information Sciences Permanence of Paper for Printed Library
Materials, ANSI/NISO Z39.48-1992.

Printed in the United States of America

# Contents

# Introduction

## *The Rise of Astro-Blackness*

## Reynaldo Anderson and Charles E. Jones

Since the last decade of the twentieth century and the beginning of the twenty-first century, following 9/11 and the crash of the 90s digital boom, the World Wide Web has transitioned significantly. From a 1.0 static read only search for content web-based driven usage, in the middle of its first decade it began to evolve into a social media driven environment characterized by entities such as Facebook, YouTube, Twitter, Google, and Wikipedia (Berners-Lee, Hendler, and Lassila 2001). Correspondingly, the 1.0 era of the web was delineated as a race and gender neutral zone with the utopian potential to transform society. Alondra Nelson noted: "race and gender distinctions would be eliminated with technology was perhaps the founding fiction of the digital age." However, scholars like Alondra Nelson (2002), Alex Weheliye (2002), Kali Tal (1996), Anna Everett (2002), Ron Eglash (2002), and others pointed out the inequities inherent in what was then referred to as the digital divide, with regard to the conventional narrative that race was a liability in the new century.

The purpose of this book is to identify the applicability of contemporary expressions of Afrofuturism to the field of Africana Studies, to connect these phenomena to other fields of academic inquiry, and to expand it to include what we refer to as Astro-Blackness. Astro-Blackness is an Afrofuturistic concept in which a person's black state of consciousness, released from the confining and crippling slave or colonial mentality, becomes aware of the multitude and varied possibilities and probabilities within the universe (Rollins 2015, 1). More precisely, Astro-Blackness represents the emergence of a black identity framework within emerging global technocultural assemblages, migration, human reproduction, algorithms, digital networks, software platforms, bio-technical augmentation and are constitutive of racialized identities that are increasingly materialized vis-à-vis contemporary technological advances or "technogenesis, the idea that humans and technics have co-evolved together" (Hayles 2012). Furthermore, this notion of Astro-Blackness suggests a shift from the modern era or nation-state bound analog notion of blackness transitioning through a digitized era toward and in tension with post-digital perspectives as a global response to the planetary and near planetary challenges facing black life in the early twenty-first century. What is presently called Afrofuturism was originally a techno-cultural perspective accompanying engagement in a form of cultural production, originating in practices of black urban dwellers in North America after World War II and popular examples emerged in the works of Jazz musician Sun Ra and artists of the Black Arts Movement like Ishmael Reed or Amiri Baraka (Anderson and Jennings 2014).

Although the practices that form the black artistic matrix and practice of what we call Afrofuturism can be traced back over 100 years; its current trajectory can be connected to literary engagement between writers Greg Tate and Mark Sinker in 1992 surrounding the relationship between science fiction and Black music. The recently popularized term "Afrofuturism" was coined in the early 1990s by writers like Mark Dery in an interview, with Samuel Delaney, Greg Tate and Tricia Rose and defines it as "Speculative fiction that treats African-American themes and addresses African-American concerns in the context of twentieth-century techno-culture—and, more generally, African-American signification that appropriates images of technology and a prosthetically enhanced future—might, for want of a better term, be called Afrofuturism" (Dery 1994, 180). In eighties and nineties England, the Black Audio Film Collective with members like John Akomfrah, and in Germany, organizations like AFROTAK also represented early impulses of late twentieth century Afrofuturism. However, their early articulation of the phenomenon was limited largely to music, art, the digital divide, the public sphere and speculative literature. Kali Tal articulated the notion of a race-less cyberspace vis-a-vis an Afrodiasporic culture analyis of W. E. B. Du Bois's notion of "Double Consciousness" as a sophisticated cyber culture critique on the tension between identity, multiplicity and postmodernity (1996). Alondra Nelson noted: "Afrofuturism can be broadly defined as 'African American voices with other stories to tell about culture, technology and things to come.'" (Nelson 2002, 9). More recently, Kodwo Eshun asserts: "Afrofuturism may be characterized as a program for recovering the histories of counter-futures created in a century hostile to Afrodiasporic projection and as a space within which the critical work of manufacturing tools capable of intervention within the current political dispensation may be undertaken" (2007).

An important distinction between concepts such as futurism and Afrofuturism is that the former began as an avant-garde movement among European intellectuals and artists, and during and after WWII in the ideas and work of Isaac Asimov, Claude Shannon, Philip K. Dick, Bertrand de Jouvenel, The Rand Corporation and others; leading to a current situation where "The powerful employ futurists and draw power from the futures they endorse" (Eshun 2007, 289), whereas the latter, Afrofuturism, has its contemporary beginnings in the North American Black Arts movement of the 1960s and 1970s among various literary figures, modern jazz musicians, R&B and pioneering hip hop performers. Recently, cultural critics like Martine Syms (2014) have asserted in "The Mundane Afrofuturist Manifesto" that Afrofuturism focuses too much on unexamined tropes, references to Egyptology, figures in popular culture, and needs to develop a new focus on black humanity and a critique on "true, vernacular reality." This is not a new argument as scholars like Ron Eglash (2002) previously made the case that Afrofuturists were ignoring the scientific sphere. Furthermore, critics like Tegan Bristow have asserted that "Afrofuturism has nothing to do with Africa, and everything to do with cyber-culture in the West". This assertion is misplaced due to the fact that 1) Africa and its diaspora are connected via cyber-culture and have exchanged ideas, art, politics and more recently remittances since the nineteenth century; and 2) the African diaspora has been institutionally designated the sixth zone of the African Union and similar to early developments of Pan Africanism starting in the African Diaspora, Afrofuturism is now a Pan African project. Moreover, this concern may reflect more of a Post-Cold War/ Post-Apartheid existential crisis of some White South Africans and some of their former "clients" living in the midst of a predominantly Black African society than the "Africanity" of an emerging global Afrofuturism. Therefore, contemporary twenty-first century Afrofuturism, or what is now called Afrofuturism 2.0, a term initially discussed at the Alien Bodies conference at Emory University in 2013, is moving in the direction of a more applied, theoretical, critical, and transdisciplinary approach in regards to the future of African peoples.

## AFROFUTURISM 2.0

A goal of this volume is to build upon the previous definition and identify the twenty-first century contemporary expressions of Afrofuturism emerging in the areas of metaphysics, speculative philosophy, religion, visual studies, performance, art, and philosophy of science or technology that are described as "2.0," in response to the emergence of social media and other technological advances since the middle of the last decade. Whereas Afrofuturism was primarily concerned with twentieth century techno-culture, the digital divide, technology, music and literature in the West; Afrofuturism 2.0 is the early twenty-first century technogenesis of Black identity reflecting counter histories, hacking and or appropriating the influence of network software, database logic, cultural analytics, deep remixabililty, neurosciences, enhancement and augmentation, gender fluidity, posthuman possibility, the speculative sphere, with transdisciplinary applications and has grown into an important Diasporic techno-cultural "Pan-African" movement (Samatar 2015). Moreover, within this Pan-African Afrofuturist movement there will be regional differences such as, and not limited to, Caribbean Futurism, African Futurism and Black futurism. Contemporary Afrofuturism 2.0 is now characterized by five dimensions, to include: metaphysics; aesthetics; theoretical and applied science; social sciences; and programmatic spaces. The first Afrofuturist dimension of metaphysics includes and engages ontology or the meaning of existence, relations between the ontological and epistemological or the truth-functional aspects of knowledge, cosmogony or origin of the universe, cosmology or structure of the universe, an example of this are naturalistic Afro-Diaspora traditions, Rational Panpsychism (or Animism) and indigenous African spiritual practices such as Okuyi or Dogon cosmology in West Africa and or Ifa in Nigeria to name a few; and the works of W. E. B. Du Bois, John Mbiti, Kamau Brathwaite, Kwasi Wiredu, Yvonne P. Chireau, Dwight Hopkins, and Albert Raboteau represent some of the scholars within this dimension. The second Afrofuturist dimension of aesthetics includes anthropomorphic art, music, literature, and performance; examples in this sphere include the performers or artists like Sylvia Wynter, Sanford Biggers, Sun Ra, Henry Dumas, John Akomfrah, Afrika Bambatta, Juan Atkins, Derrick May, Kevin Saunderson, Jimi Hendrix, Janelle Monae and others. The third dimension of Afrofuturism is in the areas of theoretical and applied science; for example, archaeology, math, physics, chemistry, biology, astronomy; and applied areas such as computer science, architecture, engineering, medicine, and agriculture"; the creations of architect Kiluanji Kia Henda, the work of ethno-astronomer Jarita Holbrook or physicist James Gates and his work with West African Adinkra Symbols, and Ron Eglash and his work in ethno-mathematics and African fractals is instructive in this area. A fourth dimension of Afrofuturism is in the social science disciplines to include: sociology, anthropology, psychology, political science, history, and are represented by scholars such as Kwame Nkrumah, Molefe Asante, James Stewart, Dorothy Roberts, C.T. Keto, Marimba Ani, Anna Everett, Alex Weheliye, Kali Tal and others. A fifth and final dimension of Afrofuturism is in the programmatic arena such as exhibitions, community organizations, online forums, and specialized salons or labs; the community work of Philadelphia Afrofuturist Affair founder Rasheedah Phillips along with the recently organized Afrofutures_UK (2015) salon organized at Mad Labs in Manchester, England, the Afrofuture festival (2015) organized by WORM in

Rotterdam, Netherlands, and the Afrofuturist series (2015) organized by The Goethe Institute in Accra, Ghana, Johannesburg, South Africa and Nairobi, Kenya are especially noteworthy in this area.

## SCHOLARSHIP

There have been several books or journals dedicated to the topic of Afrofuturism; however, most of the contributions have been outside of the Africana Studies discipline. First, one of the most prominent books on the topic was written by Kodwo Eshun in 1998, and the most prominent among journals on Afrofuturism (self-titled *Afrofuturism*) was published by *Social Text* and edited by Alondra Nelson in 2002. Eshun's book, *More Brilliant Than the Sun: Adventures In Sonic Fiction*, developed in the late 90s, was the first book-length treatment on the topic of Afrofuturism. However, its focus on music and visual culture excluded other technocultural philosophical dimensions of Afrofuturism.

Alondra Nelson's special issue on Afrofuturism that was published in the journal *Social Text* began to expand on previous work done by Eshun and others. However, its primary focus was in the technocultural aspects of Afrofuturism, in light of issues and concepts such as the digital divide, late twentieth century online black activism, and speculative fiction, sound, music, or visual art. However, when Alex Weheliye authored the book, *Phonographies: Grooves in Sonic Afro-Modernity* (2005), it was awarded The Modern Language Association's William Sanders Scarborough Prize for Outstanding Scholarly Study of Black American Literature or Culture. This work became among the first published book length treatments of work done on Afrofuturist-related work in an Africana Studies department. Finally, Marlene Barr's *Afrofuture Females: Black Writers Chart Science Fiction's Newest New-Wave Trajectory* (2008), Sandra Jackson and Julie Moody- Freeman's *The Black Imagination: Science Fiction, Futurism and The Speculative* (2011), and more recently Ytasha Womack's popular representation of the concept in her book *Afrofuturism: The World of Black Sci-Fi and Fantasy Culture* (2013) and Rasheedah Phillip's book *Black Quantum Futurism: Theory and Practice Vol. 1* (2015) have continued to introduce the concept to the broader public.

## SYMPOSIA

The last several years have seen an explosion of interest in the techno-culture sphere and Afrofuturism within the Africana Studies field. In the United States, one of the first important meetings, the eBlack Studies conference, emerged out the initiative sponsored by the National Council for Black Studies with support from the Ford Foundation. The workshop was hosted in July 24–27, 2008, by the Department of African American Studies at the University of Illinois at Urbana-Champaign.

Other black studies departments hosted or co-hosted conferences, such as: the AfroGEEKS conference (2005) at the University of California Santa Barbara; "Double-Consciousness and the Digital Individual: Reflections on Black Thought 2.0" (2012) at Duke University; "Alien Bodies: Race, Space, and Sex in the African Diaspora Logo" (2013) at Emory University; Duke University's Race in Space conference (2014); the Black Studies in the Digital Age seminar at Northwestern University; "Afrofuturism in Black Theology" (2014) at Vanderbilt University; and the AstroBlackness conferences at Loyola-Marymount University (2014–15).

These are just a few of the symposiums or conferences the Africana Studies field has organized recently to study the growing Afrofuturism movement. However, in the interest of brevity, it is important to note and articulate previous Africana formations around the concept of Afrofuturism.

## AFRICANA STUDIES AND TECHNOLOGY

During the discipline's formative stage (1968–1972), minimal attention was devoted to the relationship between scientific and technological issues and Africana Studies. By and large, black studies practically made only a passing reference to the role of science and technology in the scholarly investigation of people of African descent. However, in 1970, a year before Sun Ra's historic lecture series "The Black Man in The Cosmos" at the University of California Berkley, Nathan Hare, chair of the Black Studies department at San Francisco State University introduced a "Black Science" course that would contrast Ra's metaphysical approach and introduce science in relation to the Black studies curriculum.

For instance, in a discussion of the nation's first comprehensive black studies curriculum, Nathan Hare, the founding chair of the Department of Black Studies at San Francisco State University, sole mention of the topic was a black science course identified as an example of the pragmatic phase of the curriculum which consisted of courses producing socio-economic skills" (Hare 1970). The three credit hours course "Black Science" introduced students to "scientific development stressing the contributions of black scientists. Emphasis on the application of fundamental concepts and methods of science to the environment of black Americans" (Hare 1970).

The subsequent, albeit, limited scholarship on the discipline's scientific and technological dimension has tended to focus on curricular (Stewart 1976; Little, Leonard, and Crosby 1980; King 1992; Stewart 2004), pedagogical (Hendrix, Bracy, and Davis 1985; Herron 1984; Stewart 1985; 2003), research (Hendrix, Bracy, Davis, and Herron 1984; Stewart 2004; Conyers and McKnight 2005), and community empowerment (Anderson 1974; Stewart 1976; Johnson 1980; Jenkins and Om-Ra Seti 1997; Alkalimat 2001; Anderson and Stewart 2007, 277–303) issues.

James Stewart, the long-time black studies scholar and arguably the discipline's leading authority on the integration of science and technology in Africana Studies, has produced an impressive body of work (1976; 1985; 1988; 2003; 2004; Anderson and Stewart 2007, 277–303) spanning over thirty years (1976–2007) which proves useful in elucidating the aforementioned extant literature.

In his initial 1976 essay appearing in *Black Books Bulletin*, Stewart identified several critical future developments in black studies among which were scientific and technological concerns. Stewart's prescient essay addressed several of the salient themes which would become the focus of the subsequent scholarship on the integration of scientific and technological issues into the discipline of black studies. He contended that "the integration of instructive and research applications using modern technology is critical to the amelioration of adverse material conditions facing Black people" (1976, 24). His contention raised critical instructional, research, and liberational implications for the discipline that undergirded its future attention to scientific and technological concerns.

The discipline's attention to the importance of the relationship between black studies and scientific and technological issues underscored in Stewart's provocative essay was evident in the early effort of the National Council for Black Studies (NCBS) to develop a standardized curriculum for the discipline. In 1980, the organization's curriculum committee under the leadership of William Little included science and technology among the eight subfields of its recommended curriculum model (Little, Leonard, and Crosby 1980).

Specifically, the committee's contention was that the science and technological development subfield "examines and analyzes the development of mathematics, metallurgy and mineralogy, architecture, agronomy, etc. This area also examines the relationship of science and the application of technology in various African societies (e.g.) medicine, agriculture, architecture, education, and nutrition" (1980, 16). The curricular focus was further echoed by William H. King, the second president of NCBS. King proposed a transdisciplinary approach to explore several facets of science and technology from an Afrocentric perspective wherein the world view, normative assumptions, and frames of reference grow out of the experiences and folk wisdom of black people (1992, 25). King proclaimed that "Black Studies can play a most important role in examining the 'values and expectations' that guide science" (1992, 30).

In 2004, Stewart revisited the curricular inclusion of science and technology in Africana Studies when he proposed "a strategy to integrate the study of science and technology into Black/Africana studies and instruction" (Stewart 2004, 277). Stewart introduced a framework for developing relevant instructional and research activities," which consists of a "synthesis of Black/ Africana Studies and Science, Technology and Society (STS) perspectives" (Stewart 2004, 277).

In this landmark essay, Stewart offered several "examples of curricular strategies designed to familiarize students with the interface between black/ Africana studies and STS" (2004, 294). Examples of the curricular treatments included a comparison of ancient and/or pre-industrial African and "modern" western scientific/technological approaches; impacts of technological innovations on the lives of African Americans; medical research, healthcare policy, and quality of life of African Americans; and environmental degradation/enhancement and the quality of life of African Americans (Stewart 2004, 297–302).

Notwithstanding the efforts of NCBS and the exhortation of King (1992) and Stewart (1976; 2004), the discipline has failed to make significant inroads in incorporating scientific and technological perspectives in the curriculum of black studies academic units. Black science courses still remain a rarity in the discipline and more importantly minimal attention has been devoted to the systematic integration of science and technology in the educational orientations of black studies programs. Fortunately, the discipline has made considerable more pedagogical progress with respect to the application of scientific and technological innovations.

Furthermore, King highlighted the pedagogical applications of technological innovations, such as the computer, as a promising alternative mode of instruction in the discipline. Stewart insightfully observed that the mode of instruction "would emphasize to students that modern technological developments and concerns of black people were interwoven" (Stewart 1975, 24). He proposed that black studies scholars collaborate with those with technical expertise to address the myriad problems plaguing the black community. Finally, Stewart insightfully observed: "An expected early development will be the use of modern technology to bring Black Studies to the black community at large" (Stewart 1975, 24). He insightfully observed that the mode of instruction "would emphasize to students that modern technological developments and concerns of Black people were interwoven" (Stewart 1975, 24). Stewart's computer software package was entitled *Liberation 2000? The Black Experience in America* (Stewart 1985).

As principal investigator of a grant funded by the United States Department of Education that was designed to improve the quality of science and technology instruction for secondary urban minority students, Stewart introduces the concept of "Science, Technology and Society (STS) to enhance the instructional quality of science education" (Stewart 1988). Stewart continues his explorations of pedagogical technological application in the essay "Will the Revolution Be Digitized?: Using Digitized Resources in Undergraduate Africana Studies Courses"—in which he identifies web-based resources and Internet-based documents for use in Africana Studies coursework (Stewart 2003).

In his seminal essay which addresses both scientific and technological curriculum and application in Africana Studies, Stewart "proposes a strategy to integrate the study of science and technology into Black/Africana studies and instruction" (Stewart 2004, 277). He maintains: "There can be little doubt that the serious scrutiny of science and technology is a legitimate and logical extension of the quest by Black/Africana Studies scholar/activists to fashion a body of knowledge that can provide a foundation for developing a viable liberation strategy" (Stewart 2004, 277).

His landmark essay, *A Synthesis of Black/Africana Studies and Sciences, Technology and Society (STS) Perspectives,* describes his proposed framework for developing relevant instructional and research activities (Stewart 2004, 277). Finally Stewart's most recent contribution to this topic is the inclusion of a chapter devoted to science and technology in *Introduction to African American Studies: Transdisciplinary Approaches and Implications* (Anderson and Stewart 2007, 277–303). A chapter entitled "Science, Technology, and the Future of African Americans" examines a host of critical scientific and technological issues impacting the material conditions of African Americans including integrating science and technology studies in Africana Studies, the "Digital Divide," future studies, the scientific and technological oppression of people of African descent, and liberational uses of science and technology (Anderson and Stewart 2007, 277–303).

Many of the essays of this volume grew out the relationships formed at Astroblackness conferences and personal relationships developed within Africana Studies and what the visual artist John Jennings refers to as the Black Speculative Art Movement. Furthermore, the writers were interested in continuing the debate about the transition of Afrofuturism into other dimensions of interest or research and approach their themes from various theoretical or analytical perspectives.

Tiffany Barber explores Kenyan-born artist Wangechi Mutu's *Non je ne regrett rien* (2007) in the frame of Octavia Butler's part-science fiction, part-neo-slave narrative *Kindred* (1979), raising the question: what about black female subjectivity requires a futurist context? What are the agential possibilities for black female bodies historically represented as quintessentially other, abject, and alien? This chapter uses Dana's dismemberment in *Kindred* and Afrofuturist theorizations on blackness, technology, and female humanity to illustrate how Mutu's above mentioned collage enacts a strategy for deconstructing and reconstructing how difference becomes inscribed on black female bodies. As such, this chapter also examines how Mutu's technique of exquisite corpse—or subjecting the human body to grotesque juxta-

positions and distortions—operates as transgressive disfigurement, disman-
tling normative constructions of black female subjectivity and freedom and
literally recrafting black female bodies and new futures.

In chapter 2, Nettrice Gaskins discusses Afrofuturism as Web 3.0: "Vernacular Cartography and Augmented Space." Furthermore, the chapter critiques the use of how geometric charts or maps, virtual and real-world geographic locations of avatars, or objects such as mobile smartphones reflect
movement and migration, and how black/African artists share and exchange
cultural data. These contemporary forms do not exhaust the possibilities of
augmented space at the interaction of art, media, and vernacular cartography.
Moreover, the chapter asks whether the traditional or ancient African forms
become irrelevant and "invisible," or if artists end up creating new experiences in which the spatial and information layers are equally important. The
chapter also explores the relationship between cultural data and information
and how this might function differently in today's digital culture. Throughout
the chapter, the term augmented (space or reality) is re-conceptualized as a
concept, or a cultural and aesthetic practice rather than as new technology.

Ricardo Guthrie examines the confluence among Afrofuturism, the environment, and cyborg manifestations of twenty-first century cinema. In this
chapter, two films offer compelling opportunities for utilizing Afrofuturist
analytics to re-center the racial urban imaginary: In *DETROPIA*, filmmakers
Ewing and Grady explore the devolution of Detroit from a thriving 1.8 million-person metropolis founded on a unionized auto industry and a thriving
black professional class, to today's de-industrialized city of 700,000. *DE-
TROPIA*'s dystopic present anticipates tomorrow's urban crises, while illuminating black change agents and environmentalists who envision a new city
beyond existing racial paradigms. In *I-Robot*, the character Dell Spooner
(Will Smith) represents a type of Afro-Pessimist whose cynicism gradually
reflects a turn towards Afrofuturism's merger of black cultural ethos and
commitment to struggle. Correspondingly, this chapter examines racialized
urban geographies and develops Afrofuturist analysis to explain conflicted
racial imaginaries in dystopic Detroit and in a seemingly utopian Chicago of
2035.

In chapter 4, tobias c. van Veen takes up Paul Gilroy's call to develop an
adequate and conceptual language for Afrofuturism by undertaking a "speculative exegesis" of Mark Sinker's early meditations on black Atlantic arts
and music in The Wire. By focusing on what Public Enemy calls "Armageddon been in effect," and by reading their mediatised performances as articulating Sinker's concept of Alien Nation, van Veen explicates how both concepts address the temporal rupture of the Middle Passage and its "obliteration
of a normalized past." Germane to Africology and Africanist Studies, van
Veen argues that both Afrofuturism and Afrocentrism are differentiated, as
well as constitutively entwined, by how they utilise historical revisionism—

or what Kodwo Eshun calls their "chronopolitics"—to address the "void of origin." Emphasising how Afrofuturism focuses on open-ended temporalities rather than foreclosed pasts, van Veen turns to the transgressive music and poetry of Sun Ra, Jimi Hendrix, John Coltrane, and Gil Scott-Heron to develop a typology of Afrofuturist becomings, arguing for the ontological and political force of radical black performance in overcoming "slavery's dehumanization program."

In chapter 5, Grace Gipson explores the relationship between female android character Cindi Mayweather (aka Janelle Monáe) and her encounter with a musical market world filled with severe social stratification. Since 2007, Monáe has reenergized the Afrofuturism movement with her epic vocals, immaculate clothing style, and magical lyrics. Gipson asserts, much like her Afrofuturistic predecessors Sun Ra and George Clinton, Monáe presents a persona that can be likened to a polyvalent afrofuturistic aesthetic that embodies the desires of black feminism mixed with a futuristic sonic groove. This chapter shows how Monae strategically mixes space with racial and sexual politics, black feminism, historical narratives, and class conflicts all in a "radical visionary Afrofuturistic" perspective.

Ken McLeod explores the impact of hip hop icon Tupac Shakur in relation to technology, arguing that hip hop often refutes notions of "real time." Focusing on Tupac and drawing on concepts from Auslander, Baudrillard, Eshun, Hayles, and Weheliye, among others, this chapter analyzes the place of time-travel and immortality in Afrofuturist music. Furthermore, McLeod asserts that, rather than signaling a loss of human agency, post-human, cyborg, and/or holographic performances reinforce a collective human consciousness and therefore underline Afrofuturist ideals surrounding utopian migration and freedom.

In chapter 7, Andrew Rollins explores how Afrofuturism intersects with the historical mission of the black church in America. Although intellectuals, artists, and scholars in a broad range of fields have already generated creative or scholarly production on Afrofuturism, the black church has been silent on the subject. Rollins argues the black church is at a crossroads in its development in American society and must adapt to the challenges of the current age to remain relevant. Rollins asserts for the black church to serve the "present age" it must successfully transition, and to fulfill its calling, it must incorporate an Afrofuturist view as a guide for praxis in contemporary postmodern society.

Lonny Avi Brooks critiques his personal experience as a minority forecaster conducting ethnographies of new media and futurist think tanks in Silicon Valley from 1998 to 2011. Based on field research, Brooks developed a set of Foresight Frames. First, examining how future texts become normalized sets of expectations. Brooks collected sets of future visions produced at these elite sites in the form of future scenarios, visual trend maps, and interviews of forecasters. Second, these contemporary future visions project racial, segregated, and elite future landscapes by reinforcing notions of racial segregation and discrimination. Therefore, these Foresight processes avoid issues of latent racism that pervade the history of Futures studies, its assumptions, and future scenarios.

In chapter 9, David DeIuliis and Jeff Lohr propose communicology as a framework for understanding Afrofuturism as speculative discourse. Communicology's method of explicating "human consciousness and behavioral embodiment as discourse within global culture" allows for the study of Afrofuturism as not only "the speculative fiction of the African diaspora," but also the diasporic communication of the experience of blackness. The chapter initially frames the intellectual origins of communicology as a way to engage Afrofuturist discourse. Second, it reviews the recent literature on Afrofuturism as a critical method and liberating hermeneutic that, with communicology as a theoretical and methodological framework, can rewrite the narrative of human experience through mainstream academic discourse.

In chapter 10, Esther Jones utilizes an Africana Womanist approach to examine how black women's science fiction contributes to medical humanities discourse, particularly as it relates to the practice of empathy in medicine. Jones argues that black women's science fiction enables us to analyze the shifts that may need to take place in order to transform the current uneven medical paradigm to establish a culture of health parity. Moreover, Jones argues that science fiction writings by Octavia Butler, Nalo Hopkinson, and Nnedi Okorafor enable people to examine how human beings may be able to communicate more ethically and empathetically across differences.

Finally, in chapter 11, scholar Quiana Whitted conducts an interview with prominent Nigerian-American author Nnedi Okorafor. Okorafor's approach to speculative fiction draws upon elements of fantasy, magic realism, hard science fiction, and dystopian horror. Okorafor values the notion of Afrofuturism as a way of being for the female protagonists of her novels. Okorafor is the first Nigerian American to win the World Fantasy Award for her critically acclaimed novel, *Who Fears Death* (2010). She also received the Wole Soyinka Prize for Literature in Africa for the young adult novel, *Zahrah the Windseeker* (2005) and the Carl Brandon Society Parallax Award for best speculative fiction by a person of color for *The Shadow Speaker* (2007). In this interview, the writer and professor talks about the role of Afrofuturism in her work, including the cultural fusion of technology and magic.

*Part I*

# Quantum Visions of Futuristic Blackness

*Chapter One*

# Cyborg Grammar?

*Reading Wangechi Mutu's*
Non je ne regrette rien *through* Kindred

## Tiffany E. Barber

A maimed figure—part human, part animal, part machine—is suspended in the middle of a gray and brown, cloud-like background. Severed from its upper half and projected into a cumulous abyss, only the lower limbs of the figure remain, separated like scissors. The bottom leg extends and the top leg bends at the knee, reaching upward like a scorpion's tail or a morbidly elegant arabesque. Instead of a knee joint, the top leg is equipped with a motorcycle wheel that connects to spinal tubing. Green and gray-scaled tentacles cover its pelvic region. The right half of the picture plane is bisected by the figure's bottom leg. Instead of a foot, the end of the leg is fitted with an amalgam of animal hoof, stiletto, and blooming flower. The left half of the picture plane is dominated by a coiling serpent whose skin is imbued with violet, red, and other earthen hues.[1]

The center of the image is the most visually arresting. Occupied by black root-like structures emerging from the figure's lower excised torso, the gray background is spattered with colliding color fields of ochre, green, and pink spewing from the figure's top leg from which its foot appears to have been violently amputated. The composition is arranged in such a way that it is hard to tell whether the coiling serpent is responsible for the figure's ruptured state, or if the plant parts have caused the body to breach internally. The collage, *Non je ne regrette rien* (2007) by artist Wangechi Mutu, confronts the viewer with a complex scene that is repulsive yet seductively compelling, and the arrangement of human, animal, plant, and mechanical parts suggests a type of mutualism that results in a dismembered body. Known for her grotesque representations of black female bodies that exist between the cyborgian and the Afrofuturistic, Mutu's *Non je ne regrette rien* offers a unique approach to black female subjecthood, what I call transgressive disfigurement.[2] It pictures ways of being that are not predicated on wholeness but which instead incorporate alternate, at times violent or "undesirable" forms of transformation that serve to produce dismembered black female bodies.

In 2000, just before graduating with an MFA in sculpture from Yale University, Mutu began exploring relations between black women's bodies, female victimhood, resistance, and transformation. *Pin-Up*, two grids of twelve 13x10 and 14x10 images, was her first series of collaged female figures. It consists of images culled from pornography and health and beauty magazines mixed with ink and watercolor on paper. Mutu's collage practice has since evolved to include images extracted from automobile and motorcycle magazines as well as dated anthropology and anatomy pamphlets and textbooks. A primary component of Mutu's subject matter, the female cyborg body, brings her work into conversation with the liberatory presuppositions of posthumanism as feminist critique first theorized by Donna J. Haraway in 1985.[3]

The incorporation of various modes of technology and mechanical parts as proxies for human limbs situates Mutu's work within a posthumanist discourse of the cyborg. In "A Cyborg Manifesto," Haraway writes, "A

**Wangechi Mutu, *Non je ne regrette rien*, mixed media on Mylar, 138.4 x 233.7 cm, 2007.**

cyborg body is not innocent; it was not born in a garden; it does not seek unitary identity and generate antagonistic dualisms without end (or until the world ends); it takes irony for granted. . . . Intense pleasure in skill, machine skill, ceases to be a sin, but an aspect of embodiment" (Haraway 1991, 180). Haraway embraces technology as a way of moving away from a humanism built on normative binaries and dualisms in order to create a regenerated world without gender. For Haraway, humanism's binary system is crippling and requires a welcome incorporation of technology to negate this system: "We require regeneration, not rebirth, and the possibilities for our reconstitution include the utopian dream of the hope for a monstrous world without gender. . . . Cyborg imagery can suggest a way out of the maze of dualisms in which we have explained our bodies and our tools to ourselves" (Haraway 1991, 181).

Following Haraway, Mutu's figures revel in boundary confusion. As such, they dispel the utopian ideal of a whole, self-possessed body. This ideal is frequently associated with a modern Cartesian humanism centered on wholeness that underscores science fiction, a genre with which Afrofuturism finds kinship and comes to play in Mutu's work.[4] But where Haraway's theorizations of the cyborg neglect an explicit examination of race, the figures in Mutu's collages assail racialized dimensions of female humanity by critically emphasizing how black female bodies are seen and acquire meaning. And rather than a hopeful dream, *Non je ne regrette rien* excises the black female body as a privileged signifier or site of identification for black female subjectivity; Mutu's black cyborgian female figures are perpetually uneasy, undone.

In addition to posthumanism, because of the joining of racialized and gendered bodies with techno-mechanical parts Mutu's work has repeatedly been considered Afrofuturistic. Since its coining, Afrofuturism has been considered a revisionist discourse in which racialized and gendered bodies in the past, present, and future use technology to new reparative ends. Bringing the discourses of posthumanism and Afrofuturism into direct engagement to analyze Mutu's collages posits new conceptions of subjecthood relative to race, gender, and sexuality. Other than mentions of race as a system of domination and a call for intersectional feminist scholarship that contends that race, gender, sexuality, and class are not mutually exclusive, Haraway stops short of directly dealing with the implications of race in relation to the cyborg in her manifesto.[5] As a result, Tricia Rose questions the usefulness of the cyborg as both an imaginary and a political formation for black women in the portion of her interview with Mark Dery included in *Flame Wars: The Discourse of Cyberculture* (1994). Rose notes, "I'm not troubled by the cyborg *as* an imaginary, but by the fact that it's almost impossible for the average young woman to see herself as a person who could take up that much social space" (Tricia Rose qtd. in Dery 1994, 216).

According to Rose, the cyborg's possibilities are too fantastical to function in *actuality*; the average (black) woman, presumably unmotivated by or unaware of such possibilities, cannot imagine herself as such a transgressive figure. Here, Rose dismisses the potential for 'the average young woman' to possess agency in radically new ways, and in doing so, she refuses to acknowledge the transformative power of the cyborg. Furthermore, Rose worries that Haraway's theorizations of the cyborg reinforce gendered dynamics of technology in which machines are signifiers of an "impregnable masculinity," while flesh is coded as feminine (Tricia Rose qtd. in Dery 1994, 217). Finally, Rose contends that previous conceptualizations of femininity do not allow for racialized and gendered subjects—namely black women (Rose in fact posits herself as an example)—to exhibit power and aggression without being perceived as masculine.

Mutu herself regards her visually disturbing and disruptive collages, which picture complex, fragmented, and exaggerated black female bodies, as a way to "question the relationship between resilience and compliance," between agency and victimization (Wangechi Mutu qtd. in Murray 2005, 8). Indeed, much of the critical response to Mutu's collage practice situates her work within a redemptive paradigm. Within this paradigm, agency and resistance are linked with transcendence and transgression, despite the overt references to deviance, disease, and disfigurement that populate her collages. As such, Mutu's work is often summarily praised for what critics consider to be its staging of hybridity and multiplicity as modes of resistance; her figures are understood as adaptors and adaptations that tack back and forth between danger and reclamation, mutations of normalized ideals of femininity, beauty, and sexuality. I propose, however, that Mutu's collage practice results in something more alarming, more disturbing than this drive toward reparative resistance. Rather than claiming that Mutu's images picture repaired or reassembled bodies, I locate Mutu's work within discourses of posthumanism and Afrofuturism to depart from them. What other ways can we read Mutu's collage practice? Can the feminist theorizations that shore up discourses such as posthumanism and Afrofuturism allow us to think of Mutu's collages as repetitions of fragmentation, and further as representations of anti-healing rather than of redemption?

In this chapter, I offer a close reading of *Non je ne regrette rien* against the grain of how her work is typically theorized to claim that Mutu's project is actually to produce dismembered black female bodies. Within this framework, Mutu's *Non je ne regrette rien* dismantles normative constructions of black female subjectivity and freedom by crafting maimed black female bodies. Additionally, my analysis of Mutu's use of collage moves away from readings of the artist's own African origins and fragmentation as a feature of postcolonialism.[6] My study of Mutu's *Non je ne regrette rien* instead rejects notions of "the body" itself as a locus for identity formation.[7]

To set up this approach to Mutu's work, I read the figure at the center of *Non je ne regrette rien* alongside the protagonist in Octavia Butler's 1979 novel *Kindred* to bring new considerations to a relation between historical and discursive violence and black female bodies. *Kindred* is one of Butler's many novels considered to be a work of Afrofuturism in addition to its generic status as a neo-slave narrative. Neo-slave narratives are modern and postmodern fictional works by contemporary authors who use existing slave narratives, imagination (or what author Toni Morrison terms re-memory), oral histories, and archival research to address and often reconstruct the experiences and alienating, traumatic effects of enslavement in the "New World" (Reed 1976; Butler 1979; Morrison 1987; Rushdy 1999). Using specific instances from neo-slave narratives and how they represent dismembered black female bodies underscores a relation between physical, bodily fragmentation and a fragmented racial and gendered self that I attest Mutu explores through collage. One such instance is the self-amputation scene in *Kindred*. In this pivotal scene, Dana becomes lodged between the world of her time and the world of her ancestors. A fatal skirmish ensues, resulting in Dana's dismemberment. Her body literally becomes a battlefield on which issues of possession, ownership, and agency are played out. Dana's amputation serves as a point of entry into Mutu's collage and a way of thinking through the values and limits of fragmentation relative to race, gender, and sexuality at issue in both works. These two texts—one visual and one literary—share cyborg thematics and generic traits rooted in science fiction and fantasy as methods for imagining pasts, presents and, most importantly, alternative though not necessarily redemptive futures.

What about black female subjectivity requires a futurist context? What are the generative possibilities for black female bodies historically represented as quintessentially other, abject, and alien? What is at stake in privileging a project that ultimately produces dismembered black female bodies? Literary scholar Farah Jasmine Griffin's definitive essay (1996) on what she terms "textual healing" is an important point of reference for contemporary studies of neo-slave narratives and for my writing on transgressive disfigurement. Griffin's essay is a significant contribution to a body of literature that addresses the place of black women writers within the American literary canon and the recuperative efforts of black women's literature as a response to the legacies of slavery. In "Textual Healing: Claiming Black Women's Bodies, the Erotic and Resistance in Contemporary Novels of Slavery," Griffin discusses how contemporary black women authors rewrite dominant discourses of black bodies as ugly, inferior, and inhuman into sites of "healing, pleasure, and resistance" (Griffin 1996, 521). Griffin continues,

> I am using the term healing to suggest the way in which the body, literally and discursively scarred, ripped, and mutilated, has to learn to love itself, to func-

tion in the world with other bodies and often in opposition to those persons and
things that seek to destroy it. Of course, the body never can return to a pre-
scarred state. It is not a matter of getting back to a "truer" self, but instead of
claiming the body, scars and all—in a narrative of love and care. As such,
healing does not deny the construction of bodies, but instead suggests that they
can be constructed differently, for different ends. (1996, 521)

In this passage, crucial to the definition of textual healing, Griffin advises
literally and discursively mangled black bodies to love themselves in order to
"get along" and to guard against destruction from outside forces. Textual
healing, then, is a project of reclamation as resistance. Griffin's rhetoric is
grounded in a hope for rehabilitation and reconciliation, a return to a restored
black self through love and care in literature and in the world at large.

By contrast, *Non je ne regrette rien* centers on rupture and trauma represented by a dislocated body violently separated from its other half. How
might we begin to think of the construction and contemporary representations of black female bodies in postmodern collage and fiction apart from a
binary of slavery and freedom, trauma and reconciliation, not as sites of
reclamation but as something else altogether? This analysis of *Non je ne
regrette rien* situates fragmentation and disfigurement as epistemologies for
"reading" black female bodies that defy reparative constructions of black
female subjectivity. Departing from Griffin's notions of textual healing, I
argue that Dana's self-dismemberment in *Kindred* and *Non je ne regrette
rien* picture the repulsive effects of how difference becomes inscribed on
black female bodies. In their negation, both texts undermine Griffin's argument and demand a reconsideration of conceptions of healing, freedom, resistance, and agency.

In addition to the texts' shared themes, reading Mutu's collage through
Butler's novel also serves as a heuristic tool in considering the implications
of Mutu's work within a uniquely American imaginary in which racial discourse plays a central role. Although Mutu is originally from Kenya, much of
her work addresses articulations of blackness and black womanhood within
an American context. To this end, Mutu's practice draws equally from
African vernacular forms, modernist European collage styles, and American
mass culture, but it also follows conventions of the neo-slave narrative.

Mutu certainly distinguishes her African origins and a relation to blackness from an American black experience born out of slavery; however,
Mutu's reference to a forced creation story vis-à-vis colonialism and her
imaginative interventions into this story rhyme with the neo-slave narrative
genre. For example, in an interview with curator and critic Okwui Enwezor,
Mutu states, "[B]roaching the idea of race is very complicated because
Africans have a different historical experience to those who were abducted
and brought here to the USA. They're equal senses of alienation and exile but

the myth that's loudest is the slave narrative, which doesn't apply to a huge amount of Africans, myself included. I always say that I was racialised [sic] in America. . . . My work relates to the forced creation story that the colonialists invented us."[8] Despite Mutu's attempt to maintain a certain distance between her own blackness and the processes of racialization that form part of an American understanding of blackness, I contend that Mutu's work is informed by and reflects a politics of race and racial identification particular to the U.S. Furthermore, several of Mutu's collages and video works approximate the genre of the neo-slave narrative, a notably American literary form.[9]

For example, a number of Mutu's collages distort female reproductive organs, recurring motifs that resonate with the process, economy, and culture of production that justified and regulated sexual violence enacted toward black female bodies under conditions of slavery. *One Hundred Lavish Months of Bushwhack* (2004) features a nude female figure whose upper and lower torso is masked by a serpentine entanglement that doubles as both a labyrinthine web and an unruly pubic bush covering the figure's exposed mid-section. Mutu's *Sprout* (2010) pictures an inverted figure rendered in a pose similar to a birthing position, its feet replaced with budding branches. The figure's pubic region is soiled—stained with splotches of brown paint as well as soil as organic matter itself—and sprouting a blossoming, plant-like nest. Mutu's representations of female reproductive organs in these works recall a particular history of black female subjugation, a history rooted in black women's labor as production and reproduction in U.S. antebellum slavery. On this score, Mutu's collages share some of the imaginative and imaginary impulses of the neo-slave narrative genre in that they reimagine the forms, contours, and facilities of black female bodies. But rather than capitulate to redress, reading Mutu's *Non je ne regrette rien* through Octavia Butler's *Kindred* posits new, albeit counterintuitive and impossibly dark insights into the construction of black female bodies in Mutu's work.

## A BRIEF HISTORY OF "BLACK ART"

Before continuing with my comparative analysis, it is important to situate Mutu's artistic output within a history of black radical aesthetics in the United States more broadly. Mutu's collage practice participates in a genealogy of black artistic production in the U.S. and abroad that challenges how problematic notions of race and gender—from the Harlem Renaissance to 1990s-era identity politics—have been historically sutured to black bodies. During the Harlem Renaissance, African American artists such as Aaron Douglas were concerned with defining and representing blackness as humane, dignified, and intellectually robust—oscillating between W. E. B. Du Bois's notions of integrationism and Booker T. Washington's nationalist ideas embedded in accommodation.[10] Thirty years later, the Black Arts Movement, in conversation with the Civil Rights and Black Power Movements, established blackness as beautiful, radical, and revolutionary. Proponents of the Harlem Renaissance and the Black Arts Movement, though distinct, promoted and attempted to recover racial blackness and black bodies as powerful and worthy—dignified and tactful on one side, radical and dangerous on the other. In doing so, these movements fixed blackness—racial, corporeal, and aesthetic—as the very foundation of identity. Beginning in the late nineteenth century and into the late twentieth century, the notion of black art was nearly inseparable from a rhetoric of racial solidarity; following Du Bois, Alain Locke, and others, black art was all but required to be a project of uplift, legibility, and legitimacy.[11]

In the 1980s and 1990s, identity politics came to bear on contemporary art in such a way as to deconstruct oppressive social forces and to bring, among others, artists of color that were historically relegated to the margins to the center of the art world. A landmark example of this is the Whitney Museum of American Art's 1993 Biennial Exhibition. Fitted with a newly hired director, a fresh team of curators, and a politically correct agenda, the exhibition sought to showcase the Whitney Museum's efforts toward inclusion and diversity as a reflection of the current political climate. Instead, hitherto marginal artists such as Daniel J. Martinez, Jimmie Durham, Lorna Simpson, and others included in the 1993 Biennial Exhibition were pigeonholed and all but expected to produce work that exclusively addressed their racial, gender, sexual, cultural, or ethnic heritage. However well intentioned, the Biennial essentialized the groups it wished to celebrate: "black artists [were made to] speak only for blacks, women [were made to] speak only for women, and gays only for gays, bound by a constrained notion of community [and relegating] artists to cultural essences" (Wright 2012, 268).

In 2001, as part of her new post at the Studio Museum in Harlem, curator Thelma Golden, a member of the Whitney's 1993 Biennial team, introduced what has become the familiar definition of post-black art. The cheeky phrase describes work by artists included in Golden's blockbuster exhibition, Freestyle, "who were adamant about not being labeled as 'black' artists, though their work was steeped, in fact deeply interested, in redefining complex notions of blackness."[12] This definition, which emerged out of Golden's conversations with artist Glenn Ligon, is a response to the categorization of "black art" in the United States, a widely adopted and narrow "interpretive paradigm . . . that sees its defining task as that of establishing or indicating a proper relation between black artists and black art" (English 2007, 2). Instead of a coterminous relationship between artists' racial identities, artistic production, and a political project of racial uplift, Golden's post-blackness delinks this formulation, creating new space for artists who identify as black to make work unbound by racial responsibility and racialized looking practices if they so choose. According to Golden and Ligon, post-black artists react to a history of identity politics in the U.S. that originated in the 1960s alongside a host of liberation movements.[13] In her *Freestyle* exhibition catalog essay, Golden asks, "How could black artists make work after the vital political activism of the 1960s, the focused, often essentialist, Black Arts Movement, the theory-driven multiculturalism of the 1980s, and the late globalist expansion of the late 90s?" (Golden 2001, 14).

By the 1980s, identity politics had become pervasive and a preferred lens through which to view contemporary art produced by artists of so-called marginalized identities. Major art museums in the U.S. embraced identity politics as an exercise of inclusion, one that also spurred a series of critiques of identity as a theoretical and curatorial framework. These subsequent critiques in the 1990s became a hallmark of institutional exhibitions and art-making practices in the United States to which post-blackness responds. Within this climate of change, black artists working in the 1990s and subsequent generations invert racial stereotypes as well as assumptions about work made by black artists. In the wake of identity politics, Golden and Ligon's post-black "speaks to an individual freedom that is a result of the transitional moment in the quest to define ongoing changes in the evolution of African-American art and ultimately to ongoing redefinition of blackness in contemporary culture" (Golden 2001, 15). This version of post-blackness, therefore, celebrates individual freedom as a reaction to various iterations of identity discourse and liberation movements between 1960 and 1990 during which "black art" as a mode of racial and political solidarity was conceived.

Current manifestations of Afrofuturism share similar impulses with the expressive modes of post-blackness. Afrofuturism has become an umbrella term for considering how science fiction, fantasy, and technology can be used to imagine and reimagine lost pasts and new futures for alienated, black "others." While earlier expressions of Afrofuturism may have left notions of black identity formulated in the 1960s, 1970s, and 1980s undisturbed, current expressions of Afrofuturism center on reimagining and resignifying blackness and black identities.[14] But where instantiations of post-blackness seek to disrupt a relation between blackness and a history of racialization, particularly with regard to stringent categorizations of visual work made by black artists, Afrofuturism holds onto this history of racialization and troubles it by working within it. To this point, many Afrofuturist works relate blackness to tropes of science and speculative fiction to comment on histories of racial oppression and to propose new possibilities for engaging blackness and racial difference in the past, present, and future.

Within Afrofuturism, the realities of captive slavery and forced diaspora are likened to instances of bodily transformation and alien invasion that appear in science and speculative fiction novels and films. Robots, cyborgs, and androids such as contemporary psychedelic soul singer Janelle Monáe's alter ego Cindi Mayweather as well as interstellar adventures and time travel all feature prominently in the otherworldly, intergalactic narratives at the core of Afrofuturist visual, literary, and sonic texts. Afrofuturist works also aim to subvert science fiction tropes in order to highlight and complicate issues of racial difference and representations of blackness that are often left out of generic plots or altogether eclipsed in science fiction texts. These issues and representations include the structured absence and token presence of black characters and actors, themes of racial contamination and racial paranoia as constitutive of a post-apocalyptic future, and the traumatized black body as the ultimate signifier of difference, alien-ness, and otherness (Kilgore 2003; Nama 2008; Rieder 2008; Lavender 2011).

Linking blackness with experiences of alienation and dislocation, Afrofuturism has gained considerable currency in academic and popular discourse since the late 1990s and early 2000s. It has also served as a thematic framework for a number of recent museum exhibitions, including The Museum of Contemporary African Diasporan Arts' *Feed Your Head: The African Origins of the Scientific Aesthetic (2011)* and *Pixelating: Black in New Dimensions* (2011), The Museum of Contemporary Art San Diego's *Approximately Infinite Universe* (2013) and The Studio Museum in Harlem's *The Shadows Took Shape* (2013). Musician Sun Ra, writers Samuel R. Delany and Octavia Butler, scholars Alondra Nelson and Kodwo Eshun, and contemporary visual artists Wangechi Mutu, Sanford Biggers, and others are frequently associated with Afrofuturism.

## LOCATING THE CYBORG

Mutu's work incorporates the tenets of Afrofuturism, but with a difference; the ruptured, dismembered bodies in her collages call into question both the reparative potential of the prosthetic devices therein and the relation between the cyborg and black womanhood. Building on notions of the cyborg, Haraway's "Ecce Homo, Ain't (Ar'n't) I a Woman, and Inappropriate/d Others: the Human in a Posthumanist Landscape" (1992) acts as a postscript to her manifesto. In "Ecce Homo," Haraway seems to challenge or even correct her own cyborg provocations by adding considerations of historical intersections between gender, race, class, and sex. If a cyborg is post-gender and without history, is it also post-sex? Post-nation? Post-race? I consider Haraway's emphasis on "the body" and language, and her inclusion of Hazel Carby's description of black womanhood under conditions of slavery in "Ecce Homo" as an expanded view of the cyborg as an imaginary.[15] Referring to Carby's discussion of how a cult of true womanhood positioned black women as abject counterparts to white women, Haraway asserts, "[I]n the New World, and specifically in the U.S., black women were not constituted as 'woman,' as white women were. Instead, black women were constituted simultaneously racially and sexually—as marked female (animal, sexualized, and without rights), but not as woman (human, potential wife, conduit for the name of the Father)—in a specific institution, slavery, that excluded them from 'culture' defined as the circulation of signs through the system of marriage."[16] Thus, black women (as slaves) bear and produce property; they do not own or possess it.[17] As a result, the cultural practice of naming and valuation as it relates to legacy, inheritance, and origination bears no meaning for black women because, for them, names are merely empty signifiers granted according to a dominant discourse of the Master.[18] In other words, intelligible bodies presuppose and are contingent upon materiality, self-possession, and origination. Thus, black women, within a discourse of slavery, are alienable property as well as unintelligible and ungrammatical.[19] They are objects to be circulated and used that exist outside of a classical configuration of how matter and bodies *as matter* come to mean, originate, and generate.[20] Essentially and historically, then, black women's bodies are the stuff of un-matter.

Black female subjectivity is provocative here precisely because it is "inappropriate/d."[21] By focusing on conditions of black female slavery and Sojourner Truth's iconic transformation and speech "Ain't I a Woman?," black female subjectivity represents a site of figuration for Haraway. This figuration—a performative image—is about apprehending and escaping entrapment to "[reset] the stage for possible pasts and futures" (Haraway 1992, 36). Nameless, fugitive and mobile, sojourning black women, then, carry with them a dangerous, uncolonizable, incomprehensible, and inherent otherness.[22] I position Dana and Mutu's Afro future females in relation to and against this history, spanning the speculative landscape between neo-slave narrative and future text.[23] For if hybrid, boundary-crossing, post-gender subjects are or can be simultaneously human and animal, plant and machine, and black women in the U.S., following Carby, have been historically figured without origin, inheritance, or history, is black womanhood always already cyborgian? That is, under these conditions, black women are both neither and at once animal, human, and sexualized conduit. Therefore, black female subjectivity—its historically unintelligible, ungrammatical, and amorphous nature—is cyborgian in its conception.

## BUTLER AND MUTU'S KINDRED CYBORGS

Mutu's practice of extracting images from a collection of mass-produced publications, from *Vogue* to *National Geographic*, mirrors the very extractions of racialized bodies from "natural" matters of subjectivity discussed above and the dislocation of racial experience from Haraway's posthuman

critique of a false universalism. Her repurposing of found photographic images also speaks to discourses of representation informed by science, religion, ethnography, and other disciplines that historically contributed to a systematic oppression of otherness particular to black female bodies.[24] Indeed,
black female bodies were a central focus of nineteenth-century scientific
studies that often ended in perverse examinations and dissections—Saartje
Baartman, popularly known as the Hottentot Venus, among the most well-
known subjects of these experiments and displays.[25]

Mutu's work represents what Okwui Enwezor terms a "bold interrogation
of historicized forms of racial violence, misogyny, sexual perversion, and the
domination of black bodies."[26] Her collages recall the colonial fetishism that
resulted in Baartman's carnivalesque display and dissection, thus highlighting the literal and figurative violence enacted on Baartman's cadaver in
postmortem examinations. Curator David Moos observes, "By using collage
Mutu infuses her task with a certain violence, cutting and slicing with razor-
like precision. Her composite bodies become a merger of cultural signification, presenting a new hybrid of the female figure by blending distinctions
between parts and whole, face and limb, outside and inside, into writhing
emblems of excess and interpenetration" (Moos 2010, 17). Here, Mutu's
exaggerated, grotesque female forms violate dominant discourses of black
female subjectivity as at once exotic, fetishistic, grotesque, unnatural, diseased, and nonhuman, that is, black female subjectivity as a site of difference
par excellence. Following this claim, Mutu's collage practice acts as a tactic
for rejecting how difference—through historical and discursive violence—is
inscribed on black female bodies.

In keeping with discourses of the body and black female subjectivity, I
turn to Octavia Butler's *Kindred* to think through the image of the ruptured
body in *Non je ne regrette rien*. *Kindred* vividly depicts a contemporary
black woman's fantastical yet transformative encounters with her ancestral
past. On her twenty-sixth birthday Dana, a struggling writer who works odd
jobs at a temporary labor agency that she likens to a slave market, has just
moved into a new house with her white husband Kevin when she begins a
series of time travels between 1976 suburban Los Angeles and antebellum-
era Maryland. During her second trip, Dana realizes she has been transported
to the 1800s to intervene in her own history, to ensure that her direct ancestor
Hagar is born. Essentially, Dana is made responsible for her own production,
her own lived history. Through time travel and encounters with her ancestors, Dana must secure her own existence, an imposed, forcible re-member-
ing that is uncertain, painful, and dangerous.

As *Kindred* unfolds, Dana transforms from passive observer to active
participant in constructing and reconstructing history. Dana comes to terms
with her responsibility to Rufus, heir to the Weylin plantation who will
eventually father Hagar, and acknowledges a resonant dialectic in their rela-

tionship that is animated by gendered power relations. She and Rufus are constituted *through* each other, thus Dana is literally constituted through encounters with her own, initially unknown history. Mutu's figures, as cyborgs, are also constituted through an unknown history or origin, incorporating various image-species from animal to machine to construct new subjects whose very beings are vested in alteration and never resolved. Both cases refuse a synthetic reconciliation of difference, of the alienation produced in the space between "others." However, while Dana's history and origin is eventually known, or in some respects has been known from the outset of her otherworldly journey, the ruptured figure in *Non je ne regrette rien* remains without both origin and closure.

Near the end of *Kindred*, Dana's motivations for her actions "in the past," repeatedly saving Rufus's life and allowing her ancestor Alice to be sexually violated in order to bear her future self by way of Hagar, are hard to parse because of Dana's tenuous relationship to consent. Throughout the novel, Dana refuses to occupy a position of rape, which disjoins Dana's personhood from that of black female slaves as defined in bondage.[27] Moreover, Dana is withheld from networks of kinship that were often considered anchors for enslaved black females in bondage.[28] Twice orphaned, as a child and by her aunt and uncle's disavowal of her interracial marriage, Dana exists within a paradigm of individualism. In many slave narratives and neo-slave narratives informed by Emersonian and Jeffersonian principles of self-reliance and independence within the American literary canon, individualism is a male construct and privilege.[29] With her refusal to occupy conditions of rape, her subsequent removal from a quintessential black female slave experience, and her constructed individualism, Dana elides normative gender constructions of male and female. She is at once both and neither: a cyborg in a postgender world.[30]

Here, her character confuses boundaries and defies essentialist or archetypal conventions of both masculinity *and* femininity. *Kindred* concludes without a tangible resolution; Dana is not restored to wholeness. Like Mutu's collage, she is unresolved, undone. Instead, she is left fragmented yet literally formed by the intersubjective relationships and shared experiences that she now carries with her. Dana's dismembered black female body challenges Western concepts of subjecthood vested in a rhetoric of wholeness by forging not only a *felt* understanding of history but also an enriched self, born out of fragmentation. Dana's felt understanding of history privileges an embodied particularity that reflects the black female slave experience in the United States, an understanding and experience antithetical to an Enlightenment humanism vested in universal rationality. In the cases of Dana and *Non je ne regrette rien*, wholeness is the antinomy of brutalized black female bodies.

Griffin argues that "a discourse of black inferiority . . . stands on 'evidence' derived from cranial measurements and genital mutilation. Through these discourses the black body came to bear specific cultural meanings: These discourses constitute all black people as unsightly, deformed, diseased" (Griffin 1996, 520). Her conclusions resonate in the formations of both Dana's body and Mutu's *Non je ne regrette rien*. Similar to Dana's painful yet improvisatory resourcefulness, Mutu is clearly interested in disrupting normative associations, as evidenced in her image-form inversions, ruptures, and abnormalities. But Mutu's *Non je ne regrette rien* also departs from Dana's reconstituted body. Whereas Dana's "future" existence is formed through her encounters with history—her body literally bears the marks of her "past" experiences—Mutu's figure negates a notion of subjecthood constructed *by and through* history as well as a self and body constructed relationally or *inter*subjectively. From within *Non je ne regrette rien*, Mutu's figure contests the spatial logic of the frame that attempts to contain it. The figure's appendages spill over the edge of the work as the figure appears to hurtle through the gray abyss, a space demarcated and confined by the frame of the image.

Rather than a drive toward wholeness, healing, and a mastery of the self, Mutu's *Non je ne regrette rien* defies Western concepts of wholeness and subjecthood, formally and figuratively. Here, I emphasize that wholeness in and of itself is not the issue; in the context of black women's bodies marked by histories of violence, notions of wholeness are simply untenable. Although fragmentation can be seen as a sign of victimization, *Non je ne regrette rien* upends discursive narratives of black women as ever and only victims, injured and traumatized. For if fragmentation is always already there, Mutu refuses to deny this condition by simultaneously refusing closure. Unlike Griffin's notions of healing and rehabilitation that are focused in and on the body, then, Mutu's project is one of *anti-healing*; the goal is actually to *produce* dismembered bodies. What Griffin calls textual healing of psychic wounds, "the affirming nature of sensual touch" relative to problematic constructions of black female subjectivity suggests an irreconcilable binary between bodies in need of repair and whole bodies (Griffin 1996, 522). For Griffin, healing, though perpetually incomplete, is the operative or ideal recourse for black female bodies in the texts she analyzes. However, for Mutu fragmentation and rupture are both the given conditions and the ends.

## NO, I HAVE NO REGRETS

Mutu's practice brings the mediums of painting and collage, mediums historically dominated by the figurative, into collision, thereby literalizing the symbolic ruptures she activates. In this way, *Non je ne regrette rien* is what curator Hamza Walker describes as a resort to *dis*figuration in order "to deny easy recourse to the body as the locus of an essentialized self" (Walker 2013,

12). Mutu's choices in medium and materials attend to how race and racialized notions of sex and gender have acquired epistemological value within a Western, Eurocentric history of modernity. When looking at *Non je ne regrette rien*, viewers are forced to grapple with the amalgam of images present by bouncing between fracture and reconciliation, dismemberment and reassembly. But in the end, transgressive space in *Non je ne regrette rien* cultivates violation and repulsion, and the formal qualities of collage envelop viewers into a process of deconstruction and disordering. Just as *Kindred*'s narrative resists resolution, Mutu's collages complicate the necessity for conclusion and reconciliation. Instead of a totalizing semblance of order and resolve that is inevitably bound by a Cartesian rhetoric of subject-as-whole, Mutu constructs environments and subjects that exist in systems of counter-order, dis-order, and in-difference.

This chapter concludes with an elaboration on the shared generic traits identified in the aforementioned analysis of *Non je ne regrette rien* and *Kindred*. Cultural theorist Greg Tate claims that black science fiction texts relate "the condition of being alien and alienated . . . to the way in which being black in America is a science fiction experience" (Greg Tate qtd. in Dery 1994, 2008). For Tate, black experience *is* alien experience. In this way, Mutu's *Non je ne regrette rien* and Butler's Dana animate what sociologist Alondra Nelson terms "an appraisal of identity that does not simply look to what is seemingly new about the self . . . but looks backward *and* forward in seeking to provide insights about . . . what was *and* what if" (Nelson 2002, 3–4). *Non je ne regrette rien* and *Kindred* enact a "dialectic between defining oneself in light of ties to one's history and experience and being defined from without (be it in virtual or physical space, by stereotypes or the state)" specific to representations of black female subjectivity (Nelson 2002, 4). Neither nature nor machine nor humanity solely comprise the exploded figure at the center of *Non je ne regrette rien*. All of these elements are present and, at the same time, none are mutually exclusive or constitutive. Therefore, the future text at which we arrive in *Non je ne regrette rien* is one in which blackness, femaleness, and bodily-ness are no longer coterminous, naturally accompanying, or associated. While *Non je ne regrette rien*'s Mylar surface commands our attention, the racialized and gendered corporeality that the work's figure inhabits no longer adheres as container or contained. The black female cyborg body is pushed to its limits.

With her collaged figures, Mutu revises spaces of capital and commerce that have historically figured black female subjects as objects for consumption—from beauty magazines to science pamphlets to anatomy textbooks. Her cyborg figures represent black female bodies constituted through mutualism—uprooted plants, shiny motorcycle parts and all. However, the mutualism visualized in *Non je ne regrette rien* is a parasitic one in which the host body must be dismembered in order to exist. Thus, *Non je ne regrette rien* unhinges the black female body as a locus upon and within which normative racial, gender, and sex codes materialize. Additionally, *Non je ne regrette rien* negates a hegemonic system bolstered by a politics of looking that at once celebrates and institutionally oppresses difference. In a time of digital techno-optimism, techno–determinism, and post-identity discourses, *Non je ne regrette rien* demands that we rethink what it means to be black, woman, and human in the twenty-first century.

*Non je ne regrette rien* represents a key intervention, one that not only undermines a system by which black female bodies in the U.S. have been produced by and through a history of violence that created "natural" racial divisions as well as gender and sex binaries through material means. Mutu's collage also disorders the ways in which black women have become a specific typology involving reservoirs of difference and deviance. The figure in *Non je ne regrette rien* visually explodes and dispenses with the very matter of its black female body. Here, where the question of wholeness comes into even sharper focus. If a condition of corporeal and racialized blackness specific to U.S. black bodies has been one of disempowerment, fragmentation, and dismemberment from the beginning, then what does fragmentation yield?[31] Why not strive for wholeness and healing? Why submit to what equates to a wound rather than a scar?

*Non je ne regrette rien* intervenes into historical and essentialist understandings of black female subjectivity, targeting the black female body as the grounding of these understandings. Wholeness, then, with its foundations in reason, possession, origination, and a pursuit to overcome an alienation that follows from a separation between self and other as routes to full subjecthood, actually becomes oppressive within this formulation. In the "classical" view, the human body is positioned as an immutable foundation for identity formation. But the black female body has been historically withheld from the grammar of identity construction. Thus, in aggressively cracking open the basis—the body—upon which the self and agency come to matter and mean, particularly in the case of black female subjectivity, the ruptured body in *Non je ne regrette rien* insists that we rethink relationality, healing, and becoming.

To this point, rather than offering an escape from oppressive conditions, technology and mechanical parts in *Non je ne regrette rien* fail to protect and reassemble the ruptured black female body. In turn, the subject-object and self-subject splits that anchor myriad humanisms—from Enlightenment to anti to post—are fundamentally obliterated, and dismemberment engenders an evocative epistemology. This is not to suggest that Mutu's work represents a global black womanhood.[32] On the contrary, the individual, ruptured figure in *Non je ne regrette rien* gains more momentum here as it hurtles through space; for it is in the individual figures that proliferate within Mutu's collage practice that uneasy and undesirable expressions of black female

bodies emerge. And these expressions repeat and change, but most importantly, they remain in full view.

## NOTES

1. Nicole R. Smith notes, "[M]uch of Mutu's work[s] . . . often include a central female creature. Sometimes such figures are flanked by smaller and even more fantastical creatures—part fairy, puck, and insect. In some instances, they merely surround the main figure, while in others they take on a more sinister appearance, acting out in devilish ways" (Smith, "Wangechi Mutu: Feminist Collage and the Cyborg," *Art and Design Theses* Paper 51 (2009), 13). A portion of the left side of the female figure in *Non je regrette rien* is flanked by a serpent. For the purposes of this chapter, I focus on the central female figure in *Non je regrette rien* in order to underscore the intervention into representing black female bodies that my reading of Mutu's collage entails.

2. A portion of this chapter was presented at the 35th Anniversary Conference of the Simone de Beauvoir Institute at Concordia University in April 2013 in Montréal, Québec. Special thanks to my colleague Rachel Zellars for the many conversations that helped me clarify this notion of "transgressive disfigurement."

3. Haraway first published "A Cyborg Manifesto" as "Manifesto for Cyborgs: Science, Technology, and Socialist Feminism in the 1980s" in *Socialist Review* 80 (1985): 65–108.

4. Literary scholars Madhu Dubey and Sherryl Vint offer detailed discussions of how conventions of the genre of science fiction center on a Cartesian subjecthood rooted in wholeness. See Dubey's "Becoming Animal" in *Afro-Future Females: Black Writers Chart Science Fiction's Newest New-Wave Trajectory*, Ed. Marleen S. Barr (Columbus, OH: The Ohio State University Press, 2008) and Vint's *Bodies of Tomorrow: Technology, Subjectivity, Science Fiction* (Toronto: University of Toronto Press, 2007).

5. Janell Hobson is among a growing group of scholars who take Haraway's conceptions of the cyborg's liberatory possibilities to task for their blind spots concerning the intersectional and historical conditions of black female bodies. See *Body as Evidence: Mediating Race, Globalizing Gender* (Albany, NY: SUNY Press, 2012).

6. The title of Mutu's collage instantly alerts the viewer to the artist's interests in a politics of armed resistance, particularly within Algeria's postcolonial history. "Non, je ne regrette rien," meaning "No, I have no regrets," is a French song composed by Charles Dumont in 1956 with lyrics by Michel Vaucaire. It was made famous by Édith Piaf who dedicated her 1960 recording of the song to the French Foreign Legion. At the time of the recording, France was engaged in the Algerian War of Independence (1954–1962) and the 1st Foreign Parachute Regiment—which was disbanded after backing a failed putsch by the French military against the civilian leadership of Algeria in 1961—adopted the song when their resistance was broken. The song is part of French Foreign Legion heritage and is sung when the Legion appear in Camerone Day parades. The song's title and Mutu's appropriation of it to name her image of a fragmented, dislocated figure marks multiple meanings: French colonial history in Africa, decolonial and postcolonial conditions, the failure of the French Foreign Legion's role in a coup d'état, and the complex networks of alliance and dissent that eventually led to Algeria's independence from France. Historian Alexander Harrison offers a brief discussion of the significance of Piaf's recording within French Foreign Legion history in *Challenging de Gaulle: The O.A.S. and the Counterrevolution in Algeria, 1954–1962* (New York, NY; London, UK: Praeger Publishers, 1989). Harrison's text outlines French colonization of Algeria and the roots of the counter-revolution, with chapters on the three abortive efforts to grant native Algerians their independence and the subsequent emergence of the Organisation de l'armée secrète (O.A.S. or "Secret Armed Organization").

7. Art historian Courtney J. Martin situates Mutu's use of collage as a vehicle for theorizing the fragmented body as a metaphor for a postcolonial body politic. In "Fracture and Action: Wangechi Mutu's Collages, 1999–2010" she writes, "Analogous to collage, the composite nature of the nation is always on display despite the insistence on fluid cohesion. The nation is

always making itself as it is being remade" (50). While Martin's reading of Mutu's collage technique is certainly compelling and points to larger conversations around postmodernism and postcolonialism, I would like to interrogate the implications of Martin's relation between actual bodies and postcolonial nationhood. Mutu's work challenges systems of representation by which the black female body has become what performance artist and critic David Harradine describes as "a locus for complex processes of ideological construction that materialise the body itself in and through discourse, and that reveal the body as only the apparent base from which notions of 'identity' (such as 'race,' 'sex,' 'gender,' 'class,' or 'sexuality') can be read" (69). While Mutu's practice of fragmentation can certainly be read as mirroring the postmodern condition, instead of reflecting compositions of nations Mutu's collages also offer an ontological model of resistance vested in intersubjectivity. Instead of disabled bodies, her hybrid figures are adaptors and adaptations, mutations of normalized ideals of femininity, beauty, and sexuality. For Martin's essay; rigorous contextualization of Mutu's collage practice in relationship to Hannah Höch, Romare Bearden, and other artists who have used collage to explore issues of difference; and more on the formal qualities of Mutu's work, see *My Dirty Little Heaven*, Exh. Cat. (Deutsche Guggenheim Berlin; Ostfildern, DE: Hatje Cantz, 2010). See also David Harradine's "Abject Identities and Fluid Performances: Theorizing the Leaking Body" in *Contemporary Theatre Review* 10, 3 (2000): 69–85.

8. Mutu quoted in Okwui Enwezor's "Cut and Paste: Interview with Wangechi Mutu," *Arise Magazine* 11 (2011) http://www.ariselive.com/articles/cut-paste/87416/. Accessed 27 March 2014. Mutu's emphasis on invention parallels Hortense Spillers's opening lines in "Mama's Baby, Papa's Maybe." Spillers opens her essay "Mama's Baby, Papa's Maybe: An American Grammar Book," first published in *Diacritics* 17, 2 (1987), with the following: "Let's face it. I am a marked woman, but not everybody knows my name. . . . I describe a locus of confounded identities, a meeting ground of investments and privations in the national treasury of rhetorical wealth. My country needs me, and if I were not here, I would have to be invented" (*Black, White, and in Color*, 2003).

9. *Amazing Grace*, a 59-minute looped video work filmed in Miami, Florida, follows the artist dressed in a flowing white dress as she walks slowly along the sandy shores of the Atlantic Ocean singing "Amazing Grace" in Kikuyu with Mutu eventually disappearing into the sea. Although sung in her native language, the intertextual reference of "Amazing Grace" as both the work's title and sonic framing device, a hymnal still sung today that became an emblematic Negro spiritual in late-nineteenth century America, comments on the loss of life at sea on slave ships traveling to "the New World." It is significant that Mutu performs these actions from the edges of the U.S.'s land mass. Mutu's inclusion in the exhibition *30 Americans*, a traveling group show of select works by African-American artists held by the Rubell Family Collection, further situates Mutu and her work within a black American context.

10. See W. E. B. Du Bois's "Criteria of Negro Art," *The Crisis* 32 (October 1926), 290–97 in which Du Bois demands that all art, and in particular "black art," be seen and understood as propaganda that services a program of racial pride and uplift.

11. Margo Natalie Crawford and Lisa Gail Collins have recently published on deferred readings of the Black Arts Movement. Additionally, Crawford's ongoing research expands the limits of how we think about the Black Arts Movement as a failed, finished, and narrow project. See *New Thoughts on the Black Arts Movement*, eds. Margo Natalie Crawford and Lisa Gail Collins (Rutgers, NJ: Rutgers University Press, 2006); Crawford's "Black Aesthetics Unbound," *Nka: Journal of Contemporary African Art* 29 (Fall 2011), 8-21; and Crawford's "Baraka's Jam Session: On the Limits of Any Attempt to Collect *Black Aesthetics Unbound*," Callaloo 37, 3 (Summer 2014), 477–79.

12. Thelma Golden, "Post . . . ," *Freestyle*, Exh. Cat. (New York: The Studio Museum of Harlem, 2001), 14. *Freestyle* was presented at The Studio Museum in Harlem in 2001 and featured work by 28 contemporary black artists. The first in an ongoing series of survey exhibitions of contemporary black art at The Studio Museum under Golden's direction, *Freestyle* has since been followed by *Frequency* (2005), *Flow* (2008), and *Fore* (2012). It is important to note that there is at least one instance in which the term post-black enters art historical and scholarly discourse prior to Golden's proclamation. In "Afro Modernism," a September 1991 *Artforum* review of *Africa Explores: 20th Century African Art*, Robert Farris

Thompson writes, "A retelling of Modernism to show how it predicts the triumph of the current sequences would reveal that 'the Other' is your neighbor—that black and Modernist cultures were inseparable long ago. Why use the word 'post-Modern' when it may also mean 'post-black'?" (91). While Thompson's review appears to be the first published use of the now pervasive term, Thompson's use of post-black differs from current iterations of the term.

13. The phrase "burdens of representation" refers to how black artists and their production are enmeshed in a metonymic relation with black identity, contributing to essentialist understandings of blackness. That is, art made by black artists becomes representative of a totality of black aesthetics and representative of larger understandings of black experience and black identity. As a result of the burdens of representation, black artists can only be conceived of as making "black art," and only black artists can produce "black art." See Kobena Mercer's "Black Art and the Burden of Representation," *Third Text* 4, 10 (1990), 61–78.

14. See Cinqué Hicks's "Circuit Jamming" in *International Review of African American Art* 23, 3 (June 2011, 2–8) for an overview of how monolithic and fraught understandings of blackness between the 1960s and 1980s have shifted from Afrofuturism as a route to political solidarity (that, with the development of funk and psychedelic soul emerged alongside the Black Arts Movement) to the term's current manifestations.

15. Janell Hobson is among a growing group of scholars who take Haraway's conceptions of the cyborg's liberatory possibilities to task for their blind spots concerning the intersectional and historical conditions of black female bodies. See Hobson's *Body as Evidence: Mediating Race, Globalizing Gender* (Albany, NY: SUNY Press, 2012).

16. Haraway, "Ecce Homo, Ain't (Ar'n't) I a Woman, and Inappropriate/d Others: the Human in a Posthumanist Landscape" in *Feminists Theorize the Political*, Eds. Joan Scott and Judith Butler (New York, NY; London, UK: Routledge, 1992): 93–94. See also Hazel V. Carby's "Slave and Mistress: Ideologies of Womanhood under Slavery," *Reconstructing Black Womanhood: The Emergence of the Afro-American Woman Novelist* (New York, NY; Oxford, UK: Oxford University Press, 1987): 20–39 and Hortense J. Spillers's "Mama's Baby, Papa's Maybe: An American Grammar Book" in *Diacritics* 17, 2 (1987).

17. To be clear, white women during the years of slavery did not legally own property, except in the rare cases that they inherited it from a male relative or spouse. But, following Carby, I draw a distinction between black and white women here in order to show how black women's persons and subjecthoods were in question given the fact that they existed outside of the category of "woman." Even more radically, black women existed outside of the category of human. They were considered property, subjectless and without gender, even if over-sexualized, a drastically different mode of existence compared to white women.

18. I would like to acknowledge the students in my Fall 2013 Afro Future Females course at the University of Rochester, especially Quinlan Mitchell, for illuminating discussions and responses that helped me finesse my thinking here around a certain lineage of black female cyborg identities.

19. I use the terms ungrammatical here and grammar in the title of this essay to refer to Hortense J. Spillers's theorizations of black female subjectivity in relation to language and the law. Like Spillers, I aim to propose a new semantic field in which to discuss and understand black female subjectivity by theorizing rupture and fragmentation as productive epistemologies in themselves. Haraway also invokes Spillers's theorizations of the ungrammatical ("Ecce Homo" 92). Spillers opens "Mama's Baby, Papa's Maybe: An American Grammar Book," first published in *Diacritics* 17, 2 (1987), with the following: "Let's face it. I am a marked woman, but not everybody knows my name. . . . I describe a locus of confounded identities, a meeting ground of investments and privations in the national treasury of rhetorical wealth. My country needs me, and if I were not here, I would have to be invented" (203). See Spillers's collection of essays titled *Black, White, and in Color: Essays on American Literature and Culture* (Chicago, IL; London, UK: University of Chicago Press, 2003).

20. Judith Butler traces this classical relation of materiality and meaning to Greek and Latin origins. She writes, "The classical configuration of matter as a site of *generation* or *origination* becomes especially significant when the account of what an object is and means requires recourse to its originating principle" (*Bodies That Matter* 31; emphasis in original). For Butler, matter is either associated with reproduction or origination and causality. See Judith Butler's

*Bodies That Matter: On the Discursive Limits of "sex"* (New York, NY; London, UK: Routledge, 1993).

21. Haraway borrows theorist Trinh T. Minh-ha's sign of an impossible figure, the inappropriate/d other, to describe "New World black womanhood" ("Ecce Homo" 91). See Trinh T. Minh-ha's "She, the Inappropriate/d Other," *Discourse* 8 (1986/87).

22. Special thanks to Quinlan Mitchell for this beautiful articulation that helped me bridge my thinking around the cyborg and black womanhood.

23. Alondra Nelson develops the phrase "future text" after author Ishmael Reed's *Mumbo Jumbo* character PaPa LaBas. Nelson writes, "LaBas believes that the next generation will be successful in creating a text that can codify black culture: past, present, and future. Rather than a 'Western' image of the future that is increasingly detached from the past or, equally problematic, a future-primitive perspective that fantasizes an uncomplicated return to ancient culture, LaBas foresees the distillation of African diasporic experience, rooted in the past but not weighed down by it, contiguous yet continually transformed" ("Introduction: Future Texts" 8).

24. Social Darwinism as a theory of evolution formed a foundation for scientific examination of racial, gender, and sexual difference. Social Darwinism spawned such studies as phrenology, physiognomy, and racial eugenics among others, which informed pictorial representations of bodies in the United States—particularly in relation to a practice of photography at the turn of the twentieth century. Through these modes of study, typologies of race, gender, and class enter a broader discussion around a history of producing subjects and stereotypes informed by photography in terms of idealized and de-idealized body types. See Elizabeth Edwards' *Anthropology and Photography 1860–1920* (New Haven, CT: Yale University Press, 1994) and John Tagg's *Burden of Representation: Essays on Photographies and Histories* (Minneapolis, MN: University of Minnesota Press, 1993). For an in-depth comparative study of how black subjectivity throughout the African diaspora was constructed and subjugated through nineteenth century American and European intellectual thought as well as contemporary counter-discourses, see Michelle M. Wright's *Becoming Black: Creating Identity in the African Diaspora* (Durham, NC; London, UK: Duke University Press, 2004).

25. For a comprehensive history of how the pseudoscience of eugenics and social Darwinism was used to justify experimental exploitation and shoddy medical treatment of black bodies with the view that they were biologically inferior, oversexed, and unfit, see Harriet A. Washington's *Medical Apartheid: The Dark History of Medical Experimentation on Black Americans from Colonial Times to the Present* (New York, NY: Anchor Books, 2008). Also see Mara Gladstone and Janet Berlo's "The Body in the (White) Box: Corporeal Ethics and Museum Representation" in *The Routledge Companion to Museum Ethics: Redefining Ethics for the Twenty-First Century Museum* (New York, NY: Routledge, 2012) and Sadiah Qureshi's "Displaying Sara Baartman, the Hottentot Venus," *History of Science* 42 (2004). On cultural taxidermy see Fatimah Tobing Rony's *The Third Eye: Race, Cinema, and Ethnographic Spectacle* (Durham, NC: Duke University Press, 1996) and Tony Bennett's "The Exhibitionary Complex," *New Formations* 4 (Spring 1988), 73–102.

26. Okwui Enwezor, "Weird Beauty: Ritual Violence and Archaeology of Mass Media in Wangechi Mutu's Work" in *My Dirty Little Heaven*, Exh. Cat. (Deutsche Guggenheim Berlin; Ostfildern, DE: Hatje Cantz, 2010).

27. Farah Jasmine Griffin identifies sexual abuse and rape as primary reasons for textual healing and Dana resists these conditions of the black female slave experience.

28. In *Incidents in the Life of a Slave Girl* (1861), Harriet Jacobs's choice of a sexual relationship with Mr. Sands and her decision to hide in bondage in order to stay close to her children forces re-conceptualizations of agency, consent, freedom, and resistance. Though Jacobs chooses to remain in conditions of bondage, Jacobs experiences instances of freedom within this bondage and Jacob's formulations of self are constructed intrasubjectively; that is, through Jacobs's social networks, relations, and attachments rather than through a master-slave relation.

29. Individualism through mobility and flight as means of escape and freedom are figured as gendered tropes in *Narrative of the Life of Frederick Douglass* (1845), *Narrative of William W. Brown, a Fugitive Slave* (1847), *Narrative of the Life and Adventures of Henry Bibb, an American Slave* (1849), *Narrative of the Life of J. D. Green, a Runaway Slave from Kentucky*

(1964), and other male-centered slave narratives. In these narratives, male slaves have liberties to flee and visit other plantations that differ from female slaves who are obligated to mother-hood. The pursuit of freedom through Emersonian self-reliance requires a rejection or negation of family. See Ralph Waldo Emerson's "Self-Reliance" in *Essays: First Series* (1847).

30. While Dana's suspension between gendered identities in this scene could be read as queer rather than post-gender, I assert that this suspension follows my arguments regarding the significant, shifting, mutable relationship between technology and the body as sign, as well as historical constructions of black female subjectivity in the U.S. as always already cyborgian. While post-gender and queer identities share a politics of choice, I distinguish between the two for the purposes of this essay by considering post-gender identities in relation to histories of science and biological reproduction and, following scholars such as Judith Butler and others, I consider queer identities in relation to performativity. In a 2008 essay, bioethicists George Dvorsky and James Hughes extend Haraway's theorizations of post-gender cyborgs. Dvorsky and Hughes explain, "Postgenderism is an extrapolation of ways that technology is eroding the biological, psychological and social role of gender, and an argument for why the erosion of binary gender will be liberatory. . . . Postgenderists contend that dyadic gender roles and sexual dimorphisms are generally to the detriment of individuals and society. . . . Greater biological fluidity and psychological androgyny will allow future persons to explore both masculine and feminine aspects of personality. . . . Bodies and personalities in our postgender future will no longer be constrained and circumscribed by gendered traits, but enriched by their use in the palette of diverse self-expression" (2). See Dvorsky and Hughes's "Postgenderism: Beyond the Gender Binary" (Hartford, CT: Institute for Ethics and Emerging Technologies, March 2008): 1–18, http://ieet.org/archive/IEET-03-PostGender.pdf. Accessed 20 October 2013. On gender theory and performativity, see Judith Butler's *Gender Trouble: Feminism and the Subversion of Identity* (New York, NY; London, UK: Routledge, 1990) and *Bodies That Matter: On the Discursive Limits of "Sex"* (New York, NY; London, UK: Routledge, 1993).

31. Similar to both Carby's and Spillers's theorizations of the relations between black wom-anhood, language, and humanist thought, a protagonist in Ishmael Reed's *Flight to Canada* named Raven Quickskill describes literacy under conditions of slavery as "the most powerful thing in the pre-technological pre-post-rational age" (35). Literary scholar Thomas Foster reads Quickskill's commentary as a summation of "the different historical relation of African slaves [in the 'New World'] to Enlightenment humanism and its investment in universal rationality as opposed to embodied particularity" (*The Souls of Cyberfolk* xxv). Foster's reading translates the "pre-post-rational" into the "pre-post-human," which "signifies a shortcircuiting of the narrative teleology of the romantic subject, which exists first as an alienated and privatized—that is pre-social—individual, and only subsequently comes into contact with either society or nature as external to the self" (Ibid). Conversely in *Non je ne regrette rien*, the figure is already connected with alien experience, society, nature, and machine all in one. See Foster's *The Souls of Cyberfolk: Posthumanism as Vernacular Theory* (Minneapolis, MN; London, UK: University of Minnesota Press, 2005).

32. While this essay positions Mutu's *Non je ne regrette rien* within an American context, and uses it as a lens through which to view and understand black female subjectivity in the U.S., Mutu's work also bears relations to African mythology. For a brief discussion of African mythology and African futurism as political methodologies and rhetorical strategies, see Pamela Phatsimo Sunstrum's "Afro-mythology and African Futurism: The Politics of Imagining and Methodologies for Contemporary Creative Research Practices" in *Para-doxa: Studies in World Literary Genres* 25 (2013), 119–36. Born in Mochudi, Botswana, Phatsimo Sunstrum is also a celebrated artist who, similar to Mutu, works in drawing, collage, animation, and performance to imagine parallels between ancient mythologies and futuristic sciences. Phastimo Sunstrum has an alter ego named Asme.

# REFERENCES

Butler, Judith. 1993. *Bodies that matter: On the discursive limits of "sex."* New York, NY: London, UK: Routledge.

————.1990. *Gender trouble: Feminism and the subversion of identity.* New York, NY; London, UK: Routledge.

Butler, Octavia E. [1988] 2004. *Kindred.* Boston, MA: Beacon Press.

Carby, Hazel V. 1987. *Reconstructing black womanhood: The emergence of the Afro-American woman novelist.* New York, NY; Oxford, UK: Oxford University Press.

Dery, Mark, ed. 1994. *Flame wars: The discourse of cyberculture.* Durham, NC: Duke University Press.

Dvorsky, George and James Hughes. Postgenderism: Beyond the gender binary. Hartford, CT: Institute for Ethics and Emerging Technologies (March, 2008): 1–18. http://ieet.org/archive/IEET-03-PostGender.pdf. Accessed October 20, 2013.

Edwards, Elizabeth. 1994. *Anthropology and photography 1860–1920.* New Haven, CT: Yale University Press.

English, Darby. 2007. *How to see a work of art in total darkness.* Cambridge, MA: MIT Press.

Enwezor, Okwui, ed. 2010. *Wangechi Mutu: My dirty little Heaven.* Exh. Cat. Deutsche Guggenheim Berlin; Ostfildern, DE: Hatje Cantz.

Eshun, Kodwo. Further considerations of Afrofuturism. *CR: The New Centennial Review* 3, no. 2 (2003): 287–302.

Foster, Thomas. 2005. *The souls of cyberfolk: Posthumanism as vernacular theory.* Minneapolis, MN; London, UK: University of Minnesota Press.

Golden, Thelma. 2001. Post . . . *Freestyle,* Exhibition. Cat. New York: The Studio Museum of Harlem.

Griffin, Farah Jasmine. Textual healing: Claiming black women's bodies, the erotic and resistance in contemporary novels of slavery. *Callaloo: A Journal of African-American and African Arts and Letters* 19 (1996): 519–36.

Haraway, Donna J. 1991. *Simians, cyborgs and women: The reinvention of nature.* New York, NY: Routledge.

Harradine, David. Abject identities and fluid performances: Theorizing the leaking body. *Contemporary Theatre Review* 10, no. 3 (2000): 69–85.

Harrison, Alexander. 1989. *Challenging de Gaulle: The O.A.S. and the counterrevolution in Algeria, 1954–1962.* New York, NY; London, UK: Praeger Publishers.

Kilgore, De Witt Douglas. 2003. *Astrofuturism: Science, race, and visions of utopia in space.* Philadelphia, PA: University of Pennsylvania Press.

Lavender, Isiah, III. 2011. *Race in American science fiction.* Bloomington, IN: Indiana University Press.

Moos, David, ed. 2010. *Wangechi Mutu: This you call civilization?* Exh. Cat. Toronto, ON: Art Gallery of Ontario.

Mutu, Wangechi. 2005. Quoted in Soraya and Derek Conrad Murray's A Rising Generation and the Pleasures of Freedom. In *International Review of African American Art* 20, 2, 8.

Nama, Adilifu. 2008. *Black space: Imagining race in science fiction.* Austin, TX: University of Texas Press.

Nelson, Alondra, ed. *Afrofuturism,* Special Issue of *Social Text* 71, 20, no. 2 (2002).

Rieder, John. 2008. *Colonialism and the emergence of science fiction.* Middletown, CT: Wesleyan University Press.

Rushdy, Ashraf H. A. 1999. *Neo-slave narratives: Studies in the social logic of a literary form.* New York, NY; Oxford, UK: Oxford University Press.

Spillers, Hortense J. 2003. *Black, white, and in color: Essays on American literature and culture.* Chicago, IL; London, UK: University of Chicago Press.

Tagg, John. 1993. *Burden of representation: Essays on photographies and histories.* Minneapolis, MN: University of Minnesota Press.

Vint, Sherryl. 2007. *Bodies of tomorrow: Technology, subjectivity, science fiction.* Toronto, ON; Buffalo, NY: University of Toronto Press.

Walker, Hamza. 2013. Introduction: Domino Effect. In *Black Is, Black Ain't.* Chicago, IL: The Renaissance Society at the University of Chicago, 12.

Wright, Charles A., Jr. 2012. The mythology of difference: Vulgar identity politics at the Whitney Biennial. In *Theory in contemporary art since 1985,* Second Edition, eds. Zoya Kocur and Simon Leung. New York, NY: Wiley-Blackwell.

Wright, Michelle M. 2004. *Becoming Black: Creating identity in the African Diaspora.* Durham, NC: Duke University Press.

*Chapter Two*

# Afrofuturism on Web 3.0

*Vernacular Cartography and Augmented Space*

## Nettrice R. Gaskins

Afrofuturism fosters the artistic practice of navigating the past, present, and future simultaneously (Dery 1994). The use of quilts as maps along the Underground Railroad is one such example. Artist Sanford Biggers refers to Railroad conductor Harriet Tubman as an astronaut who traverses "the south to the north by navigating the stars."[1] Biggers reconstructs eighteenth and nineteenth century historical quilts as maps to new galaxies where passengers chart new destinations in search of freedom. The idea of Tubman as an astronaut is a good starting point for examining our relationship to the boundless dimensions of space in which people, objects, and events have relative position and direction. Tubman followed the North Star by night, making her way from the South, to and from Pennsylvania and Canada while guiding others to freedom. Passengers followed codes embedded in quilts hanging in front of the safe houses with symbols telling them where to go and when the next "train" would come. These quilt-based maps may be viewed as cultural or vernacular space that emanate from the customs and rituals of a given community.

Like many works in Afrofuturism, coded quilts are somewhere between myth and fact. Quilt codes consisted of basic shapes arranged in specific patterns to represent trails, the North Star, safe houses, and other landmarks. As vernacular maps, these artifacts are reduced representations of the physical world. The codes are similar to the symbols displayed on a Global Positioning System (GPS) or on Google Earth, a virtual map and geographical information program. Imagine that, in an alternate reality, Underground Railroad conductors and passengers used mobile phones with cameras that when pointed at coded quilts obtained information as augmented, digital overlay images.

Augmented or layered space offers us new ways to map, view, encode, or decode traditional cultural systems and symbols with dynamically changing information, sometimes digital in form and closely linked with the development of a techno-cultural network. This network is matched with vernacular to illustrate spoken, aural, or visual languages in physical and virtual spaces in this chapter. Geometric cultural maps, geographic locations, and digital media on mobile devices chart the movement, migration, or dispersal of people who share and exchange cultural data. These technologies do not exhaust the possibilities of vernacular space as the interaction of modern science, media and communication, and cultural art.

This chapter considers whether in the new media spaces, traditional or ancient African symbols and forms become irrelevant and invisible or if artists end up creating new experiences in which the cultural, spatial, and information layers are equally important. It presents creative works that explore the general dynamic between cultural data and creative expression and how this interaction might function differently in today's digital culture. Vernacular cartography and segmented space is reconceptualized as an idea, or as a cultural and aesthetic practice rather than as emerging or new technology. I make a distinction between *augmented space* as a new sensibility in creative and cultural production and *augmented reality*, which is the overlaying of digital objects onto the physical environment, viewed through camera-enabled mobile devices. This chapter proposes a new platform to engage this emerging sensibility and technology. Creative practices in mapping African cosmography, physical and virtual installations, film/video, and twenty-first century art are discussed in terms of their relation to Afrofuturism.

## BLACK FUTURISM: RACE AS TECHNOLOGY

According to scholar Patrick Manning, black culture "renews itself repeatedly through new technology, new audiences, improvisation, and continued borrowing" (Manning 2010, 34). Other scholars have explored the cultural and historical underpinnings of black vernacular and creative expression, especially as it relates to technology. Beth Coleman argues that technology's embedded function of self-extension may be exploited to liberate race from an inherited position of abjection toward a greater expression of agency (Coleman 2009). According to Coleman this function entails "the ability to move freely as a being—and it is not restricted to individuals but also includes systems: it concerns how beings are subjected in systems of power, ideology, and other networks (Coleman 2009, 70). She frames the work of twentieth century Italian Futurists who attempted to destroy Western icons and replace them with altered systems through sound, images, or text. In this reconceptualization of technology, race becomes "denatured" from its historical roots and becomes a tool for creative expression.

James Snead differentiated European artistic practices such as Italian Futurism from black cultural expression that he organized around two key principles, repetition and the "cut":

> In black culture, the thing (the ritual, the dance, the beat) is "there for you to pick it up when you come back to get it." If there is a goal in such a culture, it is always deferred; it continually "cuts" back to the start, in the musical meaning of "cut" as an abrupt, seemingly unmotivated break (an accidental da capo) with a series already in progress and a willed return to a prior series. (Snead 1984, 67)

Snead's work supports evolving modes of black techno-vernacular production—signs of change that are evident and cyclical in the art of the African Diaspora. Repetition, through techniques such as collage, sampling, and remixing, employ the "cut" as a tool to reuse portions of one or more sources as instruments and images in new work.

Artists explore how what is cut away (as a subject) from dominant culture finds its way back into the picture through layering and repetition—the transformation through language and signification—and cutting that enable artists of the African Diaspora to piece together fragments from their past of historical emigration (forced relocation), violence, and marginalization. The "cut" of blackness and the silhouette that remain are mobile, able to be collaged or layered with other things or repeated. For example, Kenyan-born artist Wangechi Mutu pieces together magazine imagery with painted surfaces and found materials to explore the split nature of cultural identity referencing colonial history, fashion, and contemporary African politics. She uses the term "augment" to describe her process of altering, disrupting, and layering images.[2]

Improvisation, call and response, hacking, and tinkering elicit the active engagement and participation of the at-large community (audience). Call and response is a form of spontaneous verbal and non-verbal interaction between speaker and listeners in which all statements (calls) are punctuated by expressions (responses) from the audience. Riffs, vamps, thematic variations, and call and response are endemic to jazz, blues music, and the visual arts. In a Johns Hopkins University study, researchers who examined the neuroscience of jazz and the power of improvisation found that the brains of jazz musicians participating in spontaneous improvisation with other musicians showed robust activation in the same areas of the brain traditionally associated with spoken language and syntax (Limb and Braun 2008). We hear these syntactic and semantic exchanges in the music of John Coltrane and Sun Ra (Rudolph 2010). In sum, combined with repetition and cutting, improvisation in music, art, and performance contributes to techno-cultural shifts that lead to the technoscape of Afrofuturism.

## AFROFUTURISM AND TECHNO-VERNACULAR CREATIVITY

Afrofuturism is not a black version of the early twentieth century Italian futurism since it is not solely concerned with the future. Instead, Afrofuturism navigates past, present, and future simultaneously. Afrofuturism is counter-hegemonic and not concerned with representing the mainstream or the canon of Western art. Afrofuturism advocates for the revision of accepted, long-standing views, theories, historical events, and movements. It retells history, altering characters and/or the environment by re-using existing artifacts, themes, and concepts such as quilt-based signposts, star charts, and even the heliocentric model of the universe. One such example of vernacular mapping is found on the cover of Sun Ra's 1965 album, *The Heliocentric Worlds of Sun Ra, Volume One.* The album cover references heliocentric theory in which jazz musician and cosmic philosopher Sun Ra (Ra being the Kemetic/ Egyptian god of the sun) positions himself at the center of other known Western cosmic philosophers and scientists.

Sanford Biggers defines Afrofuturism as "a way of re-contextualizing and assessing history and imagining the future of the African Diaspora via science, science fiction, technology, sound, architecture, the visual and culinary arts and other more nimble and interpretive modes of research and understanding" (Sanford Biggers quoted in Castro 2012, 124). Afrofuturism unleashes what theorist Arjun Appadurai identifies as the social imaginary, specifically a "technoscape" that embraces the "semantic, cultural, and creative aspects of science and technology" (1996, 31). In Afrofuturism, the technoscape is sustained through techno-vernacular creativity, and by extension, the cultural art and technology produced by African diaspora communities. Such work accepts that technological meaning is culturally and historically grounded and, as a result, becomes located within a larger social imaginary. Afrofuturism then, is an antecedent for techno-vernacular creative production. such as do-it-yourself (DIY) techno culture and the merging of cultural and religious traditions as in the case of syncretism, all of which highlight the interconnectedness of seemingly disparate practices.

Techno-vernacular creativity consists of three methods. The first, reappropriation, describes how Afrofuturists reclaim cultural artifacts, often to counter dominant social or political systems. Artists in the African Diaspora reclaim and adapt traditional symbols and systems such as the cosmogram that is a cultural map of the Universe. This universal cultural glyph represents the cycle of life, or a crossroad between the spiritual and material worlds. The second method, improvisation, is the practice of performing, creating, problem solving, or reacting in the moment and in response to one's environment and inner feelings. Improvisation results in the invention of new practices, artwork, and/or new ways of acting. Reinvention (of the self) is the third method. Identity refers to the self or essential being of a person. Artists often question commonly held assumptions and stereotypes, self-awareness, portraiture, and what it means to be an artist in their work. Sun Ra came up with the term "myth science" to explain how to re-create oneself in a place of oppression.[3] Sun Ra explored reinvention of identity through the creation of an alternate personality or avatar. Afrofuturists often use digital and non-digital avatars as tools for transcendence, reinvention, or for existing in and moving between worlds or realities.

Rayvon Fouché, a cultural historian of technology, formulated the concept of "black vernacular technological creativity," otherwise referred to here as techno-vernacular creativity (2006). Fouché references James Brown's 1969 musical anthem "Say It Loud, I'm Black and I'm Proud" as representative of the African American desire to reclaim, recover, and articulate self-claimed black identity and expression. Fouché references the late author and critic Amiri Baraka's prescient 1971 essay "Technology and Ethos" as initiating the conversation about vernacular space. Baraka called for African Americans to rethink their relationships with technology and take action to make technology more representative of their culture. He further asserted that through black technological utterances rooted within black cultures and communities, technology would be more responsive to the realities of black life in Western societies (Baraka 1971, 157). Artist and scholar Duane Deterville further builds upon this contention by drawing on "continental African cultural ethos, contemporary technology, and artistic actuation in a self-determined, representational space" that he describes as the Afriscape.[4]

Fouché describes black vernacular technological as re-deployment (reappropriation), re-conception (improvisation), and re-creation (reinvention) as a basis for creativity and innovation. Re-deployment reinterprets technology while maintaining its traditional use and form, such as using the Twitter social networking platform, otherwise known as "Black Twitters," to focus on interests of African American communities. According to a 2013 Pew Research Center report, twenty-six percent of African American Internet users tweet compared to fourteen percent of non-Hispanic white American, online users (Duggan and Brenner 2013). Reappropriation counters the hegemonic practice of reabsorbing vernacular into mass culture through commodification. Twitter hash tags #SolidarityIsForWhiteWomen and #BlackPowerIsForBlackMen encouraged many users to engage in conversations about how ideologies such as feminism often omit the voices of women of color. Through the reappropriation of online social networking, Black Twitterers have redeployed the participatory Web 2.0 platform as a communication tool more representative of black culture. Re-conception is the active redefinition of technology that transgresses its designed function and dominant meaning. DIY techno culture and aesthetics reflect the myriad social and cultural factors that shape access to technological resources. In African American and other historically marginalized communities, production reflects creativity and innovation within settings of limited technological resources. Brenda Dixon Gottschild asserts that "African American culture has always been subversive and improvisatory, by force of circumstance" (Gottschild 1996, 117). Black speculative fiction writer Octavia Butler's novels re-conceptualize notions of utopia that hinge on the belief that the progress of technology serves to advance society to a state absent of inequality. Afropunk is a multigenre platform for the African American experience and DIY technoculture is a foundation. Artist Cyrus Kabiru crafts Afrofuturistic pieces—most famously his one-of-a-kind "C-STUNNERS" spectacles—from recycled waste and objects he finds on the streets of Nairobi, Kenya. For "Blossom"—a lifesized tree constructed with a piano emerging from it—Sanford Biggers reconceptualizes the piano and programs it using a MIDI controller to play his improvisation of "Strange Fruit," an anti-lynching protest song made popular by the Blues singer Billie Holiday. Kabiru and Biggers utilize the DIY method of "making do" with found materials to create their artwork. Blossom and other examples demonstrate Afrofuturistic re-conception of and DIY improvisation with technology in ways that mirror the past and present.

DIY improvisation within the African Diaspora through music and dance is both culturally and historically significant. Yet, questions remain about improvisation through other art forms such as visual and performance with coding (programming). Many followers of Afrofuturism find the idea of coding and the re-purposing, remixing, or sampling of existing content intriguing. Passengers on the Underground Railroad looked for keys embedded in quilts to ascertain information to lead them to freedom. Artist and writer Judy Bales views the Afro-traditional quilt as a type of vernacular map that qualifies both as a contemporary art, as well as a functional object (Bales 2012). Sanford Biggers re-purposes quilts using cultural, historical, astrological, and musical visualizations. In conceiving the artworks that compromise his "Codex" series, Biggers sees himself as an intervener hundreds of years after historical quilts have been made who in the next phase, adds new layers of coded meaning.[5] The encoding and confluence of visual elements in his quilts ranging from cloud forms in Tibetan art, as a graphic device in early graffiti, and according to Biggers are "nature's own form of collectivity."[6] Janet Goleas compares Biggers' cloud formations to cloud-computing, a colloquial expression used to describe different types of computing concepts that involve a large number of computers connected through a real-time communication network.[7] It should also be noted that cloud computing reflects the development of the web from static to semantic. Today, codes are programmable scripts embedded into virtual objects. In his 2013 work,

"Vex," Biggers embeds a QR code that when scanned by a mobile device launches "Moonrising," an online music video.

Afrofuturism and the techno-vernacular are linked to the 1964–65 New York World's Fair, which depicted "The Space Age," and symbolized American culture and the coming technological age. Arguably, it also created resonances of Afrofuturism. In the early 1950s, jazz musician Sun Ra, the father of Afrofuturism, abandoned his birth name and in a process of re-creation, developed a complex persona using cosmic philosophies and lyrical poetry. Re-creation rejects traditional forms and create new ones. By one account, Sun Ra was well aware of the New York World's Fair (Sun Ra "suggested they go" there in '64) so it is highly likely that his life altering "trip to Saturn" was meant to coincide with the space race (Lewis 2008, 161). The Space Age with it heliocentric-themed Unisphere landmark heavily influenced such Afrofuturist pioneers as Sun Ra, George Clinton of Parliament-Funkadelic, and Afrika Bambaataa and the Soul Sonic Force whose works resonate with Hype Williams's music video for Craig Mack's "Flava in Ya Ear." Examples of other members of the Afrofuturist cohort include Sanford Biggers, Cauleen Smith, Erykah Badu, and Janelle Monae. The Studio Museum in Harlem's recent exhibition, "The Shadows Took Shape," borrows its title from a Sun Ra poem. Fittingly, this show chronicles the movement's ongoing relevance and its global reach from the United States to Africa and Europe.

One of the more obvious examples of techno-vernacular creativity is electronic music production. We can see re-creation and DIY improvisation in the invention of new genres or subgenres as well as the creation of new techniques and technologies. Rap music producers master techniques such as sampling, which is the art of taking a portion, or sample, of one sound recording and reusing it as instrument or a sound recording in a different song. Hip-hop pioneer Grandmaster Flash played a key role in the technical design of Race Corporation's Empath mixer. Fouché notes that Grandmaster Flash's technological rhetoric shows an "understanding of re-creation based on personal aesthetics and the use of scientific methods to develop his technique" (2006, 656). Afrika Bambaataa and others helped to invent turntablism, which is the art of manipulating sounds and creating music using photograph turntables and DJ mixing consoles (mixers). Today, interactive, augmented soundscapes combine pre-existing musical samples and whatever the software can detect from a microphone on a mobile device creates an entirely new listening experience. [8]

Semantics denotes a range of ideas about the world, from the popular to the highly technical, i.e., using devices to layer visual or aural rhythms and effects to produce complicated patterns. The semantic web is part of Web 3.0 which inventor Tim Berners-Lee describes as a platform that supports dynamic graphical applications such as virtual 3D worlds with huge spaces of data.[9] Afrofuturism on Web 3.0 is grounded in genres such as cyberpunk or postmodern sci-fi, Afropunk DIY culture, electronic music, and virtual performance. Web 3.0 combines specialized forms of representation such as alphabets, visual images, music, choreographic notations based on geometric, linguistic, and scientific formulations, programming languages, hardware (robotics or mobile devices), and software (game platforms). These forms and representational, vernacular spaces produce cultural data such as heritage artifacts, geometric motifs that depict nature and the universe, music, performance, and games. The combination of cultural data—images, artifacts, sounds, and spaces—and virtual worlds is what I refer to as Afrofuturism 3.0.

## THE SOCIAL IMAGINARY:
## VERNACULAR CARTOGRAPHY AND THE SEMANTIC WEB

Afrofuturism, an antecedent to a variety of emerging cultural frameworks, comprises what social-cultural anthropologist Arjun Appadurai refers to as a social imaginary that directs viewers to critical and new aspects of artistic and cultural production (1996). John B. Thompson explains that the social imaginary "[is] the creative and symbolic dimension of the social world, the dimension through which human beings create their ways of living together and their ways of representing their collective life"(1984, 6). Jacques Lacan presents the imaginary as one of the three intersecting orders that structure all human existence, the others being the symbolic and the real (Macey 1994, xxi). These strategies can be used to examine materials and virtual encounters in cultural art across the African Diaspora. Afrofuturists visualize the social imaginary using vernacular cartography—the study and practice of making maps—to combine techno-vernacular creativity and aesthetics to build on the premise that cultural systems and data can be modeled to communicate spatial information in unique ways.

Vernacular cartography straddles the boundaries between culture, art, information, and representational space in both the physical and virtual worlds. Mapmakers and artists share skills, materials, and techniques that have been closely linked throughout history. Resonance can be found in a variety of texts (art, media, and literature) about maps as a medium for transportation, teleportation, re-invention, communication, and representational space for re-invention. Art historian Steven Nelson describes Houston Conwill as a "careful researcher of the hybrid mysteries of African influences on American culture, from Middle Passage slave ships to plantation life, and to post-slavery, African-influenced art forms."[10] Conwill and his sister Estella Conwill Majozo developed a metaphorical, vernacular cartography as inlaid floor cosmograms. These floor maps are installed in lobby entrances of the Schomburg Center in Harlem, New York, and the Harold Washington Library in Chicago, Illinois. In "The Cartographer's Conundrum" exhibition (2012), Sanford Biggers mapped artistic, cultural, and spiritual practices, as well as other disciplines and fields, including Afrofuturism, music, and sacred geometry. Vernacular maps, as cultural art forms and technologies, straddle the boundary between art and information, and are appreciated for aesthetic qualities as well as strategic navigational needs.

Ben Williams writes that the electronic music duo Drexciya (Gerald Donald and the late James Stinson) are the water-born children of pregnant enslaved African women who were thrown or jumped overboard during the Middle Passage.[11] These deep-sea dwellers are mutated beings, cyborgs, or hybrids that now live among us, creating art in vernacular spaces. The inner sleeve notes for Drexciya's "The Quest" is a map of the African Diaspora. Artists like Ellen Gallagher use the Drexciyan origin mythology as a basis for their creative work, mapping pathways between the past, present, and future. Gallagher's "Watery Ecstatic" series (2000–2005) and "Osedax" (2010) consist of layered, multiple projections with hybrid sea organisms. Finally, Duane Deterville's analysis of director Kahlil Joseph's music video for "Until the Quiet Comes" a song recorded by electronic musician Flying Lotus underscores the image of water symbolizing the barrier between the living and the ancestors.[12] The work can best be understood by navigating the Kalunga (which is the Kikongalic word for "threshold between worlds") "aquazone" on the Kongo cosmogram. These examples help us to visualize layered, intercultural, transnational networks through movement and migration, as well as the vernacular cartographies of the African Diaspora.

Advancements in "Web 3.0" have created a new, semantic type of online space that includes software used to render digital images and objects used in new media technologies, such as virtual 3D worlds.[13] Virtual worlds are computer-based simulated environments through which users in the form of three-dimensional avatars can interact with one another and other objects. Avatars navigate the virtual 3D world of Second Life (SL) through searchable maps. The basic unit of the SL world is the map region. The Main Grid, which lays out all the map regions on one large map so that regions that are side by side and users can see across and travel between them. Avatars can also be teleported or transported around virtual 3D space using an interactive or scripted map. To teleport is to instantly change locations based on specific landmark locations that are similar to bookmarks or favorites in a web browser. Conceptually, SL teleportation is similar to the fictional transporter machine used in Star Trek that converts a person or object into an energy pattern, and then beams the pattern to a target, where it is reconverted into matter. In SL, avatars can be in many virtual locations in a short period of time, thus time and space are compressed.

From 2006 until 2010, IBM was heavily invested in Second Life as a possible platform to replace face-to-face telecommunications. Curated by

Andrew Sempere, the IBM Exhibition Space granted me an artist residency in Second Life to simulate Afrofuturist cultural production. "Alternate Futures: Afrofuturist Multiverses and Beyond" was the first of its kind and presented several themes, such as altUtopia, an imaginary and ideal universe, altDystopia, the anti-utopian futuristic reality, and the SkyWalk that provided a cultural and historical timeline for Afrofuturism. AltDystopia was characterized by a repressive social control system, with a lack or total absence of individual freedoms and expressions. Visitors encountered static and scripted objects such as a wall of virtual 3D eyes that followed the avatar to simulate constant surveillance. AltUtopia contrasted against this in an open, transparent, blue-tinted world full of Afrofuturistic models such as a double helix DNA tower and 3D objects linking visitors to online information about ancient Dogon mythology. SkyWalk spanned the length of the simulation and presented a scepter that paid homage to Sun Ra. A golden silhouette of the jazz musicians rose high above the scepter. At its center was a glowing, spinning Eye of Horus.

"Alternative Futures" presented an interactive, virtual 3D cosmogram for visitors to navigate the exhibition. Cosmograms or mandalas are flat geometric images depicting the universe and can be seen in cultures around the world, including in the African Diaspora, such as in Haiti or Brazil as the "Veve" or sacred ground drawings of Umbanda called "pontos riscados." Cosmograms traced in chalk, paint, or sand on floors become signs of spiritual invocation and encounter. Cosmograms are found in the Americas, such as the Medicine Wheel or the mandalas of Tibetan Buddhism, as well as in the hermetic system of the Tarot. According to Deterville, ideograms or symbols contained in some of these drawings are based on Kongo and Yoruba cosmology, indicating a connection to and contiguity with spirituality of African continental and representational space.[14] The cosmogram maps the crossroad between worlds and realities. By layering and texturing digital images and objects artists can create a new kind of vernacular space. In virtual 3D space the cosmogram becomes a navigational and teleportation map. Visitors to "Alternate Future" could click on scripted gold buttons embedded in a map and be transported to different locations in the virtual 3D exhibition. In addition to embedding symbolic codes in quilts, floor installations and other artwork, artists can embed QR codes or computer programming in virtual objects to navigate the virtual 3D environment.

Artists can assume any form and are limited only by their imaginations in virtual 3D space. Embodied as avatars, artists can project and insert themselves in physical, virtual, or mixed realities. Artist Jacolby Satterwhite uses Maya 3D modeling software to create virtual 3D environments as sites for his performances. Satterwhite incorporates video, performance, 3D animation, fibers, drawing, and printmaking to explore a variety of themes. In a series titled "Reifying Desire" Satterwhite takes on a performative role by including himself in his videos interacting with objects within a fantastical and natural landscape through experimental movement, modern dance, and voguing.[15] Using a green screen, he captures his real-life performances and computer-generated software to create multiples of himself that he inserts into his artwork. In her virtual photomontage series entitled "Apparition," artist Camille Norment conjures up a projected, "oscillating dream space" that exists in the social imaginary of Afrofuturism.[16] Norment's notion of virtual space includes mirrors, multiple projections, and overlays, as a mixed reality collage and "sound-mind spaces." These modes of experiencing art can also be used to demonstrate how augmented reality works. Norment's apparition weaves in and out of her dreams and virtual reality. She compares the oscillating dream space to Sun Ra's music. Although this work is technically not augmented space, it addresses the conceptual and aesthetic issues of creating layered and mixed realities.

## THE POETICS OF AUGMENTED DREAM SPACE

To augment something is to make it greater, in size, extent, or quantity. To become augmented is to add to or multiply what already exists, whether it is in physical or virtual form. Media theorist Lev Manovich asks, "How is our experience of a spatial form affected when the form is filled in with dynamic and rich multimedia information?"[17] Augmented space offers creators new and different ways to overlay, view, encode, and decode cultural systems and objects with dynamically changing information. The built environments and objects of the real world are often covered with information such as signs, flyers, and graffiti. Keiichi Matsuda writes, "Augmented Space refers to group of emerging technologies that are unified by their ability to overlay physical space with information."[18] Augmented space, which succeeds virtual reality, merges the physical (real) and virtual worlds to create a contiguous, layered, and dynamic reality. In a hyper-networked world, Afrofuturists and Afropunk DIY techno-utopists navigate in and out of realities, sometimes merging them. Their self- and computer-generated imagery and sounds reflect their personal and cultural mythologies, as well as the creative and symbolic dimensions of their social worlds. This production explores how, conceptually and technically, built environments become augmented with cultural information and how creators replicate this information through techno-vernacular creativity.

Duane Deterville notes how the use of the Internet expands the area of ritual space to include virtual reality along with metaphysical, African Continental, and African Diasporic spaces to form the Afriscape.[19] Using the Afriscape and Afrofuturism as lenses, we can understand the augmented vernacular in new ways. Afrofuturism 3.0 is a utopic vision, as a web of cultural art and data, or merely as a natural paradigm shift in the creative practices of the African Diaspora on the Web. Afrofuturism is the "Space Age," ancient African iconography, cosmology and metaphysics, psychedelic artwork, cultural heritage artifacts, and electronic soundscapes that reflect the techno-vernacular creative practices of an idiosyncratic, visionary, and creative community of makers. In theory, the practice of augmenting space can also refer to the layering of quilts with embedded codes at safe houses, using multiple projections on multiple surfaces as part of an installation, using multiple projected avatars, or combining music samples with other sounds to immerse listeners.

Sun Ra believed that sound was from the future. This was before the invention of web-based technologies that mix, layer, or combine sound and imagery. Camille Norment writes that (twenty years) after Sun Ra's passing we are now ready to teleport into simultaneously outer and inner realms of reality. Artworks by Xenobia Bailey and Saya Woolfalk explore augmented dream spaces by creating layers of digital and non-digital materials. Bailey is an American artist and designer best known for her large-scale crochet pieces and mandalas, consisting of colorful concentric circles and repeating patterns. Bailey created a sound visualization and device inspired by jazz musician John Coltrane. At one end is a "mouthpiece" where the breath goes in and at the other end is a constellation of layered two-dimensional mandalas where the "magic comes out."[20] In "The Shadows Took Shape" exhibition at the Studio Museum in Harlem, Woolfalk directed an "inspired video (with music by D.J. Spooky) that seems to capture the color-splashed rituals of outer-planetary mystics who have landed on Earth."[21] These mystics are hybridized avatars, often covered in layers of materials such as fabric, felt objects, and paint. These works represent artists' collective participation in the fabrication of alternate realities that is at the core of Afrofuturism. Augmenting space with multiple projected images, objects and personalities extend the concept of vernacular cartography.

Although he does not describe himself as an Afrofuturist, Yung Jake, like Jacolby Satterwhite, walks among us as virtual personality, the very incarnation of an avatar. Yung Jake re-conceptualizes 1960s Happenings as mixed reality performances for the Information Age (i.e., smartphones, tablet PCs). Yung Jake has been described as a "datamoshing, glitch-creating, meta-rapping artist who employs cross-genre collaborations, GIFS, and the sweet new app he and his buddies created for Sundance."[22] Augmented Real is a mobile augmented reality (AR) application and rap music video featuring a virtual 3D Yung Jake that pops out of postcards, magazines, and computer screens. The app can be downloaded on mobile devices like smartphones and iPads. Yung Jake also stars in E.m-bed.de/d, another online performance that pops up on laptops and is triggered by sitting down in front of the device. Jacolby

Satterwhite and Yung Jake represent the next generation of artists that teleport into new realms of virtual reality to perform in augmented space.

Afrofuturism, in its many forms, directly engages audiences and subtly influences us, through the layering of text, images, and sound. Filmmaker Kahlil Joseph augments his music videos with text and cultural heritage artifacts such as African masks as a way to establish and sustain a relationship between the past and the present. In his "Belhaven Meridian" music video for Shabazz Palaces (2011), a hero played by actor Ernest Wadell of HBO's television drama "The Wire" appears to be on a journey. He is walking, with some ominous figures waiting on the road ahead of him, but then an African mask appears to come down upon him from above. He eventually turns around and grabs the mask just as it begins to float away. He then runs forward, mask in hand, towards his adversaries. This is the key point in the allegory. Only when you set out on the journey, leaving behind the status quo, will you open yourself to the helping hand of the universe.[23] Joseph's films and videos reveal a sensibility of vernacular mapping, augmented space, as well as Afrofuturistic storytelling.

In "Belhaven Meridian" another scene presents a text overlay "Sheep Killer, est. 1977" that refers to Charles Burnett's film "Killer of Sheep." Kahlil Joseph uses Burnett's film as a stylistic inspiration in the blocking and shot choices in his video. A live action "Afrofuturist comic" that artist/ author/comic book creator John Jennings worked on with rapper/producer/ actor David Banner is another example of augmented space. Jennings provided artwork to the story, acting as a graphic artist on the film. His work is used to tell the tragic and epic story of Aket Heru played by Banner. "Walking With Gods" is the story of an ancient West African prince (Heru) who is being pursued and murdered over and over again by an evil spirit throughout time.[24] Like Grandmaster Flash and Yung Jake, John Jennings samples and remixes content as part of the techno-vernacular mode of production. Jennings's images are seen in flashback sequences and as video overlays. "Belhaven Meridian," "Augmented Real," "Walking With Gods," and other examples overlay and embed symbols, text, and graphics in cultural systems with dynamic content, sometimes digital in form and closely linked with the development of Afrofuturism as a semantic, cultural arts network.

Vernacular cartography can be applied to contemporary art forms that employ symbols derived from cultural diagrams and from their own collection of images, objects, performances, and sounds. Xenobia Bailey uses fiber materials to create her crocheted mandalas. Houston Conwill and Sanford Biggers also work with mandalas and materials that also serve as maps, chalk-line, or cake walks from the nineteenth century American South and break dancing surfaces. These artists demonstrate a sense of augmented space, overlaid with dynamically changing information. The use of geometric charts maps, virtual and real-world geographic locations of objects such as performers/avatars, and mobile smartphones reflects Diasporic movement, migration, and the scattering of people who often share and exchange cultural data. These examples do not exhaust the possibilities of augmented space and new technology at the intersection of contemporary art and new media. Creators of new media applications and interfaces should consider whether cultural art forms become irrelevant and invisible or if designers end up creating new experiences in which the spatial and information layers are equally important. Artists and designers can interrogate the dynamic between creative expression and information as well as how these aspects might function differently in today's digital culture.

To further explore this development artists are using open source, web-based software to design Web 3.0 applications and interfaces that draw on cultural, visual systems to design applications that trigger digital objects, patterns, and other objects. A creative collaboration between The Heavy Projects (Los Angeles) and Public Ad Campaign (New York City), Re+Public "uses emerging technologies to alter the current expectations of urban media and accomplish our core mission of re+imagining public space."[25] Instead of embedding visual codes in quilts or symbols in floor plans Re+Public uses several basic shapes that are embedded in painted murals. The Re+Public app unlocks dozens of digital variations of these basic shapes and allows users to view and randomly re-compose murals into hundreds of variations. If Underground Railroad conductors and passengers had their own mobile devices and technological skills, they could have created dynamically changing artwork and displays to represent geographical locations, constellations in the sky, or even the North Star. By applying Afrofuturism to the creation of games, art, and other cultural forms, artists and designers can engage people in diverse interactive technology experiences.

## CONCLUSION

Vernacular cartography and augmented space, as an extension of techno-vernacular creative production, challenges artists and makers with new ways to sample, remix, or re-purpose cultural artifacts or data and author Afrofuturistic narratives via science, science fiction, technology, sound, architecture, the arts, and other cultural and interpretive modes of analysis. The purpose of this essay was to explore how Web 3.0 and other technologies continue to push the boundaries of digital culture and encourage Afrofuturists to navigate these new vernacular spaces. Proto-Afrofuturists and conductors of the Underground Railroad devised clever techniques that helped make their forays successful, including quilt-based maps embedded with visual codes to guide their passengers to freedom. Today, codes are embedded in art and crafts, in virtual 3D objects through programming languages, and presented as digital overlays in videos and on camera-enabled mobile devices. Artists across the Diaspora augment images and sound to disrupt syntax and alter systems. Inspired by scientific theories and mathematical equations, artists explore the connection between cultural heritage artifacts and contemporary ideas about the structure of time, space, and the universe. Sun Ra experimented with electronic instruments to create soundscapes from the future. Mobile applications create augmented soundscapes that make us receptive to multiple dimensions of reality. Artists, makers, and designers who use the Afrofuturism aesthetic can tap into these technologies and sensibilities in their work. They are part of an evolving, global movement to sustain this aesthetic through creativity, innovation, and culture.

## NOTES

1. Tom Butter, "Interview with Sanford Biggers," *Whitehot Magazine*: http://whitehotmagazine.com/articles/2010-interview-with-sanford-biggers/2054 (Accessed November 20, 2013).

2. Robert Enright. "Resonant Surgeries: The Collaged World of Wangechi Mutu," Border Crossings: http://bordercrossingmag.com/article /resonant-surgeries-the-collaged-world-of-wangechi-mutu (Accessed March 13, 2014).

3. Dan Busheikin, "Sun Ra: Man, Myth, Alien, Angel": http://www.chartattack.com/features/2012/06/08/sun-ra-man-myth-alien-angel (Accessed December 1, 2013).

4. Duane Deterville, "Defining the Afriscape through Ground Drawings and Street Altars": http://viscrit.files.wordpress.com/2010/08/09deterville.pdf (Accessed November 30, 2013).

5. Laura Hutson, "Coded Quilt Drawings: Notes From Sanford Biggers' Art Talk": http://www.nashvillescene.com/countrylife/archives/2013/11/25/coded-quilt-drawings-notes-from-sanford-biggers-art-talk (Accessed December 1, 2013).

6. Janet Goleas, "July 2013: Sanford Biggers @ Eric Firestone Gallery": http://whitehotmagazine.com/articles/sanford-biggers-eric-firestone-gallery/2817 (Accessed November 30, 2013).

7. Ibid.

8. Eliot Van Buskirk, "RjDj's Inception App Creates Personal Movie Soundtracks with iPhone Mic": http://evolver.fm/2010/12/09/rjdj-inception-app-personal-movie-soundtrack-iphone-mic (Accessed December 1, 2013).

9. Victoria Shannon (June 26, 2006). "A 'more revolutionary' Web," *International Herald Tribune*. Retrieved November 30, 2013.

10. Steven Nelson. "Circumnavigating the Atlantic: Houston Conwill's Choreographed Diaspora" (lecture): http://gallery400.uic.edu/events/steven-nelson#sthash.33kbdNll.dpuf (Accessed November 30, 2013).

11. Ben Williams. "Black Secret Technology: Detroit Techno and the Information Age": http://isites.harvard.edu/fs/docs/icb.topic500286.files/Black_Secret_Technology_by_Williams.pdf (Accessed November 30, 2013).

12. Duane Deterville. "Kahlil Joseph's 'Until the Quiet Comes': The Afriscape Ghost Dance on Film": http://blog.sfmoma.org/2013/03/kahlil-josephs-until-the-quiet-comes-the-afriscape-ghost-dance-on-film (Accessed November 30, 2013).

13. Victoria Shannon (June 26, 2006). "A 'more revolutionary' Web," *International Herald Tribune*. Retrieved November 30, 2013.

14. Duane Deterville, "Defining the Afriscape through Ground Drawings and Street Altars": http://viscrit.files.wordpress.com/2010/08/09deterville.pdf (Accessed November 30, 2013).

15. Monya Rowe Gallery, "Jacolby Satterwhite: The Matriarch's Rhapsody (press release)": http://monyarowegallery.com/files/Satterwhite_2012_Press_Release.pdf.

16. Camille Norment. "Notes from the Oscillating Dream Space": http://www.norment.net/studio/art/oscillationDreamSpace/index.htm (Accessed November 30, 2013).

17. Lev Manovich, "The Poetics of Augmented Space": http://www.alice.id.tue.nl/references/manovich-2006.pdf (Accessed November 30, 2013).

18. Keiichi Matsuda, "Domesti/City: The Dislocated Home in Augmented Space": http://www.keiichimatsuda.com/kmatsuda_domesti-city.pdf (Accessed November 30, 2013).

19. Duane Deterville, Defining the Afriscape through Ground Drawings and Street Altars: http://viscrit.files.wordpress.com/2010/08/09deterville.pdf (Accessed November 30, 2013).

20. Xenobia Bailey, "Xenobia Bailey's Amazing Art and John Coltrane": https://www.youtube.com/watch?v=mzOa4ce5DJ8#t=16 (Accessed December 1, 2013).

21. New Yorker magazine, "Goings on About Town: The Shadows Took Shape": http://www.newyorker.com/arts/events/art/the-shadows-took-shape-studio-museum-in-harlem (Accessed November 30, 2013).

22. Skylovestoeat, Tumblr editorial: http://editorial.tumblr.com/post/41324110814/enjoyed-sitting-down-with-datamoshing (Accessed November 30, 2013).

23. Ishmaelites, "Meditations on Belhaven Meridian": http://ishmaelites.blogspot.com/2011/09/meditations-on-belhaven-meridian.html (Accessed November 30, 2013).

24. Robert Jeffrey II, "John Jennings provides his artistic talent to David Banner's 'Walking With Gods'": http://www.blacksci-fi.com/features/article/walking-with-gods/#.UptkwWRgZb4 (Accessed November 30, 2013).

25. Re+Public: "Re+Imagining Public Space": http://www.republiclab.com/about (Accessed November 30, 2013).

# REFERENCES

Appadurai, Arjun. 1996. Disjuncture and difference. In *Modernity at Large: Cultural Dimensions of Globalization*, Chapter 2. Minneapolis, MN: University of Minnesota Press.

Bailey, Xenobia. Xenobia Bailey's amazing art and John Coltrane. https://www.youtube.com/watch?v=mzOa4ce5DJ8#t=16. Accessed December 1, 2013.

Bales, Judy. Creating again and again: Fractal patterns and process in improvisational African-American quilts. *Critical Interventions: Journal of African Art History and Visual Culture* CI, no. 9/10 (Spring, 2012): 10–30.

Baraka, Imamu Amiri. 1971. Technology and ethos. In *Raise, race, rays, raze: Essays since 1965*, ed. Imamu Amiri Baraka, 157. New York: Random House.

Busheikin, Dan. Sun Ra: Man, Myth, Alien, Angel. http://www.chartattack.com/features/2012/06/08/sun-ra-man-myth-alien-angel. Accessed December 1, 2013.

Butter, Tom. Interview with Sanford Biggers. *Whitehot Magazine*. http://whitehotmagazine.com/articles/2010-interview-with-sanford-biggers/2054. Accessed November 20, 2013.

Castro, Jan Garden. 2012. Sanford Biggers: Music, afrofuturism and re-envisioning history. *Black Renaissance/Renaissance Noire*. New York, NY: New York University Press.

Coleman, Beth. Race as technology. *Camera Obscura* 70, no. 24/1 (2009).

Dery, Mark. 1994. Black to the future. In *Flame wars: The discourse of cyberculture*. Durham, NC: Duke University Press.

Deterville, Duane. Defining the Afriscape through ground drawings and street altars. http://viscrit.files.wordpress.com/2010/08/09deterville.pdf. Accessed November 30, 2013.

———. Kahlil Joseph's "Until the Quiet Comes": The Afriscape ghost dance on film. http://blog.sfmoma.org/2013/03/kahlil-josephs-until-the-quiet-comes-the-afriscape-ghost-dance-on-film. Accessed November 30, 2013.

Duggan, Maeve and Joanna Brenner. 2013. The demographics of social media users—2012. *Pew Internet and American Life Project*. Pew Research Center, February 14.

Enright, Robert. Resonant surgeries: The collaged world of Wangechi Mutu. *Border Crossings*. http://bordercrossingsmag.com/article/resonant-surgeries-the-collaged-world-of-wangechi-mutu. Accessed March 13, 2014.

Fouché, Rayvon. 2006. Say it loud, I'm black and I'm proud: African Americans, American artifactual culture, and black vernacular technological creativity. *American Quarterly* 58, no. 3 (2006): 639–61.

Goleas, Janet. July 2013: Sanford Biggers @ Eric Firestone Gallery. http://whitehotmagazine.com/articles/sanford-biggers-eric-firestone-gallery/2817. Accessed November 30, 2013.

Gottschild, Brenda D. 1996. *Digging the Africanist presence in American performance: Dance and other contexts*. Westport, CT: Praeger.

Hutson, Laura. Coded quilt drawings: Notes from Sanford Biggers' "Art Talk." http://www.nashvillescene.com/countrylife/archives/2013/11/25/coded-quilt-drawings-notes-from-sanford-biggers-art-talk. Accessed December 1, 2013.

Ishmaelites. Meditations on Belhaven Meridian. http://ishmaelites.blogspot.com/2011/09/meditations-on-belhaven-meridian.html. Accessed November 30, 2013.

Jeffrey, Robert, II. John Jennings provides his artistic talent to David Banner's "Walking With Gods." http://www.blacksci-fi.com/features/article/walking-with-gods/#.UptkwWRgZb4. Accessed November 30, 2013.

Lewis, George R. 2008. *A power stronger than itself: the AACM and American experimental music*. Chicago, IL: The University of Chicago Press.

Limb, Charles J. and Allen R. Braun. Neural substrates of spontaneous music performance: An fMRI study of jazz improvisation. *PLoS ONE* 3, no. 2 (2008): 2–9.

Macey, David. 1994. Introduction. *Jacques Lacan, the four fundamental concepts of psychoanalysis*. London: Penguin.

Manning, Patrick. 2010. *The African Diaspora: A history through culture*. New York, NY: Columbia University Press.

Manovich, Lev. The poetics of augmented space. http://www.alice.id.tue.nl/references/manovich-2006.pdf. Accessed November 30, 2013.

Matsuda, Keiichi. Domesti/City: The dislocated home in augmented space. http://www.keiichimatsuda.com/kmatsuda_domesti-city.pdf. Accessed November 30, 2013.

Monya Rowe Gallery. Jacolby Satterwhite: The matriarch's rhapsody (press release). http://monyarowegallery.com/files/Satterwhite_2012_Press_Release.pdf.

Nelson, Steven. Circumnavigating the Atlantic: Houston Conwill's choreographed diaspora (lecture). http://gallery400.uic.edu/events/steven-nelson#sthash.33kbdNll.dpuf. Accessed November 30, 2013.

New Yorker. Goings on about town: The shadows took shape. http://www.newyorker.com/arts/events/art/the-shadows-took-shape-studio-museum-in-harlem. Accessed November 30, 2013.

Norment, Camille. Notes from the oscillating dream space. http://www.norment.net/studio/art/oscillationDreamSpace/index.htm. Accessed November 30, 2013.

Re+Public. Re+Imagining Public Space. http://www.republiclab.com/about. Accessed November 30, 2013.

Rudolph, Adam. 2010. Music and mysticism, rhythm and form: A blues romance in 12 parts. In *Arcana V*. New York, NY: Distributed Art Publishers.

Shannon, Victoria. 2006. A "more revolutionary" Web. June 26, 2006. *International Herald Tribune*. Accessed November 30, 2013.

Skylovestoeat, Tumblr editorial. http://editorial.tumblr.com/post/41324110814/enjoyed-sitting-down-with-datamoshing. Accessed November 30, 2013.

Snead, James A. 1984. Repetition as a figure of black culture. In *Black literature and literary theory*, ed. Henry L. Gates, Jr., 59–80. London: Routledge.

The Laundromat Project. Creative conversations 2013: Sukjong Hong and Kameelah Rasheed. http://www.laundromatproject.org/blog/2013/11/29/creative-conversations-2013-sukjong-hong-kameelah-rasheed. Accessed December 1, 2013.

Thompson, John B. 1984. *Studies in the theory of ideology*. Berkeley, CA: University of California Press.

Williams, Ben. Black secret technology: Detroit techno and the information age. http://isites.harvard.edu/fs/docs/icb.topic500286.files/Black_Secret_Technology_by_Williams.pdf. Accessed November 30, 2013.

Van Buskirk, Eliot. RjDj's Inception App creates personal movie soundtracks with iPhone mic.
    http://evolver.fm/2010/12/09/rjdj-inception-app-personal-movie-soundtrack-iphone-mic.
    Accessed December 1, 2013.

*Chapter Three*

# The *Real* Ghosts in the Machine

*Afrofuturism and the Haunting of Racial Space in*
I, Robot *and* DETROPIA

## Ricardo Guthrie

In many documentary and sci-fi films of the last twenty-five years, urban America is depicted as a site of decay, degradation, and disease—overrun by savage hordes who destroy civilization or worse: persisting as the hapless inheritors of urban jungles in which no "white" citizen can survive. Heroic reconquests by whites yield semblances of hope for the future, but only if savages, robotic droids, or miscreant machines can be subdued, reprogrammed, or destroyed. Future urban life is clearly a white projection of racial fears and hopes of conquests to come, but Afrofuturists (Dery 1995) might offer a different take on these racialized geographies. In fact, Dery defines Afrofuturism as:

> Speculative fiction that treats African-American themes and addresses African-American concerns in the context of 20th century technoculture . . . and, more generally, African-American signification that appropriates images of technology and a prosthetically enhanced future. (Dery 1995)

I extend this discursive line of inquiry by examining the presence of Afrodiasporic peoples within the space/time continuum generally described as the "future." The persistence of "race" as a haunting feature of modern and postmodern societies—yes, even extended into future space or science fiction imaginaries—is interrogated (Gordon 1997). Thus, my comparison of thematic racial hauntings within a Hollywood sci-fi drama and an independent documentary film of the early twenty-first century is based on fundamental antagonisms described by Afro-Pessimists (Jules-Rosette 2002; Sexton 2010; Wilderson 2008; 2010) which are also addressed by Afrofuturists such as Dery (1995; 2007), Nelson (2002), Bould (2007), Everett and Wallace et al. (2007)—but with far more optimism, or at least the possibility of emancipation through an embrace of technology and the elevation of an Afrofuturist awakening.

The two films which offer compelling opportunities for utilizing Afrofuturist analytics to re-center racial urban imaginary are *I, Robot* (2004) and *DETROPIA*. In *I, Robot*, director Alex Proyas creates a futuristic "thriller" in which black detective Del Spooner (Will Smith) challenges the logic of creating a new class of robot/slaves to liberate humankind from mundane lives, while investigating the death of a robotics scientist in 2035 Chicago. Spooner represents a type of Afro-Pessimist (Wilderson 2008) whose cynicism is gradually replaced by a soulful, Afrofuturist merger of black cultural ethos and commitment to struggle. In *DETROPIA* (2012), independent filmmakers Heidi Ewing and Rachel Grady explore the devolution of Detroit from a thriving 1.8 million-person metropolis founded on a unionized auto industry and a strong black professional class, to today's de-industrialized city of 700,000 residents with a shrinking tax base. In this bleak environment, black residents are under siege, while white professionals do battle to resuscitate the city. *DETROPIA's* dystopic present anticipates tomorrow's urban crises, while illuminating black change agents and environmentalists who envision a new city beyond existing racial paradigms. This chapter examines racialized urban geographies and develops Afrofuturist analytics to explain conflicted racial imaginaries in dystopic Detroit and in a seemingly utopic Chicago of 2035. If, as Gilbert Ryle (1949) asserted, "there have always been 'ghosts' in the machine," can technological progress really eliminate the haunting of race in the future? What cultural and political aesthetics can help us imagine racial and urban geographies of the future?

## THE REAL AND THE IMAGINARY FUTURE/PAST

> Black culture, as reflected in the white eye, is about gritty reality, not virtual reality; jacking your body, not jacking your mind into the mediasphere. Blacks, like Latinos, are mythologized as living links to the lost world of unmediated spontaneity, deeply felt physicality, and social connectedness— the rapidly receding Real, for which the white digerati feel a Baudrillardian nostalgia as they spend more and more of their lives working and playing in cyberspace. (Dery 2007, 34)

American science fiction (sci-fi) has traditionally been accepted as a valid imaginary zone for conceiving possible futures and performing thought experiments to solve social, environmental, and/or technological problems that continually vex "modern" society (Sobchack 1997). Sci-fi films, in particular, have provided a compelling arena for visualizing solutions—and continuing problems—that make the human experience "legible" to viewers of the current age. The problem with sci-fi, as expressed extensively by numerous writers, pop cultural and cinematic critics, is that the future seemingly expunges race—and in particular, African-diasporic peoples—from the equation (Bould 2007, 177). More problematically, American sci-fi futures include racialized beings who have not really solved the problem of racial hierarchy and white dominance. Even as the writers, directors, and producers of a theorized, futurist liberal society in which all men, women, animals, and plants live in post-racial, feminist, or anti-classist societies in the cosmos, they, nonetheless, unwittingly replicate existing hierarchies and subsume racial problematics through technological and/or biological assimilation under white humanitarian regimes.[1] The converse is also true: problematic racial underclasses, robots, androids, and/or rebellious beings of color exist as problems to be solved; felons, terrorists, or monsters to be subdued; or intelligent but emotionally unstable martyrs to be admired beyond the grave.

In many ways, race fills the future space as yet another "ghost" in the machine, haunting the paradigmatic ethos, revealing a problematic core in fantasies which reveal themselves as extensions of today's dominant white imaginary in society and culture. These technological machinations prove yet again unable or unsuitable to put to rest the haunting of racism that shapes modern and seemingly post-modern worlds. Modernity, however, requires abject peoples and beings to compare to our future heroes and heroines. Afrofuturist writers and critics, however, provide an antidote to these white imaginaries. Their Afro-diasporic heroes and sheroes move from the "pit" to the "tip" of racial intervention—providing skepticism, cyncism, or homeboy/girl cosmopolitan intellectualism to resurrect the ghosts, and foreground race as a place for solving social ills and persistent inequities over time and space (Bould 2007). Problematics continue, of course, within even these Afrofuturist realms: feminist *sheroes* are in limited numbers—often taking a backseat to male heroes who are sensitive "roughnecks" ready to do the job, sacrifice themselves for family and progeny, or elevate sexual tension between black men and white females—yet again the object for the male gaze.

## THE CLEAN MACHINE VS. THE MEAN MACHINE: DEL SPOONER, CHICAGO FUTURIST

Unwilling Afrofuturist Del Spooner—skeptical of robotic utopianism in 2035 Chicago—displays a knowing cynicism of future logics that will supposedly emancipate all urban denizens. Detective Spooner, assigned to investigate the death of robotics scientist Dr. Alfred Lanning, who was also his mentor, fears the rampant commodification and distribution of robot servants will not only create a new class of slaves, but will forever enslave humans as well. Deeply committed to keeping it "real," Spooner is outfitted with retro-cultural accoutrements of the 1970s (his JVC player pulses out Stevie Wonder's *Superstition* as well as Fontella Bass's 1965 R&B hit, *Rescue Me*). In the opening scenes, Spooner dresses in black leather trenchcoat and gazes lovingly at his black hightopped "Chuck Taylor All-Stars" basketball shoes before taking to the gritty streets of futurist Chicago.

Spooner displays distrust and prejudicial anger against robots—who are lauded as modernity's greatest innovation. He distrusts robots because they have no "soul": *"They are just clockwork and gears to me!"* he declares early in the film. He also questions the programming laws that control the robot machines: *1) A robot may not injure a human, or through inaction, allow a human being to come to harm; 2) A robot must obey the orders given to it by human beings, except where such orders would conflict with the First Law; and 3) A robot must protect its own existence, as long as such protection does not conflict with the First or Second Law* (Asimov 1950). Inspired by the 1950s sci-fi short stories by Isaac Asimov, *I, Robot* the film is an interesting exploration of the themes of humanity vs. mechanization, utopian vs. dystopian cities, and the future vs. the past—while employing a noted black film star (Will Smith) to interrogate quandaries about race and technology in the near future.

Spooner is perhaps an unwilling Afrofuturist because of his cynicism and reservations about imposed technology; however, he is not nostalgic about the past. Rather, Spooner is concerned with the present because of the way robots (and corporate marketers) have taken over society. He uses music and commodities from the twentieth century to recenter his body and mind in the midst of rampant consumerism. Recalling Gilbert Ryle's philosophical critique of the Cartesian split between body and mind, Spooner wrestles with the possibility that there has always been a "ghost in the machine"—his ghostly soul echoes a dual consciousness that harks back to an era in which disaster capitalism was exposed and under siege by liberation struggles of the 1960s and 1970s. Such movements were derailed, destroyed, or co-opted by COINTELPRO tactics, the logic of advanced consumerism and the seemingly universal freedoms offered through electronics and the Internet. Nevertheless, the essence of those social movements lives on in music and cultural artifacts of the future. In Spooner's world, they are echoes, ghosts of the past, residing in a twenty-first century society that uses technology to improve human potential (Wilderson 2010).

Spooner's pessimism (cynicism) is well-deserved. He survived a devastating car crash and near-drowning only because a robot chose to rescue him rather than an injured 12-year-old girl, who was also trapped in her car. The robot made the wrong decision, according to Spooner, because it had no empathy for rescuing a young girl, whose odds of survival were less than

Spooner's—the robot calculated that Spooner would survive, thus it pulled him from the wreckage, and left the girl to die. Spooner also encountered a sentient computer and a robot programmed to experience emotions; both prove to be unpredictable and unstable—leading to the death of Spooner's mentor and the near-death of Spooner himself. The ironic relationship of Spooner to sentient, non-human beings (robots) is revealed early on (the robotics scientist heals the badly injured Spooner by surgically providing him a prosthetic arm, shoulder, and ribs that make him part-robot); however, the detective still harbors prejudicial hate (or fear?) of robots in general, referring to them as "canners," and degrading them at every opportunity. He exists as a "prosthetically enhanced" futurist, but fails to note the irony until very late in the film.

The utopian logic of future cities like Chicago remains a central feature of the film, while still reifying white domination and confirming black degradation. The ghetto remains, even in the face of technological advances which are designed to improve life for the masses. The urban residents are unwitting consumers, trapped into a multicultural future in which racial enclaves and class divisions remain solidly in place. Stigmatized urban blacks are still information "have-nots" (Everett and Wallace 2007, 3) who stand to benefit from techno-consumption. At one point, Spooner tackles a robot whom he mistakenly believes had stolen a purse; he learns that the robot was running the purse out to a large, asthmatic black woman who had left her inhaler at home; she insults and derides Spooner for his mistaken assumption that the robot had committed a crime—an interesting displacement of the presumption that young black males running through the streets might encounter today.

In the "space where the future takes place" (Rose 1994, 215), Spooner lives a double life: he detests the abjection imposed by commodified technology, but his life and career are dependent upon that technology—both to survive and to work as a police detective committed to protecting life and property. Although he remains deeply skeptical about the corporate motives behind mass robot production and distribution, he is pledged to defend their right to continue selling robots, even as they prove to be unstable and/or dangerous.

The haunting of race remains, and is sustained, as Spooner attempts to solve the murder of Dr. Lanning, the robotics scientist, and is perceived by others as an "angry Black man." Spooner is also viewed as a bigoted technophobe. In this film the discursive embodiment of blackness (or Afro-diasporic consciousness) comes at a risk. Spooner can attest to his soulful authenticity (cynical or pessimistic about the benefits of commerce-driven technology) in the face of mechanized progress and alienation. His sleep is interrupted by repeated nightmares of his near-death drowning, while his robotic counterpart—a blue-eyed, plastic-skinned robot nicknamed "Sonny" by the scientist-mentor—dreams of man/machine mass unification, under the guid-ance of an unnamed hero, who could be a robot, or another human. He first says the hero figure is Spooner, but by the end of the film, it is revealed to be Sonny himself—an uncomfortable transposition between Spooner and his robot "peer" whose future is yet unclear. These two threads problematize the film's attempt to portray Spooner as an out-of-control, angry black man who is paranoid and phobic about technology, but there's more. Can urban envi-ronments of the future be sustained by massive investments in labor-saving technology? What is technology's price to society, and how do we avoid mass alienation and/or disruption of human relations? Are human beings (blacks and others) similar to robot machines—invested with "souls" and emotions to guide and protect human "masters"?

Spooner reflects an overwhelmingly cynical outlook throughout the film, and—because he remains constrained by his ironic relationship to property, technology, and policing the future—remains an ambivalent hero. Perhaps there's truth to the prophetic words of The Last Poets (1971), that "automat-ic, push-button, remote-control; Synthetic, Genetics [will] Command your Soul!" This outlook is very similar to what Wilderson (2008) and others have described as "Afro-Pessimism," in that he continually seeks a pathway to legibility—striving to be heard and understood, first, and then to possibly correct society's errant ways. According to Wilderson:

> Afro-Pessimists are framed as such . . . because they theorize an antagonism, rather than a conflict—i.e., they perform a kind of 'work of understanding' rather than that of liberation, refusing to posit seemingly untenable solutions to the problems they raise. (Wilderson 2008)

The antagonism in Wilderson's theorization is the continued "natal aliena-tion" (social death through enslavement) of African-descendant peoples in modern society. Wilderson, drawing on Orlando Patterson's study of slavery, and Frantz Fanon's psychoanalytic assessment of black nonsubjectivity de-scribes the hypocrisy of democratic societies which were founded on the subjugation of people of African descent through slavery and its afterlife (Fanon 1967; Patterson 1982; Sexton 2010; Wilderson 2008; 2010). In this framework, the "ontological" dimensions of blackness within modern (and future) societies remain antagonistic because black life and labor are structu-rally positioned "outside of humanity and civil society" (Wilderson 2010, 1). Black life/labor remain subordinate to whites, and available for capital accu-mulation—in other words, the very idea of what it means to be free, and human, is predicated on what it means to be unfree, and black.

Afro-Pessimists would go so far as to say that black people are sentient but dead to the dominant society—available for labor but constrained through gratuitous violence within civil society. Within the logic and political economy of the American cinema, black characters are similarly constrained—existing mainly to advance plot and dramatic consequences for whites, their emotions, conditions, and dilemmas. Even today's movie stars and producers such as Oprah Winfrey, Denzel Washington, and Forest Whitaker find it difficult to evade the entrapment of natal alienation that provides mythic entertainment for audiences concerned with the "trauma drama" of slavery, abject black behavior, and the persistence of racial animus. Even in historical dramas brought to the screen by Winfrey, Washington, and Whitaker to remind Americans of the impact of slavery and its afterlife, there is a recurrent sense that "we can feel good about feeling bad about what has happened in the past"—as if the racial antagonisms are no longer present or significant (Guthrie 2012; 2013).

Detective Spooner addresses the antagonism within a society which is dependent upon robot/slave labor for the creation of wealth and consumer progress in the midst of racial subjugation, economic division, and impending insurrection of subordinate beings. Spooner believes nothing good can come from slave/robots serving humankind, and falls victim to the prejudice against sentient "beings who have no soul." It is an ironic, disturbing awareness that he develops over time. Still, Spooner is not a revolutionary, and he offers no solutions to the technological challenges of future society; but he does take action to seek justice on behalf of the murdered scientist. It is his action in the face of an "irreconcilable encounter" with the collapse of "civil society" that is key to his transformation, and—by extension—the possibility of emancipation for Afro-descendant peoples.

According to Wilderson, however, such actions may be inadequate to arrest racial oppression because they merely expose limitations within civil society, rather than eliminating racial division:

> a revolution that would destroy civil society, as we know it, would be a more adequate response. Afro-Pessimists [Hartman, Spillers, Marriott . . .] would argue there is no place for blacks, only prosthetics, techniques which give the illusion of a relationality in the world. (Wilderson 2008)

Afrofuturists, however, would stop short of destroying civil society; they would settle for "legibility," and attempt to halt the erasure of black contributions to society. They act, not because they are trying to "save" society, but because they have nothing to lose (Wilderson 2010). Spooner, for instance, was selected by Dr. Lanning to solve his "suicide/murder" because Lanning realized that Spooner was a black man who yet remained skeptical of the allure of technology and capital accumulation. Lanning understood that Spooner was prepared to make visible his belief that mass production of robot/slaves would lead to disaster, and that the "Tip of white, posthuman, posthistorical" transcendence was an illusion (Bould 2007, 183) that could be

challenged by the "Pit of black, material, human, and historical being"—
represented by the "real" agent of change, Del Spooner.

This is the main lesson of the film: Spooner's Afro-Pessimism, which
provides an optic for visualizing the irreconcilable antagonism of race, is
gradually transformed through action into a type of Afrofuturism. Spooner
reveals the problematics of blacks, art, and technology in a future that echoes
racial hierarchies of "the past." He does not have "the answer," but he,
nevertheless, reckons with the "ghosts in the machine"—black people, and
their racialized past/present as well as the persistence of racism that can
never be fully erased. Spooner helps put down the mass robot insurrection,
which ironically parallels fears of slave uprisings during America's antebellum period—but he remains unable to resolve antagonisms between his own
role as a police agent and stand-in for sentient robot servants.

*I, Robot* provides a rich visual terrain of 2035 Chicago that curiously
reflects key antagonisms and conflicts of today. Three features of the film's
cinematic and literary design might be summarized by the following:

a. Racial Ethnoscapes are structural features of urban life and American
   civil society. (Despite the presence of improved robotics, the basic
   racial hierarchy and function of civil society remains the same in the
   future: blacks are still marginalized and made "invisible" by their
   "otherness," or violently suppressed should they assert their "real" or
   authentic selves. This is both a theme within Hollywood films and a
   crisis of modern society.)
b. The Relationship of Disaster Capitalism to urban social decay is a
   persistent feature of modernity, post-modernity, and future civiliza-
   tions. (The "logic" of rampant consumerism is presented as the chief
   component of "emancipation" for oppressed communities of color—
   *everyone* can enjoy the benefits of robot servants, it seems, even as
   class and social stratifications, and the profit logic of capitalism, lead
   once again to social disruption, violence, and further chaos.)
c. The Remnants of these irreconcilable antagonisms remain as "ghosts"
   in the machine (modern society—which cannot function without significant presence of "real" black, or robotic, Others!); Del Spooner's
   heroic actions help save civil society, but his skepticism is not recognized for its valuable critique. He does not fit the role of liberator, but
   his Afrofuturist vision provides unique insights and a "re-centering"
   through black music and cultural artifacts emanating from the Civil
   Rights/Black Power eras.

At the end of the film, after a violent robot insurrection, the troublesome
sentient computer is destroyed, and the Nexus-5 robot/slaves are decommis-
sioned. The future role of robots is unclear, but the prosthetically enhanced

Detective Spooner is vindicated for his skepticism. He becomes a mentor for Sonny, the remaining sentient robot, and develops a possible romantic partnership with Dr. Susan Calvin (Bridget Moynahan)—the AWF (attractive white female) who is in awe of his surgically reconstructed physique. How can this fictional sci-fi film about future Chicago help us comprehend the reality faced by other cities today? The tribulations evoked in *DETROPIA* (2012) provide ample opportunities to examine Afrofuturist visions that might offset the tremendously pessimistic depictions of a rapidly declining American metropolis—felled by disaster capitalism at its worst.

## THE ARREST OF DEVELOPMENT:
## DETROIT AND THE ANTI-UTOPIAN MOVEMENT

In this documentary film, the moribund city of Detroit stands on the verge of destruction as urban planners, politicians, labor leaders, business entrepreneurs, artists, and residents attempt to "re-purpose the city" for the future. The sustainable city can only be preserved if black populations are divested of control, made invisible or obsolete by financial restructuring of jobs, housing, city services, and redefining what it means to be a resident of Detroit. A young black videographer creates digital blogs for the Internet—capturing images of Detroit's decaying splendor: a concert hall that has fallen into disrepair; empty luxury apartments and overgrown vacant lots, as well as dilapidated former worksites are all extensively photographed and forlornly depicted, while she traverses the city. Other Detroit pioneers attempt to arrest the destruction around them, acting as squatters, performance artists, union organizers, and activists seeking to restore Detroit to its former prominence. However, it is all, seemingly, for not.

These "techno-change" agents (Dery 2007) confront the "techno-determinism" that seemingly condemns the city to destruction. Since the auto industry began laying off thousands of workers in the late-twentieth century—replacing them with machines, and relocating production facilities to other countries and to non-union shops down South—Detroit has become an anachronism, unable to finance city services through a greatly reduced tax base, and unable to invest in new businesses and industries that might replace the one-time great auto industry. Yet, in 2009–2010 the *automakers* were bailed out by President Obama and Congress, who restructured and then encouraged them to make unprecedented profits over the last few years. Although American automakers still maintain a growing market share of the global industry, the jobs and financial benefits have not returned to Detroit workers and residents, who largely remain unemployed.

*DETROPIA* is the answer to the question posed by "disaster" capitalism: Is black labor anachronistic in the post-industrialized urban core? *DETRO-*

*PIA* is a documentary that feels like a disaster sci-fi film—only its reality is "mythic"—based on the "real," the authentic re-working and re-wiring of economic and technological relations between past and present. Is it the "Future" within our grasp? The filmmakers create a running sequence of stories featuring a labor leader, a retired educator turned bar owner and entrepreneur, a video blogger, and white performance artists—all depicted without voice-over narration. The filmmakers' presence is revealed in short captions and intertitles that provide shocking statistics and historical background, while the cinematography moves about the city. The respondents provide a type of chorus of archetypal dimensions: Labor, Entrepreneurship, Youth, and White Urban Pioneers to address the various aspects of Detroit's mythic rise and fall. The "extras" in the film are city residents who express their hopes and dreams for the future. There are several confrontational scenes between residents and a beleaguered Mayor Dave Bing, who appears helpless to stop the flight of businesses and taxpayers from the city.

*DETROPIA* portrays the nightmare existence of urban residents who have been abandoned by businesses and city politicians. The title of the film comes from a reworking of a sign above an abandoned autoparts store—combining "Detroit" and "Utopia" into a filmic symbol. The film itself represents a "shock" to the system—the logical end-result of white flight/white fright from a city that was once a "Utopia" for scores of people. According to the filmmakers, a combination of two major riots (1943 and 1967) and endemic government corruption, spurred the exodus of white as well as black professionals. The subsequent downsizing of the auto industry in the 1980s sealed the city's fate. Presently, Detroit is perceived as an "interesting Petri dish"—an ongoing experiment in social engineering (Ewing 2012). Notwithstanding the city's dismal outlook, there are respondents in the documentary who echoed the possibilities of resurrecting black cultural capital to restore the city to its former greatness. They desired to attract new residents who could build nimble alternatives of cooperative farming, reduce carbon imprint of businesses, and restructure arts, sports, and cultural industries within the region.

*DETROPIA* examines the very real possibility that business and political leaders might resurrect the city by purging it of black residents—under the guise of eliminating abandoned housing and combating crime. Since Detroit has such a rich history and holds a key position in the Midwest, city elites hope to create a gleaming, white metropolis dispersed of abject blackness. This trope fits most of Hollywood's futurist imaginations. Moreover, it embodies the fears and concerns of Afrofuturists that black people will be divested of their future role in urban America, and reduced to abject, symbolic representatives of a post-Apocalyptic present. Afrofuturists would applaud the innovative spirit of those who have been abandoned in the urban core, yet remain as essential features of the ethnoscape.

For the "Afrofuturist," the apocalypse has already happened (Bould 2007, 181). In the words of Public Enemy: "Armageddon been in effect!" Those who remain behind, goes the popular sentiment, are the detritus of a failed social, political, and economic system that collapsed because of corrupt black politicians. Despite the ahistorical logic of this sentiment (the city was already in decline by the time Mayor Coleman Young came to office in the 1970s, and white flight had been steadily increasing since the 1950s), the film replicates the view that black nostalgia (music, sports, arts, and labor) are features of the past—the "new" Detroit, it seems, can display black culture in museums, but "real" black people have got to go because they have failed to embrace the future. As Alondra Nelson notes: "Western culture generally constructs Blackness . . . as always oppositional to technologically driven chronicles of progress" (Nelson 2002, 1).

Labor leader George McGregor, president of United Auto Workers Local 22, argues persuasively on behalf of his union members for a living wage, but in so doing, fails to prevent one of the key businesses, American Axle, from leaving town. McGregor explains his dilemma: "I asked . . . 'How do I sit down with one of my members, who is already scuffling and making $14.35, sit at the table with their family and got to tell them that my Union and I agree to take a $3.35 pay cut?" Ultimately, the UAW did agree to take a 50 percent wage cut for all new hires, and the incoming wage went from $28 per hour to $14. The union has grown leaner as jobs have fled overseas and have been replaced by mechanization. McGregor remains diligent about providing benefits, support, and counseling to fellow workers; however, it is clear that he no longer has any bargaining power while passing blocks of abandoned auto factories and empty lots of buildings being stripped of copper and other metal fittings.

Although Detroit's "ethnoscape" is being transformed into dreamscapes for white fantasy, white visionaries, and for pioneers of profit, black entrepreneurs still remain. One such example is retired schoolteacher Tommy Stevens, who owns a bar, The Raven Lounge that sponsors local bands and offers good food and music. Stevens recognizes the economic inequalities yet persists in running his business. He explains "Capitalism is a great system. I love it. But it exploits the weak. It always does. It always does, unfortunately" (Ewing and Grady 2012). Later in the film, he challenges automakers to develop better cars to compete with foreign automakers, and then decries the growing income disparity between middle and lower-income residents. Cognizant of the steady disappearance of his middle-class clientele, Stevens is determined to make the Raven Lounge a successful business venture. Heidi Ewing, one of the films two directors, observes:

> Tommy Stevens is the heart and soul of *DETROPIA*. . . . He is a Black middle
> class man who could leave Detroit but doesn't. He owns the last Black-owned

blues bar . . . on the eastside of Detroit. . . . He ends up saying that if there is no buffer between the rich and the poor the only thing left is revolution. That is his big line in the film. He's not calling for revolution or riots. The man is observing that at some point this is going to break . . . . He said this a year before Occupy Wall Street. (Ewing 2012)

Stevens's dogged perseverance stands in sharp contrast with that of two young white urban transplants—Steven and Dorota Coy—who settled in Detroit because of the cheap and plentiful housing and warehouse lofts. The couple reflected upon their decision to relocate to Detroit in search of an exciting urban setting to perform their art installations:

We had a project that we wanted to do like street art, public installation, and so we just started evaluating, we looked at Baltimore, we were looking into New York City, and Detroit came up. I would never be able to afford to own a home as an artist. And here I am with a studio and an apartment in, a major city you know, functioning for like $700 or less a month. We can . . . experiment here because if we fail, we haven't really fallen anywhere. (Steve Coy qtd. in Ewing 2012)

As performance artists, the Coys appear throughout the film in various costumes—wearing gold-colored masks, luxurious suits, and fur coats—to lampoon the disruption of the natural environment and the corporate abandoned cityscape of overgrown lots and uninhabited housing. While they share a powerful message, Ewing is not sure the influx of young white transplants represents a sustainable trend:

what we're seeing is young college-educated, mostly Caucasian kids who would've moved to Chicago or New York or Philadelphia or Los Angeles, but can't afford it because they're not finding employment. But a place like Detroit is a place that needs them. They can sort of make a mark . . . I just don't know if it's a trend that's going to be long term. (Ewing 2012)

Nevertheless, Detroit remains an attractive destination for young migrants—black and white—in that an estimated 50,000 people have relocated to the "Motor City" during the past five years.

However, Detroit residents refuse to give up. One survivor, Crystal Starr, is a young black woman employed as a barista at a coffee shop, who creates videoblogs of the city's splendor gone to pot. Like Stevens and McGregor, she recognizes that while something is broken in Detroit, black people are not the problem:

History is just one of my things, even since grade school. That's a passion. What was there? Who was there? Wow, it's amazing where you see where they just ripped out a wall because there is copper piping right there . . . Motown right up the street. Hmm. Can't fucking leave. I feel like I was maybe here a little while back. Or I'm older than I really am but I just have like this young, this young body and spirit and mind but I have the memory of this place when it was banging. That's how I feel. (Crystal Starr, in Ewing 2012)

In her sentimental yearning to resurrect the lost glory of Detroit's history— its greatness—Starr reflects an Afrofuturist sensibility on a declining urban landscape. She refuses to yield her place in "Zion," even as the "Sentinels prepare for a final onslaught" (Bould 2007). Similar to the underground residents of Zion in *The Matrix*, Detroit's underclass has retained its spirit of resistance while the rest of the population has already yielded to the machine. The acknowledgement that the "Apocalypse already happened" does not absolve residents like Starr from relinquishing their place in the space that once created one of the largest black professional classes in America. The cultural contributions of Motown and the mythic symbolism of the auto industry, remain hallmarks of Detroit's historiography. Indeed, Crystal Starr vehemently adheres to the central fact of the persistence of black existence in any future of Detroit.

Sadly most observers—including filmmaker Heidi Ewing—do not believe that Detroit can be restored to its former prominence. This is where the archetypal chorus comes together in a final poetic summation of *DETRO-PIA*'s significance: "culture is embodied—and history is bodies. And maybe that color-blind future can still be told so long as it is motley, mottled without hierarchy, rather than blanketed in whiteness" (Bould 2007, 184). The sci-fi future of Detroit has yet to be fully described, but as the city re-works itself by purging the "ethnoscape" of black residents, key threads from both science fiction and the documentary film converge. Namely, modern life is contingent upon black, subservient others. The error of most sci-fi futurists is that black people are not conceived as part of the solution to disaster capitalism, except as elements of the commodified ethnoscape—surplus labor/ surplus flesh that can always be erased or re-purposed. African Americans who migrated from the Jim Crow south during the twentieth century created a black utopia in Detroit, but are now part of the nightmare of abandonment. They are residents who might rebel and create insurrections against the machine, but if their bodies are displaced, what remains? Borrowing from Zuberi (2007), I suggest that black bodies in these declining urban spaces appear to others as haunting specters—ghosts in the imagination of Detroit's aging greatness; remaining behind, to disrupt the technology that does not yield progress:

The ghost exists now, a shadow or trace of a body that once existed. But it is not the same thing as that once live body or its dead remains. Because its uncanny interruption complicates a linear sense of time and therefore historicism, the ghost is a suggestive figure for Sci-Fi. (Zuberi 2007, 284)

# CONCLUSION

No return to normal is possible: what "normal" is there to return to? Part of the
story . . . has always been this—that losing everything except basic dignity and
decency is potentially a survivable disaster. (Sinker 2007/1992, 33)

Hollywood sci-fi thrillers such as *I, Robot* and disaster capitalism documen-
taries like *DETROPIA* provide extended dialogues between Afro-Pessimism
(black people are ontologically "dead" to Western society) and Afrofuturism
(Afro-diasporic presence in the future will be predicated on a positivist appropriation and mastery of technoculture—with good and bad outcomes).
This chapter outlines the seeming contradiction between sci-fi's post-racial
future and the nagging persistence of racial themes, hierarchies, and displace-
ments that foreground a black presence—perhaps as "ghosts" in the machine,
or as hapless residents of declining urban ethnoscapes. In both scenarios,
however, it is suggested that "race is a place" in cinematic imaginings—both
fictional and documentary—that allows blacks to stake a claim. Not as commodified denizens for capitalist *accumulation* (Afro-Pessimism), or capitalist
*exploitation* (Afrofuturism), but as techno-change agents whose actions will
transform and disrupt the space/time continuum. *Black people what ya'll
gon' do?*, as the Last Poets demanded in the 1970s.

Yet unclear, however, is whether Afro-diasporic Others can escape the
poverty of imagination that renders them illegible characters trapped within
the cinematic gaze, while subconsciously projecting white emancipatory
dreamscapes—both now and in the future (Guthrie 2012). Theorists have
pondered the utility of black rebellion, while positing the benefits of action
(highlighting the crises of capital accumulation and exploitation in the midst
of technological progress), compared to the very real dilemma of simply
describing that which has heretofore been "invisible." Most notably, the
novelist Ralph Ellison effectively described the uncanny prescience of a
previously abject black hero who developed a techno-mastery of sound, music, and machinery. As Dery stated, Ellison's protagonist is the "proto-cyber-
punk . . . a techno-bricoleur," who understands that racial space exists/per-
sists outside of linear time, and that race, technology, and space are intertwined. By using music, electronics, turntables and lights, Ellison's *Invisible
Man* predicted the sonic apparatuses of the post-industrial 1970s created by
other New Yorkers who proclaimed their techno-wizardry and new musical
styles that have since been adopted, and appropriated, by pop cultural consumers (Dery 2007, 30; Yaszek 2005).

As a masterful cyberpunk, however, Ellison's invisible man never moves
beyond his "hole" beneath New York City. He proclaims his desire to take
action, but remains trapped, as he attempts to rewire the relations between
past and present, and between art, music, and technology (Yaszek 2005). He

doesn't take action—unlike fictional Detective Del Spooner, and Detroit videoblogger Crystal Starr, who provide descriptive analyses that something is seriously wrong within the urban technoscape, but all is not lost, if we heed the warning signs and express ourselves beyond the "grammar of suffering" and illegibility (Wilderson 2010). Sci-fi's colorblind future remains a fictive imaginary, as both films demonstrate. Neither cinematic artifact provides a fully enabled strategy for success; however, to survive as techno-bricoleurs is a viable first step out of the "pit" of black invisibility, and cinematic abjection. Embracing the "real" does not necessarily mean succumbing to nostalgic reifications of black culture, but it may suggest a way to elevate "technological interactions inherited from jazz and now rap avant garde" that can "reintegrate humanity with the runaway machine age" (Bould 2007, 181). And that, one might say, would be a first step towards escaping invisibility and the ghostly haunting of race.

## NOTE

1. The examples are too numerous to cite here, but include *Star Trek*, *Star Wars*, and their formulaic offspring that are earnest in their attempts to promote a multiculturalist, non-sexist, anti-classist, pluralist universe—pristine, gleaming white prosthetics, *clean-machine imagery* that typically replicates Anglos in leadership roles.

## REFERENCES

Asimov, Isaac. 1950. *I, robot.* New York: Doubleday.

Bould, Mark. The ships landed long ago: Afrofuturism and black SF. *Science Fiction Studies* 34, no. 2 (2007): 177–86.

Dery, Mark. 1995. Black to the future: Afro-futurism 1.0. Reposted rumori Mailing List, 2002. http://www.detritus.net/contact/rumori/200211/0319.html. Accessed Jan. 5, 2014.

Dery, Mark. 2007. Wired man's burden: The incredible burden of being digital. In *Afro-GEEKS: Beyond the digital divide*, 29–48. Center for Black Studies Research, Univ. of California at Santa Barbara.

Ellison, Ralph. [1952] 1980. *Invisible man.* New York: Vintage.

Everett, Anna, and Amber J. Wallace, eds. 2007. *AfroGEEKS: Beyond the digital divide.* Center for Black Studies Research: Univ. of California at Santa Barbara.

Ewing, Heidi. 2012. Q&A: Heidi Ewing on C-SPAN. Morningside Partners, October 28. http://www.q-and-a.org/Transcript/?ProgramID=1415. Accessed March 2, 2014.

Ewing, Heidi, and Rachel Grady, dirs. 2012. *DETROPIA.* Docurama Studio.

Fanon, Frantz. 1967. *Black skin, white masks*, trans. Charles Lam Markmann. New York: Grove Press, Inc.

Gordon, Avery. 1997. *Ghostly matters: Haunting and the sociological imagination.* Minneapolis: Univ. of Minnesota Press.

Guthrie, Ricardo. 2013. Oprah Winfrey and the trauma drama: What's so good about feeling bad? In *Presenting Oprah Winfrey, her films, and African American literature*, ed. Tara T. Green, 45–78. New York: Palgrave Macmillan.

———. 2012. Minstrelsy & mythic appetites: *The Last King of Scotland*'s heart of darkness in the jubilee year of African independence. In *Hollywood's Africa after 1994*, ed. MaryEllen Higgins, 110–24. Athens: Ohio Univ. Press.

Jules-Rosette, Bennetta. Afro-pessimism's many guises. *Public Culture* 14, no. 3 (2002): 603–5.

The Last Poets. 1971. *This is madness*. Douglas Records.

Nelson, Alondra. Introduction: Future texts. *Social Text* 20, no. 2 (2002): 1–15.

Patterson, Orlando. 1982. *Slavery and social death: A comparative study*. Cambridge, MA: Harvard University Press.

Proyas, Alex, dir. 2004. *I, robot*. 20th Century Fox Film Corp.

Rose, Tricia. 1994. *Black noise: Rap music and black culture in contemporary America*. Hanover, N.H.: Wesleyan University Press.

Sexton, Jared. People-of-color-blindness: Notes on the afterlife of slavery. *Social Text* 28, no. 2 (2010): 31–56.

Sobchack, Vivian. 1997. *Screening space*. New Brunswick, NJ: Rutgers Univ. Press.

Wilderson, Frank B., III. 2010. *Red, white & black: Cinema and the structure of U.S. antagonisms*. Durham, NC: Duke University Press.

———. 2008. Afro-pessimism. *Incognegro, A Memoir of Exile and Apartheid*, website. Boston, MA: South End Press. http://www.incognegro.org/afro_pessimism.html. Accessed Jan. 5, 2014.

Yaszek, Lisa. An afrofuturist reading of Ralph Ellison's *Invisible Man*. *Rethinking History* 9, no. 2-3 (2005): 297–313.

Zuberi, Nabeel. Is this the future? Black music and technology discourse. *Science Fiction Studies* 34, no. 2 (2007): 283–300.

# Part II

# Planetary Vibes, Digital Ciphers, and Hip Hop Sonic Remix

*Chapter Four*

# The Armageddon Effect

*Afrofuturism and the Chronopolitics of Alien Nation*

tobias c. van Veen

It is not possible to *become* cultured in this culture, if you are *naturally* alien to it.—Gayatri Chakravorty Spivak, *A Critique of Postcolonial Reason* (1999, 12)

In 1992, all but the name of Afrofuturism had been elaborated in a detailed and esoteric—if not philosophical and prescient—article in *WIRE* magazine entitled "Loving the Alien in Advance of the Landing—Black Science Fiction" (Sinker 1992).[1] Though it is Mark Dery who would coin "Afrofuturism" in a roundtable with Tricia Rose, Samuel R. Delany, and Greg Tate in 1993 to name the themes and concerns of twentieth-century African-American speculative fiction, music, comics, film and arts (1994a),[2] Sinker's essay is deserving of a speculative exegesis for its attention to the *conceptual* dimensions of the Afrofuturist arts and culture of the black Atlantic. In this chapter, I mobilize Sinker's nascent concepts to explore Afrofuturist aesthetic praxis, distinguishing at the same time their cultural deployment from— but also entwinement with—Afrocentric usages.

Arguably building upon the earlier reflections of Amiri Baraka on futurism and Sun Ra and John Coltrane's interstellar jazz (1999), Samuel R. Delany on black science fiction (2012), and Greg Tate's music and cultural criticism that traversed poststructural theory, semiotics and hip-hop (1992), Sinker was one of the first cultural critics to identify an array of science fictional tropes resonating throughout Afrodiasporic cultural production and practices.[3] Sinker emphasized the latter's reconceptualization of slavery under the science fictional trope of alien abduction, and its decisive outlook:

that there is no "normal" to return to, no untainted origin but the "Alien Nation" of post-abduction existence.

> The ships landed long ago: they already laid waste whole societies, abducted and genetically altered swathes of citizenry, imposed without surcease their values. Africa and America—and so by extension Europe and Asia—are already in their various ways Alien Nation. No return to normal is possible: what "normal" is there to return to? (Sinker 1992)

What is the meaning of "Alien Nation"? Sinker writes the split sign but once; its meaning is inferred and all but hermetic. My intention below is to tease out the resonances and ramifications of such fragmentary tropes and descriptive signs and to construct a conceptual grammar forged from its works.

In *Between Camps*, Paul Gilroy underscores the "absence of an adequate conceptual and critical language" for addressing the "density of today's mixed and always impure forms" of Afrodiasporic—and Afrofuturist—belonging (2004, 251). Yet the positing of an absence betrays the "operational concepts" at work in the thick of the Afrofuturist milieu. These concepts inhabit practices that transform technologies in their mis-use, amplify individuated becomings through technique and affect, and reconstruct master languages in the forging of idiom. There is a need, then, to turn to a number of science fictional motifs and tropes and to transpose them from descriptions into verbs: to read them not just as allegories for the traumas of oppression and slavery elsewhere and elsewhen, but as operational concepts articulated through Afrodiasporic (and planetary) practices and becomings. As well as developing an "adequately conceptual" and "critical" language, such a lexicon needs to be able to address the *imaginative, futurological* and *speculative* dimensions of Afrofuturism. It needs to undertake its conceptual labors within discourses and practices however impure, however fantastical—precisely because such impurities challenge readymade futures and whitewashed pasts that constrain the possibilities of the present (and which is to say, police their impossibilities).

Sinker's brief 2,415 word article contends with a complexity of thought drawn from Afrofuturist media. My intention here is not to explicate Sinker's argument per se—for as a music journalist, it operates by way of inferences and observations—but to unfold two of his Afrofuturist samples. The first is from Public Enemy: "Armageddon been-in-effect." The second is of his own coinage: "Alien Nation." Both concepts address the rupture of transatlantic slavery in cultural memory, or rather, the way slavery has been reassembled, reinterpreted, and historicized by Afrofuturology. While the Armageddon effect signals the temporal rupture of black Atlantic slavery and its obliteration of a normalized past, positing a void of origin that is as enabling as it is a locus of trauma, the second rupture is coterminous in its uncanny unhomeliness, or rather un-Earthliness. Since slavery's dehumanization program, Afrodiasporic subjects live in Alien Nation.

Sinker amassed several concepts from what he called "Black Science Fiction," a naming that, like Dery's usage, included multiple modes of Afrofuturist cultural production. Writing for the *Village Voice*, Greg Tate had also identified similar strains of black futurism. In fact, the two honed in on a phrase from militant hip-hop outfit Public Enemy (PE), a phrase that in itself is a temporal concept: *Armageddon been in effect*. In "Yo! Hermeneutics!," Tate had taken to task Henry Louis Gates, Houston Baker and David Toop for neglecting what he saw as "futuristic black contemporary variants on the blues and signifying tradition"—turning to the work of emcee, sculptor and graffiti artist RAMM:∑LL:Z∑∑, among others, to exemplify the complexities and intensities of Afrofuturological *slanguage*—writing at the very end of his essay that "that the half ain't yet been told" of what was to come (Tate 1992, 158). What wasn't yet told was the full explication of the meaning of PE's phrase. In an essay on PE's *It Takes A Nations of Millions To Hold Us Back* (1988), Tate wrote that "*Nation of Millions* is a will-to-power party record by bloods who believe (like Sun Ra) that for black folk, it's after the end of the world. Or, in PEspeak: 'Armageddon has been in effect. Go get a late pass" (1992, 123).

*Like Sun Ra, after the end of the world.* Both Tate and Sinker would draw a connection between Public Enemy, whose visual and dancefloor aesthetics took their cue from the Black Panther Party—embodied in the urban warfare attire of the Security of the First World (S1W), PE's bodyguard and breakdance troupe headed by Professor Griff—and Sun Ra, the jazz composer and musician, philosopher poet and self-proclaimed ancient alien deity from Saturn who—in 1971 and while teaching a course on "The Black Man in the Cosmos" at Berkeley (Szwed 1998, 294)—had stayed in an Oakland house provided for *by* the Panthers (Kreiss 2008).[4]

Public Enemy, "like Sun Ra," says Tate, already examined the world through a post-eschatological timeline: total cultural destruction and dehumanization under slavery had already happened. What comes after the End Times? In the 1974 Sun Ra film *Space Is the Place* (SITP), Ra attempts to save Earth's inhabitants by offering them offworld employment with Outer Spaceways Incorporated, but seeing that the position provides no pay and requires giving up Earthly pleasures and vices, only a handful take him up on the offer.[5] At the close to the film, planet Earth is destroyed, ambiguously so.[6] But for Ra as for PE, Earth and its inhabitants are already dead: the End Times had already taken place. Earth, according to Ra, was already out of place as it was out of tune with the cosmos (2005b).

Sinker would call this state of perceiving a temporal extension beyond its finitude—of a history-less history where "the ships landed long ago"—the lived experience of Alien Nation. Tate connects the phrase "Armageddon been in effect" to the conclusions of historian Eugene Genovese, who in *Roll, Jordan, Roll* (1976) argues that enslaved Africans in North America did not revolt because of a stillborn timeline:

> Genovese offers that the failure of mainland blacks to sustain a revolutionary tradition during slavery was due to a lack of faith in prophets of the apocalypse. This lack, he says, derived from Africa's stolen children having no memories of a paradise lost that revolution might regain. (Tate 1992, 124)

Genovese' assumption that enslaved Africans failed to revolt has since been challenged (Higginson 1998; Hart 2002). Stephen Hahn has argued that revolts were more widespread than previously thought, suggesting that Reconstruction-era accounts downplayed black insurrection to further conciliatory interests (2009). That the recounting of the past has been tampered with reinforces the need to re-evaluate the conceptual trajectories of Afrofuturism that reconceptualise the past—and what is to-come. From the beginning of a lost history, then, "Armageddon been in effect" has affected historical recounting by erasing the records of revolt. In 1978, Samuel R. Delany noted that there were very few black sf authors, prompting him to write that "We need images of tomorrow; and our people need them more than most" (2012, 14). However, such images, shapes, narratives, rhythms are not just of tomorrow, but draw from and redraw the past, a past that begins with its terminus in armageddon, a terminus that is the origin of erasure.

## BLACKSKINS: ROBOT RACE

> Slavery is perhaps the most important sf theme of all time. . . . As an sf theme, robot slavery—redundant, given the word's root in forced labor—is usually but not always transparently readable as race slavery. (LaBare 2014)

As Kodwo Eshun outlines in "Motion Capture," the interview that bookends his evocative exploration of Afrofuturist sonicultures, *More Brilliant Than The Sun: Adventures in Sonic Fiction* (1999), "Mark [Sinker] made the correlation between *Blade Runner* and slavery, between the ideas of alien abduction and the real events of slavery" (1999, A[175]).[7] Sinker's reading of "armageddon been in effect" emphasizes that the End Times occur in the past tense: the slaveships beached upon the shores of the "dark continent," unloading an arsenal of cultural, economic, and epistemic destruction: what Marx called the "primitive accumulation" of forced slavery.

As Marx writes in volume one of *Capital*, along with the conquering of the Americas and India, including "the extirpation, enslavement, and entombment in mines of the indigineous population [of the Americas] . . . the conversion of Africa into a preserve for the commercial hunting of black-skins, are all things which characterize the dawn of the era of capitalist production" (1990, 915). Marx's use of "blackskins"—as if Africans were the trade equivalent of Canadian beaver pelts in the establishment of economic and territorial dominion—signifies the *ontological* conversion already in effect.[8] The blackskin is living monetary value. The blackskin marks not a human, but a living product to be commercially hunted.[9]

By raising the question of ontology, I wish to underscore how slavery converted the "human being" to a strictly monetary sign: *subject $*. Viewed from the vantage of human exceptionalism, slavery attempts to obliterate the ontological capacity of human subjectivity: that the human being, exceptional to all other species, is the unique entity irreducible to exchange value. Yet, such absolute commodification is at the very core of slavery. Under such logic (and law), slaves are not human: they are private property.[10] The labouring body becomes absolute property, pure finance, what Ian Baucom describes as the "suffering human body incessantly attended by an equal sign and a monetary equivalent" (2005, 7).[11] This is not to say that the obliteration of a subject's "humanity" was complete.[12] Despite systemic violence, the plasticity of "human" ontology—or rather, from an Afrofuturist perspective, how *becoming* reveals the "human" as but one particular modality, what Sun Ra called a Living Myth that attempts to usurp all others as the "master race"—offers means of escape, exodus, and resistance. Uncovered histories of Civil War-era slave rebellions, for example, attest to this capacity to revolt even under the most dire circumstances (Higginson 1998; Hart 2002; Hahn 2009).

Nonetheless, slavery by its very nature strives to displace even the very memory of "being human."[13] Such is the *de jure* principle of instituting slavery; that the slave is not a human subject. The violence of enslavement sought to erase the past, its rituals, religions, and languages, so as to remake living labour, what Baucom calls "the subject $," without memory or attachment. Public Enemy's dystopian soundscapes strive to imagine these traumas of the Middle Passage. Whether the individuated condition of slavery was a result of war, kidnapping, or unfortunate birth, once unloaded in the New World the "cargo" were accounted for, numbered, shackled and sold as commodities, their names and identities stripped, their cultures, histories and languages (all but) banished.[14] With the genesis of the Atlantic slave trade in the 16th century, what had yet to emerge as industrial capitalism had nonetheless already achieved the ultimate commodification of labor.

The long sixteenth to nineteenth centuries of the Atlantic slave trade (*Maafa*, or "Great Disaster" in Swahili) cannot be comprehended without taking into account the destruction wrought upon the ontological certitude of being *human*. For it is with this erasure, itself an effect of prolonged dehumanization—an erasure that assumes the positive valence of humanism, of an essential human "kernel," as it were, to the dehumanized slave—that the Afrofuturist undoing of slave consciousness commences: what worth is there in what Eshun calls the "pointless and treacherous category" of the human when the "real conditions of existential homelessness, alienation, dislocation, and dehumanization" have forever rendered modernity and its Enlightenment project suspect? (1999; 2003, 288). The stakes of this question are outlined by Eshun as well as novelist Toni Morrison:

> In an interview with critic Paul Gilroy in his anthology *Small Acts*, novelist Toni Morrison argued that the African subjects that experienced capture, theft, abduction, mutilation, and slavery were the first moderns. They underwent real conditions of existential homelessness, alienation, dislocation, and dehumanization that philosophers like Nietzsche would later define as quintessentially modern. Instead of civilizing African subjects, the forced dislocation and commodification that constituted the Middle Passage meant that modernity was rendered forever suspect. (Eshun 2003, 288)

What avenues of available existence are there if modernity is forever rendered suspect? How does one respond when faced with one-size-fits-all Enlightenment humanism that excludes those others—as dehumanized enlaved Africans—to improve the conditions of some "real" humans? If there is no "normal" to return to, what options are left? Where does one go, and what does one become, if the subjectivities available all lead towards the very ontology that instituted slavery?

## ARMAGEDDON BEEN IN EFFECT

> The central fact in Black Science Fiction—self-consciously so named or not— is an acknowledgement that Apocalypse already happened: that (in Public Enemy's phrase) *Armageddon been in effect.* (Sinker 1992)

In his link-up of black science fictions and Afrodiasporic sonicultures,[15] Sinker mapped the tropes of armageddon and alien abduction as they shaped the shared imaginaries of the dispersed, yet connected cultures of what Paul Gilroy would memorably theorize—in nearly the same year—as the black Atlantic (1993). Sinker observed how a number of Afrodiasporic cultural productions embraced alien, outerspace, and off world tropes. Central to these science fictional tropes was an account of the Atlantic slave trade, narrativized and reimagined as the armageddon of alien abduction: "The central fact in Black Science Fiction—self-consciously so named or not," writes Sinker, "is an acknowledgement that Apocalypse already happened: that (in Public Enemy's phrase) *Armageddon been in effect.*" (1992). For Sinker, the very genesis of Afrofuturism develops from the tension that "Armageddon been in effect."

Armageddon commences with Africans abducted by aliens to a strange land; everything that follows is played out in a post-apocalyptic dystopia. The phrase is taken from "Countdown to Armageddon," the dystopic, shell-shocked opening to *It Takes A Nation Of Millions To Hold Us Back* (1988). Recorded live at a London BBC Television concert with sirens screaming, Professor Griff unleashes the flow: "Armageddon been in effect. Go get a late pass. Step! / This time around, the revolution will not be televised. Step!." For Sinker as for Public Enemy, the alien ships had already landed.

In the opening to Public Enemy's "Can't Truss It" (1991), a collage of samples bombards the listener in an audio flashback of dystopia. The Armageddon effect is rendered audible through an atmosphere of what Steve Goodman identifies as *dread* (2010), as the collage construction of the Bomb Squad production is laden with low bass frequencies and rumbling reverb. The Bomb Squad sampled from news broadcasts, Civil Rights-era speeches, and field recordings to construct an ominous sound collage that collapsed the traumas of the past into the acoustic environment of the present. The collage begins with Terminator X scratching samples of Malcolm X: "*It started in slave ships . . .* [record scratch] *slave ships*. There are more records of slaveships than one would dream." As the record is spun, the sound of a helicopter buzzes overhead. Malcolm X continues: "It seems inconceivable until you affect that for two hundred years ships sailed carrying cargos of slaves." The sounds of people screaming now startle the collage, as a final and decisive record scratch reveals the now unobfuscated voice of Malcolm X: "Be non– non– be nonviolent." Malcolm X continues: "In the face of the violence that we've been experiencing for the past four hundred years, it's actually not equal to a disservice, in fact it's a crime—it's a crime—." Finally, Chuck D from Public Enemy announces the sonic war machine of what follows: "HERE COMES THE DRUMS!"

*Armageddon—in the past tense.* Professor Griff signifies that with the event of slavery, armageddon has already taken place for Afrodiasporic populations. The timeline is not as it should be. Something awry has taken place: time is (to rephrase Shakespeare's Hamlet) "out of joint." The Apocalypse has already happened: its effects have *been*, past tense. Everything else that follows is but an *effect* of armageddon. We live in a post-apocalyptic future; this future is but an *Armageddon-effect*. Consequently, everyone else, audience included, needs to go to school—in short: to get schooled. The rest of us—those unschooled in the Afrodiasporic apocalyptic experience of the armageddon-effect—are all late to the effects of armageddon, though we live its effects (blindly). Catch up to the future that has been. Go get a late pass.[16]

*This time around, the revolution will not be televised.* The 1960s protest slogan was put to poetic use by Gil-Scott Heron of the Last Poets; it first appeared on the 1970 album *Small Talk at 125th and Lenox*. The Last Poets presage the breaks of hip-hop, combining poetic flow with percussion and rhythmic accompaniment (Baraka 1999). Griff's citation links Public Enemy to the Last Poets, hip-hop to the 1960s Black Arts Movement.[17] Scott-Heron's flow underscores his use of repetition. In his live recordings, Heron slows the tempo down, pausing for effect. In the break—an aesthetic of the pause or caesura, that space in-between the drums, the circuit of the call-and-response between audience, performers, remixers (Moten 2003)—the audience calls back. "The revolution will not be televised" is structured as a series of negations: the revolution will *not* be televised, *nor* appear alongside advertising, *nor* appear to be selling products of any kind (Moten 2000, 77). The revolution will not be televised, says Scott-Heron, because there will be no audience to watch television: *you become the revolution.*

The poem's opening line affirms the revolutionary subject of history by removing the audience from the Nielsen ratings: "You will not be able to stay at home, brother. / You will not be able to plug in, turn on and cop / out." "The revolution *will* put you in the driver's seat"; "The revolution will be no re-run, brothers. / The revolution will be LIVE" (2000, 79). In an interview with PBS Television in the 1990s, Scott-Heron explains how the poem's catchphrase was meant to reinforce the transformative aspect of revolutionary subjectivity:

> You have to change your mind before you change the way you livin' and the way you move. So when we said that "the revolution will not be televised," we were saying that the thing is going to change people. There's something that no one will ever be able to capture on film. It will be something that you see and all of a sudden you realise, I'm on the wrong page. Or I'm on the right page, but on the wrong note. And I've got to get in sync with everyone else to understand what's happening with this country.[18]

Griff's rephrasing implicitly states, however, that the revolution *was* televised—the "first time around." Griff underscores the poem's paradox: that once the subject acts—gets off the couch in protest—the subject is televised regardless, caught up within the media apparatuses of representation, the "subject" of the nightly newscast and it spectacle. Griff's announcement that "this time around it won't be" is both threat and promise of an impossible act of negation in the cyclicity of revolt. Black out the networks.

But just as the symbols of black nationalism are recontextualized by Public Enemy in their lyrics, videos, and imagery—the raised fist of black power, samples of Malcolm X and Louis Farrakhan, phrases from the Nation of Islam, the S1W breakdancers garbed as Black Panthers—Public Enemy likewise reposition Nation Time within hip-hop, and hip-hop within a mediatized environment, suggesting that the televisual apparatus negated by Scott-Heron can be "revolutionised" by the force of content that depicts what a future revolution might look like.

The 1989 video for Public Enemy's "Fight The Power" appears to stage the question: "what would revolt look like today?"—a question that manifested itself in the wake of the 1992 Los Angeles South Central riots, a six-day uprising that exploded after a trial court acquitted four police officers of the beating of Rodney King. Commissioned by Spike Lee as the anthem for his film *Do The Right Thing* (1989), the video for "Fight the Power" suggests an alternate course of action, in which the Brooklyn-filmed block party— held in Bed-Stuy, no less—blends dance party and street protest into a carnivalesque atmosphere of insurgent politics.[19] In a powerful essay for *Salon.com*, Laura K. Warrall argues that

> "Fight the Power" pushed audiences to question authority, and said what we were too afraid to say about American society. The song came at a time when young people, who were being cast aside as gangstas or slackers, were hungry for meaning and connection. Not since the idealized '60s had there been such a force in music toward action. Music fans were reminded of their political strength and their right to defy the establishment. When Public Enemy called us to battle, it revived the notion that it just might be possible to fight the system. At the very least, we knew it was necessary. (Warrall 2002)

Yet the consumer cycle does not end here, and the process of capture by which such edgy representations are again recycled into marketing and consumer capitalism have become staples of the latter.[20] Beginning with the Rodney King amateur video and CNN's invention of the 24-hour news cycle during the 1990 Gulf War, the advent of mobile recording, broadcast devices and digital telecommunications have engendered an even more complex interrelationship wherein advertisers and broadcast corporations alike profit from the amateur production and consumption of revolt, violence, and military operations.[21] Identifying modes of "resistance" to representation has likewise revealed its inadequacy when facing the complexities of capitalist appropriation. The moral panics over the explosion of "gangsta'" but also militant "conscious" hip-hop in the late 1980s and early 1990s—with Public Enemy, along with N.W.A., Wu-Tang Clan, Sunz of Man, Jeru the Damaja, KRS-One and Eric B. and Rakim, at the forefront—have long since receded, precisely because mainstream hip-hop has been codified into established traits of misogyny, sexism, and black-on-black violence that remains comfortably ensconced within the narrative of consumer capitalism.[22] As Asante, Jr. writes:

> Although hip hop was founded on the principles of rebellion, over the past decade [2000–] it has been lulled into being a conservative instrument, promoting nothing new or remotely challenging to mainstream cultural ideology. Even in the midst of an illegitimate war in Iraq, rap music remains a stationary vehicle blaring redundant, glossy messages of violence without consequence,

misogyny, and conspicuous consumption. As a result, it has betrayed the very
people it is supposed to represent; it has betrayed itself. (Asante Jr. 2008, 10)

There are, of course, counterexamples to such betrayal, and Asante Jr.
focuses upon recovering and exploring these alternative avenues—as does
Afrofuturism, an oft-neglected component of hip-hop's political and revolutionary imaginary. But rather than pursuing the critique of appropriation,
authenticity, and representation—whose cycles are well worn—I wish to
return to Public Enemy's focus on *why* the problematic of representation and
its circuit of commodification continue to undermine efforts of socio-politi-
cal and economic change (or, more militantly, revolutionary agency). By
juxtaposing "Armageddon been in effect" with a clarification of Scott-Heron's phrase—*this time* the revolution will not be televised—Public Enemy
demonstrate how the former affects the conditions of the latter. The "Armageddon effect" signifies the *persistent* effects of slavery in rendering contemporary conditions dystopic. But what re-cycles these persistent effects? The
"Armageddon effect" suggests a rather more pernicious re-cycling of slavery: the commodification of black revolutionary cultures through the media
apparatus of representation. James Baldwin summarizes this condition:
"Now, as then, we find ourselves bound, first without, then within, by the
nature of our categorizations" (qtd. in Asante Jr. 2008, 1).

We may now summarize "Armageddon been in effect" as follows: whereas Public Enemy's flow depicts how *absolute* commodification began with
the slave ships—the enslaved African as the commodified "subject $"—
Scott-Heron's rap describes the paradox of commodified televisual representation, underscoring how PE represent an escape effort that remains caught in
the very Armageddon effect they dramatize. The revolutionary content that
decries the very history of enslaved commodification, in short, is caught in
the very form of commodification that profits from the vending of resistance.

Public Enemy's self-reflexive performance of the paradox of commodified resistance suggests that it is only through spectacular dramatization—a
Sicilian embrace of televisualization and consumerized means of communication—that the Armageddon effect can be rendered visible.

The mediatised era that renders revolution as televisual spectatorship is
*also* but an effect of the system of absolute commodification that turns all
that is solid into spectacle and $. In Professor Griff's brief two phrases,
Public Enemy connect slavery to the commodification of (black) revolutionary culture, while self-reflexively demonstrating, through the resampling of
Scott-Heron, how the Armageddon effect undermines, in advance, the place
of a non-mediatised outside to revolutionary activity. Public Enemy suggest—or rather self-reflexively perform—that it will only be through television, or rather through the Armageddon effect at large that the latter's forces
can be countered.

# ENCOUNTERS WITH ALIEN NATION

> . . . the planet, already turned Black, must embrace rather than resist this: that back-to-nature pastoralism is intrinsically reactionary, that only ways of technological interaction inherited from the jazz and now the rap avant garde can reintegrate humanity with the runaway machine age. (Sinker 1992)

The figure of the alien is pivotal to Afrofuturism: it is the point at which Afrofuturism articulates its imaginaries to an embodiment in a "subject" that implicates itself within mediatisation only to undermine its certitude as human. The subject $ produces an alienating effect of its own absolute commodification by undermining the guarantees of its Earthly subjectivity. Rather than struggling for (white) humanism, Afrofuturism rejects its supposed necessity as the certitude of ontology. The Armageddon-effect produces Alien Nation—not just as the effect of being estranged by foreign forces, but of strategically mobilizing estrangement towards becoming.

In what follows, I will outline three alien embodiments, or figurations of an Afrofuturist typology: the ancient alien deity (Sun Ra); the cosmic messenger (John Coltrane); and the electric Afronaut (Jimi Hendrix). [23] There is no better place to begin than with "Egyptian deity, cosmic explorer [and] mystic messenger" Sun Ra, otherwise known as the bandleader of the "Myth-Science Arkestra," prolific jazz composer, avant-gardist keyboardist, pamphleteer, and philosopher poet. We encounter Ra as he is narrating his abduction by outer-space aliens—with red glowing eyes and antennas—to Mark Sinker.

*The ancient alien deity.* "I went up at terrific speed to another dimension, another planet," says Ra to the British journalist, the latter self-describing his 1989 Philadelphia encounter with Ra as "a middle-class English kid, self-defrocked punk rocker" meeting the "prophet of a space between worlds in collision," now "in his mid '70s . . . his touchstones '40s pulp SF, '30s big band music, '20s conspiracy-theory pseudo-Egyptology" (2014). Replying over the course of two hours to Sinker—who had asked him what the link was between music and magic—Ra continues: "Anyway, they talked to me about this planet, and the way it was headed and what was going to happen to teenagers, and governments, and people. They said they wanted me to talk to them. And I said I wasn't interested" (Ra qtd. in Sinker 1992).

In his 1992 article, Sinker elicits little surprise at Ra's disinterest—because Sun Ra is, after all, an alien Egyptian deity, it is entirely natural that he turns down "the offer of Messiahship." "They wanted me to be one of them," says Ra, addressing his alien captors (or colleagues?), "and I said no, it's natural for you to be like that, but it might hurt me if you gave me some" (qtd in Sinker 1992). It is worth reflecting on the possible moral of Ra's tale in which he turns down the alien abduction: as he is already alien, he can no longer be abducted.[24] Yet is not the double-meaning of this tale, told to Sinker, that Ra cannot be abducted—which is to say, appropriated—by an alien (white) journalist? For Ra is telling something else: that as an alien, he occupies a critical position capable of countering the Armageddon-effect: he is able to deflect abduction, precisely because he has abandoned the human, including demands that he answer interview questions within the human coordinates of planetary belief structures.

Reflecting upon this interview some twenty-odd years later, Sinker writes of Ra: "He had stood on a soapbox on Chicago street-corners, in a fez, just along from where Elijah Muhammad was fashioning the Nation of Islam, creating a cosmology of his own, with himself at its centre—and he had asked people to travel with him. And many had" (Sinker 2014). But was Ra really at the centre of his own cosmology? This is a perception reinforced by Kodwo Eshun, who characterised Ra as identifying "with the Pharoahs, the despots, the ancient oppressors, by seceding from America" (1999, 09[154]). Ra's poetic philosophy, however, reveals a much more complex Afrofuturist cosmology. He does not just secede from America, but from Earth. In addition, Ra does not *identify* with the Pharoahs, but transforms the figure of the Pharoah just as he transforms himself into an ancient alien deity (Ra 2005b). It is this esoteric yet powerful theo-cosmology, and not Ra's prospects as a despotic auto-theocentrist, that garnered him "followers." One such fellow traveller was Ra's greatest jazz disciple, John Coltrane.

*The Cosmic Messenger.* In the recording of Coltrane' final album, the "interminable and maddening" *Interstellar Space* (1967/1974), 'Trane "warp-drives to the core of the galaxy and the core of the soul," writes Sinker (1992).[25] Both Sinker and Eshun work with metaphors of the cosmic and the alien to imprint Coltrane's music into language, stretching the capacities of the text in its encounter with Coltrane's "interstellar" jazz. Eshun writes that "the merciless monotony" of *Interstellar Space* "reactivates the predestination of astrology. Energy Music becomes Universal Sound which makes audible the cosmic order, fore hears the master plan in an act of clairaudience" (1999, 10[173]). In short,[26] Coltrane's efforts to blast through jazz notation with the sheer force of his instrument alone can be heard as an attempt to escape from the Earthly conventions of jazz performance. "Energy Music" is a term coined by avant-garde jazz saxophonist and Coltrane collaborator Albert Ayler, and is used to describe the forceful playing of multiphonic, free improvisation that emphasizes timbre over harmony and melody.

Eshun describes how Coltrane's raw style of overblowing his saxophone enters into a cosmic realm: that of Universal Sound, the sound of *om*, which Coltrane had earlier explored with the spiritual chants of *A Love Supreme* (1964).[27] It is the forceful style of Energy Music combined with the cosmic spirituality of Universal Sound that leads to Eshun's "clairaudience," in which *clairovoyance* and *audience* merge into a spiritual-sonic feedback loop. Coltrane carries the audience into this act of making "audible the cosmic order"; Coltrane's music becomes an act of audible, astrological "predestination" in the "forehear[ing]" of the cosmic "masterplan" of Universal Sound. But this is the first stage of Eshun's *om*: the second will be its transformation by electricity to *ohm*, as the Universal Sound shifts from the cosmic jazz player to the figure of the psychedelic Afronaut.

*The Afronaut.* Sinker writes that Coltrane cannot be thought without hearing Afronaut Jimi Hendrix, for both pushed the limits of instrumentality and music into cosmic realms: "the utterly fluid space poet glided somewhere beyond black and white, masculine and feminine, noise and grace," writes Sinker (2014). The lithe, manic, intense figure of Hendrix, thrusting into his amplifiers and burning his guitar at the 1967 Monterey Pop Festival, or savagely spraying the audience with sonic bullets during his rendition of "Machine Gun" with the Band of Gypsy's in 1969 at the Fillmore East in New York, was not quite human. Hendrix was an in-between, near androgynous figure that complicated notions of blackness as he transgressed race, his subjectivity reflecting the in-betweeness of his music that combined blues riffs and psychedelic noise, just as it mixed up his audience and Experience band, black and white. He embodies the "Afronaut," crafting a cosmic alter-ego, undertaking a transformation of self in becoming the spacepoet of cosmic feedback. Sinker's allusive point is that years before David Bowie's Ziggy Stardust persona, it was Hendrix who had landed on Earth as the androgynous and shifting star child. This cosmic in-betweenness was nowhere more contentious than with Hendrix's ambiguity toward race. Hendrix transgressed the racialized expectations endemic to American culture—that he remain a "black" performer. Cultural critics eager to defend traditions of black authenticity have often seen Hendrix as an apostate to black culture; critic Nelson George conservatively "expell[ed] the innovative guitarist from his canonical reconstruction of the black musical idiom," writes Gilroy (1993, 94).

Nonetheless, this excommunication, notes Gilroy, made his "racial alienation literal"—and it is precisely here that, using Sinker's text, we are able to read "alienation" as "Alien Nation." Hendrix had embraced something other than black nationalism in his move beyond the categories of gender and color, just as he had pushed, like Coltrane and Ra, the boundaries of black music into cosmic and alien realms. Had Hendrix embraced an unearthly ex-nationalism, the figure of Alien Nation? This question is perhaps best addressed by a detractor: "Jimi's music was, if not from another planet, definitely from another country," writes George (qtd. in Gilroy 1993, 94). Indeed, the thrust of George's criticism is that because Hendrix developed his sound in London, rather than the United States, and save for the Band of Gypsys, played with white musicians as The Jimi Hendrix Experience, he

"whitened" his music, abandoning his blues (read: black) roots to psychedelic (read: white) extravagance; in short, he was not an "authentic" black
performer. It is precisely this Alien Nation that Hendrix embraced, and that
posits Hendrix as an Afrofuturist Afronaut. Hendrix alienated himself from
the very categorical constraints, racial and otherwise, of American culture
that were constitutive of George's attempt to construct an "authentic" black
canon.

By connecting Coltrane to Hendrix, forever two figures entwined with the
1960s, one can trace the movement of Eshun's mantra, wherein the universal
chant of *om* becomes the Universal Sound of *ohm*. "Tomorrow every Afronaut and every hippie wakes up to a Universal Sound," writes Eshun of
Hendrix (1999, 10[172–73]). With electrified, cosmic blues, the "Universal
Sound" of *om* becomes that of Electricity's *ohm*. Hendrix calls home to the
heavens with his electrified, left-handed guitar, in explaining how the new
Church—its meaning here resounding with the black gospel tradition—is
that of Electric Religion:

> Everything is electrified nowadays. That is why the name Electric Sky Church
> flashes in and out. I am Electric Religion. We're making music into a new kind
> of Bible, a Bible that you can carry in your hearts. One that will give you a
> physical feeling.—Jimi Hendrix. (qtd. in Eshun 1999, 01[11])

Hendrix the Afronaut embodies the Electric in-between of the outerspace.
Electricity reaches its most superb *ohm*-state of Universal Sound with his
abstract, yet *affective* outburst of cosmic psychedelia—that "physical feeling"—"And The Gods Made Love" (on *Electric Ladyland* [1968]). Consis-
tinge of a wash of feedback that explodes into cosmic noise, Eshun writes
that it "psychedelicizes cybernetics by turning the guitar into a jet stream
engine: a 90-second painting of the heavens, a tone generator of sound spec-
tra" (1999, 01[11]). Eshun's use of "cybernetics" is an apt descriptor. Hendrix's use of feedback creates a "cybernetic system" between the guitar and
the soundsystem. Second-order cybernetics is the modelling of feedback systems, and with "And The Gods Made Love" Hendrix turns the "circular
causal" relationships of Norbert Wiener into a cosmic encounter with sound
by rendering audible cybernetic recursivity.[28] Hendrix cranks the pick-up on
his guitar until its microphones register the soundsystem's speakers: what
Hendrix plays is not so much the guitar as the entire soundsystem as it feeds-
back into itself, a performance of electricity in a technicosmic feedback
system.

*Outerspace Alien.* The Afrofuturist alien invokes a multiplicity of figures,
yet almost all tend toward the black alien of outer space.[29] What I first wish
to underscore is the differentiated alien figuration of the Afrofuturist. Sun Ra
embodies the alien Pharoah, while his music transports the big band jazz

tradition into outer space, his fellow jazz musicians an interplanetary "Arkes-tra." Coltrane embodies the cosmic mystic, his life a spiritual journey that takes him off planet toward the stars, his instrument the means to overblow Universal Sound, to undertake astrological journeys that reveal the cosmic order (*Maat*). Hendrix embodies the Afronaut space poet, the space race that floats in-between color and gender, just as he electrifies the Church of the blues, transporting the sounds of black authenticity into a technicosmic futur-ism. In each description above, a novel conceptual grammar is necessary to signify why each of these figures is an *Afrofuturist*, why each figure has undertaken a transformation of the self, in different ways and varying de-grees, toward the figures of the interstellar, the cosmic, and the alien.

The second aspect of this alien figuration emphasizes its temporal inter-vention. The very figure of the Afrofuturist alien is already an embodiment of a historical anomaly: an interruption of something-other than the accept-able paradigm of not only "authentic black existence"—as seen in Hendrix's expulsion from the "authentic" black canon—but something other to human existence, that stretches or, at the limit, abandons the figure of the human. This abandonment likewise transforms the inverse of the human in the en-slaved subject $. This becoming-other-than-human, a becoming-alien, under-takes a passage through the subject $, and suggests a temporality lived other-wise: an impossible (alien) future revealed in the destabilising of the present by revisioning the coordinates of the past.

Sun Ra is an ancient black alien deity: by entering from the Kemetian past as an alien figure of the future, he is able to posit an alternate timeline in which the fall of Egypt never happened, and in which, to sample Eshun, "the West is just a side-effect" (1999, 09[156]). Coltrane seeks to blow into the future of jazz, but does so by rewinding the past and time-travelling to before the big band era, before Louis Armstrong, and embracing an alternate time-line of jazz development in which free improvisation never gave way to formal composition.[30] Hendrix appears to erase his immediate past; he aban-dons the American order of "the Negro," departs to London, and refashions a future-self that eschews racialized baggage just as it founds a new Electric Religion. My point here is that Afrofuturist transformations of the "subject" are always temporal interventions: they necessarily break with, remodel, or revise the timeline to remake a recursive future, one that rewrites its own past, in the present. Unquestioned "tradition" is oft challenged, rewrit, or discarded. As can be seen with the criticism of Hendrix (or the general dismissal of Sun Ra by "traditional" jazz critics, the same who tend to dis-miss the "later" Coltrane) such transformative strategies are seen as pro-foundly impacting the boundaries of "authentic" black culture. But here we must re-pose Sinker's question: what "normal" is there to return to? By abandoning the "normal" and embracing the alien, the figure of the Afrofu-turist revisions the past—that "undiscovered country" all but erased during the Middle Passage. Each alien becoming suggests an alternate timeline to Western history, a recasting of temporal and cosmic possibilities. [31]

Alondra Nelson writes that Afrofuturist "works simultaneously referenced a past of abduction, displacement and alien-nation, and inspired technical and creative innovations in the work of such artists as Lee 'Scratch' Perry, George Clinton and Sun Ra" (2000, 2). Nelson articulates the prevailing vision of the Afrofuturist refashioning of the past that I have been tracing here: it is a temporality of "abduction, displacement, and alien-nation," and as such, it is entirely unnatural: there is no "normal" to return to. This has led to two divergent, yet parallel strategies in combatting the Armageddon-effect, in particular the erasures of Afrodiasporic history and the inheritance of cultural trauma. The first strategy emphasizes traditionalism, and the rebuilding of an "authentic" black culture, a movement that finds its apex in black nationalism (Nationtime) and Afrocentrism. The second utilizes many of the same tools (a revisioning of the past, a radicalism of creative black production), but tends toward exodus: it remakes black culture by pushing its boundaries, by questioning the value of "authentic" blackness, finding its most extravagant expression in Afrofuturism, in which "Earth" and "human" are abandoned apace. It is tempting to oppose these strains to each other—the traditional against the futurist, the static against the dynamic, the conservative against the progressive—but this would conflate how each embrace the invention of the other. Both strategies revise the past and construct alternate futures through creative intervention in the timeline. Both are also historically entwined with each other.

Yet there is a distinction to be made in how each strategy encounters the figure of the alien. Both view the events of slavery as abduction, as founding the system of Alien Nation. Poet and critic LeRoi Jones, who in 1965 changed his name to Amiri Baraka after the assassination of Malcolm X, [32] straddled both strategies, adopting at various times beatnik, black nationalist, and Marxist positions. [33] Baraka was also an ardent supporter of Sun Ra. [34] Writing of James Brown, Amiri Baraka identifies "a system governed by 'aliens'" in which black cultural and spiritual expression "transcends the physical-mental 'material', finally alien system-world it has to go through" (1999, 190). Yet while Afrocentrism and black nationalism battle Alien Nation with the "historical recovery" of cultural authenticity and tradition, Afrofuturism *embraces* its science fictional production. Afrofuturism thus operates by way of paradoxically embracing figures of the past while eschewing claims to authenticity or tradition. But with both strategies, acknowledged or not, the past is but an archive for repurposing, a timeline to be sampled, a chronology to be upset with intervention. Sinker underlines precisely this point:

The triumph of black American culture is that, forcibly stripped by the Middle Passage and Slavery Days of any direct connection with African mother culture, it has nonetheless survived by syncretism, by bricolage, by a day-to-day programme of appropriation and adaptation as resourcefully broad-minded as any in history. But still, the humane tradition—of warmth, community hope and aspiration—central to the gospel roots soul of the southern black tradition is, if treated as the principle that underlies all, a way of hiding from these facts in plain sight: that this tradition is no more uniquely "African" than the Nation of Islam is "Islamic," that this culture is still—in its constituent parts—very much a patchwork borrowing; necessary of course for physical and psychic survival, but not an unarguable continuity. (1992)

For Sinker as for Gilroy, Afrodiasporic culture is but an invention, "very much a patchwork borrowing," cobbled together to fill a cultural and historical void left behind by the Middle Passage. Yet this constituent mixology—its *bricolage* of sampled concepts and practices—reflects a shared project of cultural re-construction, wrought through the criss-crossing of the black Atlantic network by its cultural exports: radio and television transmissions, sound recordings (from vinyl to digital formats), film, video, literature, and the journeys of performers and participants, migrants and travellers themselves.[35] Black Atlantic cultures have evolved through the call-and-response of aesthetic production, in the reimagining of contested yet shared historical themes and ties, of which one of its most intriguing, challenging, and complex assemblages is Afrofuturism. But what are the effects of Afrofuturism's temporal operations, in the invention of shared imaginaries? Pursing this vein of thought further, how does Afrofuturism, with its parallel strategies that refashion and inform the past, present, and future, engage with chronopolitics, as the political structuration of time?

## THE MANUFACTURED HISTORY: CHRONOPOLITICS OF PAST AND FUTURE

The manufactured history . . . The manufactured history!
How came the manufactured history?
Because of the void . . . The manufactured history was
substituted for the void in order to keep man from feeling empty
And without foundation.
—Sun Ra, "The Invented Memory" [1968] (2005b, 218)

The Afrofuturist imaginary reaches into the past to reimagine a future otherwise. It upsets what Greg Tate calls the "black reverence for the past [that] is a reverence for paradise lost" with "a vein of philosophical inquiry and technological speculation that begins with the Egyptians and their incredibly detailed meditations on life after death" (in Dery 1994a, 210–11). Afrofuturism recodes the past out of a contemporary urgency to deal with the historical void left by the Middle Passage and the enforced erasures of slavery—and thus to project a futurity otherwise. The past is barely known, "a past gleaned from discussions," argues Tate, and thus open to its revisioning (qtd. in Dery 1994a, 211). In this closing section, I turn to chronopolitics and its theorization in Eshun's 2003 essay, "Further Considerations of Afrofuturism."

Eshun argues for the political efficacy of temporal strategies that not only revision the past, but upset programmatic schemas for the future:

> The field of Afrofuturism does not seek to deny the tradition of countermemory. Rather, it aims to extend that tradition by reorienting the intercultural vectors of Black Atlantic temporality towards the proleptic as much as the retrospective. It is clear that power now operates predictively as much as retrospectively. Capital continues to function through the dissimulation of the imperial archive, as it has done throughout the last century. Today, however, power also functions through the envisioning, management, and delivery of reliable futures. (Eshun 2003, 289)

It is my intention here to explicate the operational characteristics of chronopolitics so that, as a concept descriptive of a set of temporal practices, it can be put to effective use. Through chronopolitics can be found in the work of Paul Virilio, my reading here is specifically oriented toward Eshun's deployment, keeping in mind how Eshun develops an "Afrofuturist hermeneutics of (temporal) suspicion" that, in its recursive cyclicity, autonomizes the concept from its theoretical antecedents. Nearly all of Afrofuturism's effects are "chronopolitical." Afrofuturism is thoroughly invested in either imagining alternate futures or rewriting the past so as to change the present (from which futures are imagined).

At stake is a recovery of past cycles of futurity and the derailing of whitewashed cycles currently in effect. These processes have been described, to a limited extent, in the performative practices above that dramatise, but also conceptualize, the Armageddon effect and Alien Nation. To wit,

(i) Chronopolitics intervenes in the production of collective memory—institutional, pedagogical, epistemic and museological histories, oral traditions and myths—as well as in the schematic projections of the future. This collective memory is inscribed in texts, cultural practices, and technological objects.

(ii) Chronopolitics is the temporal production of countermemories and counterrealities to combat corporate, whitewashed, or technocapitalist futures of dystopia. It is also a historical recovery operation, in which erasures and evacuations of the unwanted, insurrectionary, or traumatic past are uncovered and put to use, in the "responsibility . . . towards the not-yet" (Eshun 2003, 289). The emergent force of chronopolitics can be read in Ra's words, when he writes that: "If a man can be tempted to think, thereby a better memory can he / create than the one implanted in his mind from the / So-called past" (2005b, 219).

In his 2003 essay, Eshun explores how chronopolitics extends the terrain of political agency to the field of temporality. Eshun's concept of "chrono-politics" echoes similar strategies developed by utopianist texts and the mechanisms of time-travel in science fiction (sf).[36] Fredric Jameson, in his study of the "utopian desire" in sf, *Archaeologies of the Future*, discusses how (modern) narratives of progress are "now seen as attempt[s] to colonize the future, to draw the unforeseeable back into tangible realities, in which one can invest and on which one can bank, very much in the spirit of stock market 'futures'" (Jameson 2005, 228).[37] Jameson concurs with Walter Benjamin's observation that "not even the past will be safe" from the "conquerors" of history, adding that "the future is not safe either" from "the elimination of historicity, its neutralization by way of progress and technological evolution"—the latter which he names "the future of globalization" (Jameson 2005, 228). Drawing closer to the notion of a synchronic historicity that animates his study, Jameson argues that the "antinomies of cause and effect are today exasperated by the emergence of the notion of system," whereby he traces a "gravitational shift from diachronic thinking (so-called linear history) to synchronic or systemic modeling" (2005, 87).

Chronopolitics, as a conceptechnics, partakes of the latter synchrony, amplified into a strategy. Jameson applies this strategy himself by rewriting Asimov's periodized history of sf into "so many possible dominants which form different functional constellations" (Jameson 2005, 92). The latter sf assemblages are developed and critiqued throughout the remainder of Jameson's text. Jameson does not, then, read "utopias" as "in" the future, but rather undertakes a chronopolitical revisioning of past utopian futurisms and alternate-utopian timelines that reveal a plurality of elsewhere/elsewhens.

As if to acknowledge the precedents set elsewhere for chronopolitics, Eshun's text opens with a science fictional narrative describing Afrofuturist time-travellers returning to our forgotten past:

> *Imagine a team of African archaeologists from the future—some silicon, some carbon, some wet, some dry—excavating a site, a museum from their past: a museum whose ruined documents and leaking discs are identifiable as belonging to our present, the early twenty-first century.* (Eshun 2003, 287)

Eshun's concept of chronopolitics has a specificity, however, and that is its articulation with Afrofuturism, or rather, its theorization through the latter. Eshun explains that the chronopolitical field has two interconnected vectors: that of the past (retrospective) and that of the future (proleptic). The stuff of the past is produced: it is interpreted from artifacts, institutionalized in museums, scripted into technologies, and synthesized into what Ra calls "the manufactured history" that shapes the collective memory of the subject (and what Bernard Stiegler calls *mnemotechnics* (1998). The stuff of the future is predicted: it is charted, mapped, and rendered numerical by algorithms, based upon "the manufactured past" (to use Foucault's term, it is *biopolitical*, in the statistical analysis of population timelines [2003]). The future is all but programmed into the subject through a pedagogy of the past.[38] Thus, for Afrofuturism, the stakes of chronopolitics are entwined with upsetting the Armageddon-effect. Chronopolitics are mobilized to revision accounts of slavery and colonialism and to rewrite its trauma by seeding not only alternate futures but recursive pasts for Afrodiasporic subjects who have been overdetermined by "the manufactured past."

The retrospective interventions of chronopolitics can produce as well as disassemble manufactured histories that reinforce ethnocentrist narratives. In a passage concerning "museological" interventions, Eshun writes that "for contemporary African artists, understanding and intervening in the production and distribution of this [temporal] dimension constitutes a chronopolitical act" (2003, 192). "Revisioning" the past is part of Afrocentrism's arsenal of historical reconstruction just as it is a strategy of Afrofuturism:

> By creating temporal complications and anachronistic episodes that disturb the linear time of progress, these [Afro]futurisms adjust the temporal logics that condemned black subjects to prehistory. Chronopolitically speaking, these revisionist historicities may be understood as a series of powerful competing futures that infiltrate the present at different rates. (Eshun 2003, 297)

Upsetting received narratives of the past constitutes not just an intervention that deprograms the coordinates of the present, but reprograms the future. Sometimes, the best way to reimagine the future is to alter the past. The insertion of a counter-narrative into the constitution of the past releases the trajectories of an unpredictable futurity. The same can be said in its inverse: depicting an alternate futurity can lead to a questioning of received narratives of the past. Science fictional futures that depict successful Afrodiasporic subjects imply a rejection of contemporary raciology.[39] But, crucially, Afrofutures repurpose, and do not reject, motifs of the past. The synthesis of past revisionism and science fictional futurism can be seen in the Kemetian symbols of Sun Ra. Ra is both a Pharoah and an alien, an ancient Kemetian deity and a futurist space traveller. In comparison to futurisms that dismiss the past as anachronistic, arcane, or unsophisticated, Afrofuturism repurposes the past. Moreover, Afrofuturist chronopolitics draws from the past, making use of its symbols and tropes, to reinvent futuria. Eshun's chronopolitics, then, acknowledges the debt it has to sf as a *practice* that, in its chronopolitics, "was never concerned with the future, but rather with engineering feedback between its preferred future and its becoming present" (Eshun 2003, 290).

*Stolen Legacies*. Strategic use of chronopolitics is at work in both Afrofuturism and Afrocentrism, traversing the two cultural and political strategies. The parallelism of Afrocentrist historical revisioning to Afrofuturist chronopolitics is noted by Eshun:

> Revisionist logic is shared by autodidact historians like Sun Ra and George G. M. James of *Stolen Legacy*, and contemporary intellectuals such as Toni Morrison, Greg Tate, and Paul D. Miller [a.k.a. DJ Spooky]. [Morrison's] argument that the African slaves that experienced capture, theft, abduction, and mutilation were the first moderns is important for positioning slavery at the heart of modernity. The cognitive and attitudinal shift demanded by her statement also yokes philosophy together with brutality, and binds cruelty to temporality. The effect is to force together separated systems of knowledge, so as to disabuse apparatuses of knowledge of their innocence. (Eshun 2003, 297)

Afrofuturism is as much a recovery project of a revisionist past as it is an imaginary of a future otherwise. Afrofuturism seeks to displace temporality from its whitewashed visions, the latter of which Mark Dery calls "the unreal estate of the future already owned by the technocrats, futurologists, streamliners, and set-designers—white to a man—who have engineered our collective fantasies" (1994a, 180). The figure of Sun Ra embodies this cross-wiring of the futurist, technologically-advanced alien into the past *mythos* of Pharoahnic Kemet, treading a path that parallels—for historical, political, as well as aesthetic reasons—the black nationalism of Afrocentrism. [40]

One of the key MythSciences advanced by Afrocentrism is its historical revisioning of a black Pharoahnic philosphical heritage stolen by Greek culture (for example, in James 2001), or what Eshun outlines as the "reactionary Manichaenism of the Nation of Islam, the regressive compensation mechanisms of Egyptology, Dogonesque cosmology, and the totalising reversals of *Stolen Legacy*–style Afrocentricity" (Eshun 2003, 297). By contrast, Afrofuturism grasps the same symbols, but infuses them with science fiction. Afrocentrism's Kemetianism is transfigured by Afrofuturism into conceptual matter for new belief-systems, new MythSciences capable of upending and challenging the timeline. The *mythos* of Kemet replaces Greece and the Enlightenment project, but in place of Afrocentrism's battle for truth, Afrofuturism reimagines the Pharoahs as black aliens, the pyramids as black secret technologies. Whereas Afrocentrism seeks to prove the veracity of its historical claims, Afrofuturism utilizes historical revisioning to reimagine alternatives to the timeline in the production of counterrealities.

## CONCLUSION

In closing, I return to Ra, who incants his distrust for the past in a text entitled "The Invented Memory" (2005a, 60). What is intriguing about this text is how it elaborates the impure origins of memory: that at first, in the beginning, memory was never bare, never scrubbed clean, but already invented, manufactured; for Sun Ra, these invented memories keep the hueman[41] "from looking / backward into a void . / . . Because of what has happened" (2005b, 218).

The Afrofuturist genesis of invented memory begins with the trauma of the Middle Passage and slavery: this is the "manufactured history!" of the Afrodiasporic subject. But the Biblical invention of memory—a reading that Ra develops at length—begins with the Genesis myth: Adam and Eve are given "unschooled conceptions and beliefs" by the creator. These beliefs are challenged, and revealed as the inventions that they are, when the couple attain self-knowledge—in short, Eve was "schooled" when she bit into the apple.[42] This self-knowledge, of course, results in the expulsion of Adam and Eve from the Garden.

Ra continues, elaborating the symbolic emptiness and yet the potential of the memory void: "The word man is but an / image-symbol / Thus man is striving to be the idea of himself" (2005b, 218). The question is who/what determines the meaning of the image-symbol of "man"? *What* mnemotechnical systems manufactures the invented memories of the subject? This question itself blurs the boundaries of the *who* to the *what*, the subject to cyborg, system to memory flesh. For Eshun, as undoubtedly for Ra, this "idea" is but implanted by what Eshun calls an "imperial racism [that] has denied black subjects the right to belong to the enlightenment project" (Eshun 2003, 287). Afrodiasporic subjects are forever unable to live up to such an "idea of Man," resulting in the perpetuation of what W.E.B. du Bois named "double-consciousness" (1994). However, it is this very emptiness of "the idea of Man" that opens upon the chronopolitics of Afrofuturism and its production of MythSciences and their unhuman becomings.

## NOTES

1. Sinker's article was followed by Mark Dery's edited volume *Flame Wars: The Discourse of Cyberculture* (1994b) and took place concurrently to Greg Tate's investigations of black sf and hip-hop in *The Village Voice* (collected in 1992).

2. An ethnonationalist containerisation that was to continue in Americocentric definitions. Alondra Nelson, for example, re-cites Dery in her introduction to the 2002 issue of *Social Text* on Afrofuturism—"Afrofuturism can be broadly defined as 'African American voices' with 'other stories to tell about culture, technology and things to come'" (2002, 9). Even as Nelson expands the definition's coordinates to the diaspora, the uncritical deployment of the phrase has erected checkpoints that contain the diasporic complexity of the concept.

3. Nonetheless, it was Sinker who arguably crystallized a number of fragmented observations. Though the concept of "Afrodiaspora" is nowhere to be found in Sinker's article, Gilroy's elaboration of the black Atlantic cultural network accurately describes Sinker's approach to Afrofuturism. The Afrodiaspora traces "lines of affiliation and association which take the idea of the diaspora beyond its symbolic status as the fragmentary opposite of some imputed racial essence," underlining the "rituals of performance that provide prima facie evidence of linkage between black cultures" (Gilroy 1993, 95, 101).

4. At least until Ra and the Arkestra was expelled for what Szwed calls "an ideological split within the Panthers . . . ('we got kicked out by Eldridge Cleaver or somebody')" (1998, 330). Taking the 1974 film *Space Is the Place* as a response to the split with the Panthers—the narrative is situated in Oakland and includes Panther-like characters and community programs—Kreiss speculates that "Sun Ra ultimately finds limited value in terrestrial community programs, an allusion to the Panthers, and posits that only the band's use of technology and music will liberate the people by changing consciousness" (2008, 75).

5. An offer not unlike that of joining the Arkestra itself.

6. For an analysis of the film in relation science fiction, technology, and the musical, see Zuberi 2004.

7. It's worth noting that nowhere does Sinker mentioned Ridley Scott's 1982 film *Blade Runner*; the connection is Eshun's. However the underlying motif is clear: Sinker connected the alien-android motifs of Afrofuturism, of creative explorations of nonhuman subjectivity, to the historical dehumanisation produced by slavery.

8. In Akiva Schaffer's film *The Watch* (2012), in which four men band together in a neighbourhood watch only to fend off an alien invasion, the "blackskin" is literally embodied in the character of Jamarcus (Richard Ayoade). Jamarcus is revealed to be an alien wearing the skin of a deceased black man (and whose actual person/body is never dealt with). A running gag in the film concerns the superficiality of Evan's (Ben Stiller) "multicultural friendships" with people of non-white ethnicities. The film's brilliance lies in the self-reflexivity of this searingly critical gag that comes to be embodied in Jamarcus (in this 99 percent-white town of middle-America, even the black guy isn't black, nor is he a black alien: he's an alien wearing blackskin: for this alone I refuse IMDB.com's rating of 5.6 stars and give it a 9).

9. This (de)valuation also reflects upon the ways in which the animal is categorised as nothing other than resource property in Marx's analysis (even if cynically).

10. This argument also goes for the (ongoing) patriarchial violence that treats women as private property. It also extends to the treatment of animals, and life as such, including the Earth, as nothing but privatised property ripe for exploitation and profit.

11. In this respect, we can engage with a little Lacanian play: from subject to object, the African subject $S = \$$.

12. Gates, Jr. argues precisely for the transmission of various pan-African cultural narratives, in song and ritual, down through slavery (see 1988).

13. Such programs were also instituted in Canada's aboriginal Residential schools, for example, where pupils were taken from their families, forbidden to speak their native languages, and schooled in Eurocentric history that devalued their aboriginal culture. Many students were physically and sexually abused. I note this, while reading Fanon on colonial pedagogy in the Antilles (2008), because too often slavery is considered an event of American history. Its mechanisms take many forms. They persist to this day. Hence the relevance of this work.

14. Which is not to say, as Sinker emphasizes, that humans forcibly thrown into slavery were not struggling to retain all that was in the process of being erased: "part of the story of black music (the affirmative, soul-gospel aspect) has always been this—that losing everything except basic dignity and decency is potentially a survivable disaster" (1992).

15. I deploy the portmanteau of *soniculture* to signify all that falls under a "music culture": a combinatory of cultural practices grouped around an ever-modulating set of musical motifs that nonetheless are headlined by an all-purpose descriptor such as jazz or hip-hop; soniculture encompasses performance, composition, listening practices (including dancing), and codes of critical appreciation (what constitutes "good" music). The term is inclusive of the music's production and recording techniques, its distribution networks, preferred avenues of transmis-

sion (digital, vinyl, CDs) and experience (concert halls, late-night smoke-filled clubs, raves, but also headphones, etc.). See van Veen 2010.

16. In interpreting the *flow* of the hip-hop emcee, we are reminded of Tricia Rose's analysis that "rap music is, in many ways, a hidden transcript. Among other things, it uses cloaked speech and disguised cultural codes to comment on and challenge aspects of current power inequalities"; particularly in the case of Public Enemy, hip-hop is "engaged in symbolic and ideological warfare with institutions and groups that symbolically, ideologically, and materially oppress African Americans" (1994, 100–101). And in this case: with the timeline itself, with history as a mutable object, including its past revolutions and insurgencies. (Rose is evidently echoing aspects of Gate's thesis of *Signifyin'*—see (Gates 1988).)

17. Scott-Heron has likewise been sampled in house music with the percussive, deep mini-malist jam, "The Revolution Will Not Be Televised (Lunar Disco Mix)" by the Soul Rebels (Defected 067, 1999). The track samples from a live performance of the poem, including its preamble and the audience's cheering and clapping. Scott-Heron's voice has been electronical-ly processed, resulting in a transient pitching of its harmonic components, not quite roboticized, but not quite human, either. What are the effects of rendering quasi-machinic a classic black power poem? Weheliye argues that such electronic techniques "reconstruct the black voice in relation to information technologies," thereby historicizing the enunciation of "soul" through technology (2002, 10, 33). I agree, but would extend Weheliye's argument, that (a) "soul" is transformed in the process, and that (b) "soul" is not just in the supposedly human, but an effect of the machine. (This discussion will have to be further elaborated at another place and time.)

18. "Race and Racism—Red, White, and Black," Episode 306 of *The '90s*, PBS Television, KBDI. Produced by Tom Weinberg and Joel Cohen, 4/19/91. Archived at: http://media-burn.org/video/the-90s-episode-306-race-and-racism-red-white-and-black/. This episode is well worth viewing as an incredible piece of independent television. It begins with a white metalhead defining "a black person" vs. a "nigger." Its subjects include the Klu Klux Klan (during which the producers scroll a sickening list of KKK attacks across the bottom of the screen), Mandela and apartheid in South Africa, the Mohawk Warriors of the Oka Crisis, the Black Panthers and COINTELPRO, and the framing of Panther Dhoruba al-Mujahid bin Wa-had. The producers also interview numerous scholars who discuss capitalism as the structural cause of racism.

19. Apparently the filming of the video (directed by Spike Lee) nearly transformed into what it sought to represent (see Chang 2005: 280; see Myrie 2009, 169). It is unclear whether the police filing by at 5:15 are actors (by the look on Chuck D's face), and the closing two minutes of the video depict this undecideability between revolt / representation, from the call-and-response crowd chants of "Don't Believe The Hype" led by Flavor Flav to an increasingly energetic street march. It is just this line that Public Enemy plays, as its S1W dancers bust moves underneath portraits of Louis Farrakhan. This video also pre-dates the "carnival against capitalism" and other such actions by Reclaim The Streets (RTS) in which soundsystems and electronic music from hip-hop to techno combined to create a musicotechnico assemblage of political agency that blended protest and occupation with circus, celebration, and electronic dance music culture (EDMC).

20. In a way somewhat dismissive of efforts to revitalize hip-hop's political force—such as Dead Prez and Kanye West—as well as ignoring the fragmentation of nearly all "mainstream" broadcast models, Warrall nonetheless convincingly writes that "we're even more inundated with commercialism and the market's skewed view of what's controversial. 'Urban' culture has become a trend factory, and hip-hop's dependence on faux shock has reduced the complexity of the art form. Rebellion has been commodified, a fact that is perfectly illustrated by the prolife-ration of rap stars' clothing labels. Dissent itself has become unthreatening" (2002). But is selling threads all that?

21. This point was highlighted during the Gulf War, during which CNN created the format of the 24-hour news cycle and its streaming broadcast of "real time" television. These events prompted Baudrillard to pen his infamously controversial series of three articles (published in 1991 before, during, and after the Gulf War), collected under the title *The Gulf War Did Not Take Place* (1995). Baudrillard's polemic was squarely aimed at demonstrating how actual revolutionary events had fallen entirely into spectacle.

22. M.K. Asante, Jr.'s book *It's Bigger Than Hip-Hop: The Rise of the Post-Hip-Hop Generation* lays out this deadlock of politico-cultural representation, wherein "hip hop's dive into the mainstream was a win for the handful of corporations and artists who grew rich, but a significant loss for those who it is supposed to represent" (2008, 3).

23. All of whom are male—which is not to neglect the likes of Grace Jones, Donna Summer, or Janelle Monáe, but rather to trace a particular line of sonic effects that is also reflective of structural patriarchy. For a thorough meditation upon Monáe as android Cindi Mayweather (and Detroit techno composer Jeff Mills), see van Veen 2013.

24. Ra is also not so much an abductee as a contactee: he is one of few reported cases to have successfully resisted efforts of abduction.

25. Drawing a connection that few in conventional jazz have cared to note, Sinker writes that "Coltrane is incomprehensible unless you see him as Ra's greatest pupil, terminally impatient with limits, with the trivial categories and opposites within Earthly language, and yet inhumanly patient with the fact that such things won't be transcended down here on this plane" (1992). John Corbett notes that Coltrane distributed copies of Ra's esoteric Afrofuturist pamphlet, "Solaristic Precepts" (in Ra 2006, 6); Sinker writes that Ra "weaned [Coltrane] off his addiction, or anyway rerouted it from chemistry to metaphysics."

26. But in reality at length: we will need a paragraph to explicate Eshun's single sentence.

27. Amiri Baraka writes of Coltrane that "The titles of Trane's tunes, 'A Love Supreme,' 'Meditations,' 'Ascension,' imply a strong religious will, conscious of the religious evolution the pure mind seeks. The music is a way into God. The absolute open expression of everything" (1999, 196). This evolution would lead Trane to *Interstellar Space*.

28. Norbert Wiener, 1894–1964, was an American mathematician who developed the principles of system feedback known as cybernetics. His application to social systems is perhaps emblematic of what Foucault would call biopolitics. See, in particular, *The Human Use of Human Beings: Cybernetics and Society* (1988).

29. Such as in John Sayles' 1984 film, *The Brother From Another Planet*, wherein the mute Afro-alien communicates by way of hieroglyphic graffiti. The conceit of Sayles' film is that unlike his musical compatriots—Ra, George Clinton, Coltrane, Hendrix, etc.—the black alien is mute; he communicates not through music but symbolic pictograms: alien hieroglyphs.

30. Amiri Baraka argues that "the *solo* . . . as first exemplified by Louis Armstrong, is very plain indication of the changed sensibility the West enforced. The return to collective improvisations, which finally, the West-oriented, the whitened, says is chaos, is the *all-force* put together, and is what is wanted. Rather than accompaniment and a solo voice, the miniature 'thing' securing its 'greatness'. Which is where the West is" (1999, 197). This critique sidesteps two points: (1) that both the solo and collective free improvisation are inventions of "the West" just as they are of "Black Music"; and that (2) resistance was not only to be found among white listeners and critics to the "chaos" of free improvisation (or Ra's eclectic, outerspace composition, which are rarely improvised), but among black traditionalists. Baraka, who himself inhabited multiple types of black culture, nonetheless distinguishes among them, critiquing those who adopt the "unswinging-ness" of "contemporary European and white Euro-American music" (1999, 192).

31. As Rollefson writes in a similar vein, Afrofuturism is struck by a "tension between fantasies of both 'the past' and 'the future'" (2008, 90).

32. And whose passing on January 9th, 2014, I mark here.

33. For a critical overview of Baraka's position-taking, as well as his anti-Semitism and heterosexism, see Iton 2010, 81–100.

34. This particular incarnation of Baraka stands both inside and out of Afrofuturism. Though a herald of jazz experimentation in Sun Ra, Ayler, Coltrane, and Ornette Coleman, his position implicitly disavows what would follow with hip-hop, techno, and house, all of which sampled or were in-part inspired by white European artists such as Kraftwerk. While the Arkestra played the Black Arts Repertory Theater/School (BARTS) and led the opening parade across 125th street in full outer space regalia, with Ra a prominent figure during the short-lived heyday of BARTS (1965–66) that nonetheless politically radicalised his music, see Szwed 1998: 209–12, Ra played for all audiences, remained "downtown," and collaborated with white artists (such as Phill Niblock). By Szwed's assessment, Baraka's "nationalism was too earthly

and materialistic" for Ra (1998, 212). For his part, Baraka acknowledged that Ra sought to expand both black *and human* consciousness (in Ra 2011: viii). As Baraka later reflected, "Sun Ra had a larger agenda [than black nationalism]" in Szwed 1998, 211.

35. As I will return to elsewhere, Gilroy writes that "This reciprocal relationship [between audience and performer] can serve as an ideal communicative situation even when the original makers of the music and its eventual consumers are separated in space and time or divided by the technologies of sound reproduction and the commodity form which their art has sought to resist" (1993, 102–3). Of note, Gilroy echoes Derrida here, who argues that such reciprocity is the very *condition* of the sign, including its technical networks of communicability, see Gilroy 1997.

36. This claim is novel neither to politics nor to science fiction in general. That history is written by the victors is a worn but truthful cliché of history. It is part of Sun Tzu's general strategy: "to subdue the enemy without fighting is the acme of skill" (1971, 77). Chronopolitics is the Supreme in nonfighting strategy. Time-travelling to divert a conflict before it begins is the acme of chronopolitics.

37. In a similar vein, Eshun writes: "Science fiction is now a research and development department within a futures industry that dreams of the prediction and control of tomorrow. Corporate business seeks to manage the unknown through decisions based on scenarios, while civil society responds to future shock through habits formatted by science fiction. Science fiction operates through the power of falsification, the drive to rewrite reality, and the will to deny plausibility, while the scenario operates through the control and prediction of plausible alternative tomorrows" (2003, 291).

38. A point made by Frantz Fanon (2008) (among many others) but also Paolo Freire, who criticizes the "banking" approach to education, where "education thus becomes an act of depositing" (1970, 58).

39. One such example noted by Samuel R. Delany is in Robert Heinlein's *Starship Troopers*, where in the midst of this "boy's book, a book about the way warfare can mature a young man," some 200 pages in, "our young hero . . . goes into the bathroom to put on his makeup—for in this future world all men use makeup—[and] as he looks in the mirror, he makes a passing mention of the nearly chocolate brown hue of his face" (2012, 9). Delany says that he "did a strange double take." The hero of the book was not white, but Filipino. As Delany remarks, more to the point is that the "racial situation . . . had resolved itself to the point where a young soldier might tell you of his adventures for 200 pages out of a 300-page novel and not even *have* to mention his ethnic background—because it had, in his world, become that insignificant!" (2012, 9). Unfortunately, the 1997 film, directed by Paul Verhoeven, eschews Heinlein's Afrofuturist trajectory and presents an all-white leading cast.

40. Eshun writes that "Ra zooms this lost Africa into a lost Pharoahnic Egypt" (Eshun 1999, 09[156]).

41. The "hue-man" is Ra's inscription (among others) for the construction of the human through the raciological "colour line." It signals the colour-line otherwise erased in the Enlightenment category of the (whitewashed) "human."

42. In "The Tree is Wood" (Ra 2005a, 192), I here note the "wormwood" or "spiritwood/would" implied by biting into the apple.

# REFERENCES

Asante, Jr., M.K. 2008. *It's bigger Than hip hop: The rise of the post-hip-hop generation*. New York: St. Martin's Press.
Baraka, Amiri. 1999. *The LeRoi Jones/Amiri Baraka reader*. Edited by Harris, William J. New York: Basic Books.
Baucom, Ian. 2005. *Specters of the Atlantic: Finance capital, slavery, and the philosophy of history*. Durham: Duke University Press.
Baudrillard, Jean. 1995. *The Gulf War did not take place*, trans. Paul Patton. Seattle: University of Washington Press.

Chang, Jeff. 2005. *Can't stop won't stop: A history of the hip-hop generation.* New York: St. Martin's Press.

Delany, Samuel R. 2012. *Starboard wine: More notes on the language of science fiction.* Middletown: Wesleyan University Press.

Derrida, Jacques. 1997. *Of grammatology (Corrected Edition),* trans. Gayatri Chakravorty Spivak. Baltimore and London: Johns Hopkins University Press.

Dery, Mark. 1994a. Black to the future: Interviews with Samuel R. Delany, Greg Tate, and Tricia Rose. In *Flame wars: The discourse of cyberculture,* ed. Mark Dery, 179–222. Durham: Duke University Press.

Dery, Mark, ed. 1994b. *Flame wars: The discourse of cyberculture.* Durham: Duke University Press.

Du Bois, W.E.B. [1903]1994. *The souls of black folk.* New York: Dover Publications.

Eshun, Kodwo. Further considerations of afrofuturism. *CR: The New Centennial Review* 3, no. 2 (2003): 287–302.

———.1999. *More brilliant than the sun: Adventures in sonic fiction.* London: Quartet.

Fanon, Frantz. [1952] 2008. *Black skin, white masks.* Trans. Richard Philcox. New York: Grove Press.

Foucault, Michel. 2003. *"Society must be defended:" Lectures at the Collège de France, 1975–1976.* Trans. David Macey. New York: Picador.

Freire, Paulo. 1970. *Pedagogy of the oppressed,* trans. Myra Bergman Ramos. New York: The Seabury Press.

Gates, Jr., Henri Louis. 1988. *The signifying monkey: A theory of African-American literary criticism.* Oxford: Oxford University Press.

Genovese, Eugene D. 1976. *Roll, Jordan, roll: The world the slaves made.* New York: Vintage Books.

Gilroy, Paul. 2004. *Between camps: Nations, cultures and the allure of race.* London: Routledge.

———. 1993. *The black Atlantic: Modernity and double consciousness.* Cambridge: Harvard University Press.

Goodman, Steve. 2010. *Sonic warfare.* Cambridge: MIT Press.

Hahn, Steven. 2009. *The political worlds of slavery and freedom.* Cambridge: Harvard University Press.

Hart, Richard. 2002. *Slaves who abolished slavery: Blacks in rebellion.* Jamaica: University of the West Indies Press.

Higginson, Thomas Wentworth. 1998. *Black rebellion: Five slave revolts.* New York: De Capo Press.

Iton, Richard. 2010. *In search of the black fantastic: Politics and popular culture in the post-Civil Rights Era.* Oxford: Oxford University Press.

James, George G.M. [1954] 2001. *Stolen legacy.* Sauk Village: African American Images.

Jameson, Fredric. 2005. *Archaeologies of the future: The desire called utopia and other science fictions.* London: Verso.

Kreiss, Daniel. Appropriating the Master's Tools: Sun Ra, the Black Panthers, and Black Consciousness, 1952–1973. *Black Music Research Journal* 28, no. 1 (2008): 57–81.

LaBare, Sha. 2014. Slaveship earth. In *Other Planes of There—Afrofuturism Collected,* ed. Tobias c. van Veen.

Marx, Karl. 1990. *Capital, Vol. 1.,* trans. Ben Fowkes. London: Penguin.

Moten, Fred. 2003. *In the break: The aesthetics of the black radical tradition.* Minneapolis: University of Minnesota Press.

Myrie, Russell. 2009. *Don't rhyme for the sake of riddlin': The authorized story of public enemy.* London: Canongate Books.

Nelson, Alondra. Introduction: Future texts. *Social Text* 71 (Summer 2002): 1–15.

Nelson, Alondra and Paul D. Miller. 2000. About afrofuturism. *Afrofuturism.net* Accessed 27 May 2004: http://afrofuturism.com/text/about.html.

Ra, Sun. 2011. *This planet is doomed.* New York: Kicks Books.

———. 2006. *The wisdom of Sun-Ra.* Edited by John Corbett. Chicago: WhiteWalls.

————. 2005a. *The immeasurable equation: The collected poetry and prose of Sun Ra*, ed. James L. Wolf and Hartmut Geerken. Norderstedt: Waitawhile.

Rollefson, J. Griffiths. The "robot voodoo power" thesis: Afrofuturism and anti-Anti-essentialism from Sun Ra to Kool Keith. *Black Music Research* 28, no. 1 (2008): 83–109.

Rose, Tricia. 1994. *Black noise: Rap music and black culture in contemporary America*. Middletown: Wesleyan University Press.

Scott-Heron, Gil. 2000. *Now and then: The poems of Gil Scott-Heron*. Edinburgh: Payback Press.

Sinker, Mark. 2014. A splendidly elaborate living Orrery: Further thoughts on black science fiction and transplanetary jazz. Unpublished paper.

————. 1992. Loving the alien in advance of the landing—Black science fiction. *WIRE* 96 (February). http://www.exacteditions.com/read/the-wire/february-1992-35378.

Spivak, Gayatri Chakravorty. 1999. *A critique of postcolonial reason: Toward a history of the vanishing present*. Cambridge: Harvard University Press.

Stiegler, Bernard. 1998. *Technics and time, 1: The fault of epimetheus*, trans. Richard Beardsworth and George Collins. Stanford: Stanford University Press.

Szwed, John F. 1998. *Space is the place: The lives and times of Sun Ra*. New York: De Capo Press.

Tate, Greg. 1992. *Flyboy in the buttermilk: Essays on contemporary America*. New York: Fireside.

Tzu, Sun. 1971. *The art of war*, trans. Samuel B. Griffith. Oxford: Oxford University Press.

van Veen, tobias c., ed. 2014. *Afrofuturism and (un)popular music*. Unpublished manuscript.

————. Vessels of transfer: Allegories of afrofuturism in Jeff Mills and Janelle Monáe. *Dancecult: Journal of Electronic Dance Music Culture* 5, no. 2 (2013): 7–41.

————.Technics, precarity and exodus in rave culture. *Dancecult: Journal of Electronic Dance Music Culture* 1, no. 2 (2010): 29–49.

Warrall, Laura K. 2002. Fight the power. *Salon.com*. June 03 http://www.salon.com/2002/06/03/fight_the_power/. Accessed 05 August 2009

Weheliye, Alexander G. "Feenin": Posthuman voices in contemporary black popular music. *Social Text* (Summer 2002): 21–48.

Wiener, Norbert. 1988. *The human use of human beings: Cybernetics and society*. New York: Da Capo Press.

Zuberi, Nabeel. 2004. The transmolecularization of [black] folk: *Space is the place*, Sun Ra, and Afrofuturism. In *Off the Planet: Music, Sound and Science Fiction Cinema*, ed. Phillip Hayward, 77–95. Bloomington: Indiana University Press.

*Chapter Five*

# Afrofuturism's Musical Princess Janelle Monáe

*Psychedelic Soul Message Music Infused with a Sci-Fi Twist*

## Grace D. Gipson

It's the year 2719, female android Cindi Mayweather (aka Janelle Monáe) has encountered a musical market world filled with severe social stratification. Thus, it is no mystery how race, gender, and sexuality have found themselves orbiting around each other overlooked until they reach this Afrofuturistic realm. Imagine the literary genius of Octavia Butler fused with the musical artistry of Prince and together they birthed the darling, psychedelic soul that is Janelle Monáe. Since 2007, Monáe has reenergized the Afrofuturism movement with her epic vocals, immaculate clothing style, and magical lyrics. As a result, her musical talent is by no means generic or monotonous, in fact no one definition can describe this musician activist. As a Grammy-nominated hardcore genre-crossing diva artist, Janelle Monáe has reinvented what it means to musically travel through space in order to capture her freedom. Much like her Afrofuturistic predecessors Sun Ra and George Clinton, Monáe presents a persona that can be likened to a polyvalent Afrofuturistic aesthetic that embodies the desires of black feminism mixed with a futural sonic flare. She goes beyond the outer limits of storytelling providing a signature sound, which critiques the monotone concept of punk, and clearly addresses the complexities of race, gender, and sexuality at the same time. Essentially, Monáe speaks to a subject that is transformed by law, yet does not exist within it through each musical lyric and note, and nurtures responses to presumptions of racialized and sexualized criminality (Nyong'o 2005). Through songs like her first single "Many Moons" to the controversial hit "Cold War" to her latest track with fellow soul sista Erykah Badu "Q.U.E.E.N.," this essay attempts to shows how Monae strategically inter-mixes space with racial and sexual politics, black feminism, historical narra-tives, and class conflicts all in a "radical visionary Afrofuturistic" kind of way.

*So what is Afrofuturism?* Music critic and writer Mark Dery (1994) coined the term "Afrofuturism" to describe the self-conscious appropriation of technological themes in Black popular culture, particularly that of rap and other hip-hop representations. The term is more than just being "weird," "out there," or "high." It is not an elitist movement. It's not about having different tastes or following different trends, but it is as sociologist and Afrofuturism scholar Alondra Nelson says "to explore futurist themes in Black cultural production and the ways in which technological innovation is changing the face of Black art and culture" (Nelson and Miller 2006). The appropriation of science and technology by marginalized groups has always been an essential component of resistance, and its significance in the black diaspora all the more so because of the extremes in brutality, subjugation, and geographic scope (Eglash and Bleecker 2001). As a whole, Afrofuturism is a genre that allows artists, such as Janelle Monáe, to present new and innovative perspec-tives and pose questions that are not typically addressed in canonical works. Afrofuturism is a free space that allows the option to explore, imagine, and discover blackness and womanhood (in the case of Monáe) side by side. Afrofuturism much like cyberfeminism uses science fiction and cyber culture in a speculative manner to escape the traditional definitions of what it means to be black or African (in exotic terms) within western culture (Bristow 2012). These stories of aliens and cyber beings that can be found in Afrofu-turism literature, film, and music are essentially metaphors that speak to real life experiences of blacks in the diaspora. Using these various avenues, Afrofuturism continues to redefine black culture and notions of blackness for today and the future. Musically, one could say that Afrofuturism had its start in the 1940s, 1950s, and early 1960s with the likes of jazz musicians such as Lee "Scratch Perry" and Sun Ra who portrayed themselves as an extension of all African Diasporic people as they would envision themselves as descen-dants of intelligent life forms who came to Earth to prepare the human race for its eventual destiny among the space realm. As a growing and popular aesthetic movement, particularly in the music genre, Afrofuturism continues to evolve technologically but also in terms of its political mission. Afrofutur-ist artists like Janelle Monáe, seek to disrupt, challenge, and transform the visions of tomorrow with fantastic stories that as Ruth Mayer (2000) puts it, "move seamlessly back and forth through time and space, between cultural traditions and geographic time zones" and thus between blackness as a dys-topic relic of the past and as a harbinger of a new and more promising alien future" (556). In some ways Afrofuturism exhibits this feminine aspect of humanity, a level of intuition, as it constantly gives birth to a future that is in need of reclaiming.

Interestingly enough there is this relationship between black feminism and Afrofuturism in that both have connections (feminism, science-fiction, technology) that were initially dominated by white patriarchal standards; however both are now vehicles that are being used as liberating voices to express public consciousness. This is one of the ways Janelle Monáe intertwines fantasy, her musical talents, and intellect to discuss this future reality. Monáe's work is quite compelling in that it highlights the past, present, and future within the African American diaspora. In a sense, she is exemplifying this musical resistance legacy that has been already laid out by other artists such as Afrika Bambataa, Soul II Soul, George Clinton, Sun Ra, and Grace Jones. Her music redefines essentialist notions of Black culture in music. August Wilson speaks of this notion in how our leaders of the '60s have set a tone for today's new leaders, "What blacks were doing in the '60s is coming to some fruition . . . we have the framework and the orientation to take things further."[1] And Monáe does just that as she picks up the torch to light the way for the future generations. Through each album, song, lyric, and musical note, Monáe gives freedom to that "other" (marginalized victims within the world) or segregated minority that is often discussed in Afrofuturism. Instead of them being minimalized, she maximizes their existence and breathes this sort of life. It is as though she elevates this state of consciousness that surpasses the misfortunes that one may visually perceive in today's society.

## AN AFROFUTURIST IS BORN . . . JANELLE MONÁE

Born to working class parents, her mother who worked as a janitor and her father as a sanitary/garbage collector, in Kansas City, Kansas, Janelle Monáe Robinson would learn at a very young age the value of hard work. Coming from a stressful and painful background along with early experiences dealing with perils of drug addiction, Monáe would use those factors as a source of inspiration to succeed. As a result of their hard work and dedication to survive, Monáe throughout her career has created her own niche not just through her music, but in her appearance as well. She even goes as far as creating a distinct and unique uniform. Monáe's signature uniform of a black-and-white tuxedo is her way of paying homage to her parents. Not only is her uniform a tribute to her parents, but it is also a compliment to the Gatsby-era as it simultaneously acknowledges this "post-human" androgynous symbol of class and mobility.

From a black feminist perspective, artists like Janelle Monáe have been able to use Afrofuturism to explore the boundaries of race, class, and gender and begin offering some sort of solution. Monáe is very attentive to her positionality in the musical marketplace, particularly as a black/African American woman who comes from working-class roots, even as she manipulates that marketplace in the name of future justice. Since coming to the music scene she has been able to disrupt this notion that Ytasha Womack has stated in that "fatalism is equated to blackness." Monáe's gift of song (via her lyrics) provides a message of hope, empowerment, and femininity all through an Afrofuturistic lens. Essentially, through song Monáe can travel through time and space recapturing and reclaiming what was taken, and then presenting it back to future generations. Monáe has been very successful in writing her own story and becoming a social change agent, much like her Afrofuturistic predecessors Sun Ra, George Clinton, and Octavia Butler. As Monáe would tell in an interview to the Quietus, "I learned to embrace things that make me unique even if they make me uncomfortable sometimes" (Calvert 2010). This lack of comfort would introduce us to Monáe being known for appropriating historically "non-black" genres of rock, punk, electronica, orchestra, and folk music, which then allows her to surpass sociopolitical borders.

Furthermore, her music as a platform analyzes the dynamics of race, gender, and culture at the same time incorporating them with other controversial topics like class and spirituality. Through her musical lyrics and even her music videos she offers an alternative critique regarding issues of race, class, homophobia, and sexism. Her contribution to the music world, and more importantly to the genre of Afrofuturism, is quite energetic and purposeful. Monáe provides a brown-girl narrative that is scarce and unique in today's popular recording industry. She is not necessarily the sister-girl/homegirl from the project stoop, or the high profile city girl, but more of a cyber girl sent to shake up the present day musical landscape. All in all, Monáe takes an active role, as a public image artist, in the cultivation of black women centered spaces within mass and popular culture that serve to address the concerns of not only black women but the larger black community.

## So Who Is Cindi Mayweather?

Since the inception of Monáe's recording career, she has initiated the possibility of the human, particularly of the black female body all through this narrative arc about an imagined android alter ego, Cindi Mayweather (English and Kim 2013).

> Cindi is an android and I love speaking about the android because they are the new "other."[2] People are afraid of the other and I believe we're going to live in a world with androids because of technology and the way it advances. The first album she was running because she had fallen in love with a human and she

was being disassembled for that. (according to Monáe as reported to MTV in 2010)

Monáe as an android highlights this idea of artistic freedom in that she embraces this idea of celebrating femaleness, freedom, and otherness through song. Cindi Mayweather as this android is much like Donna Haraway's "cyborg manifesto" (1991) in that it exhibits this speculative criticism that has been manipulated by this onset of a global technology culture. Monáe embraces this idea of stepping outside the box of what is considered normal by further pushing the envelope and redefining what it means to be a minority or other. Thus, Cindi Mayweather and Janelle Monáe serve as a hybrid between fantasy and human/alien boundaries. Furthermore, considering herself as an android is significant in that she reclaims this gender agency within a male dominated musical culture, where she does not have to identify as male or female.

Cindi Mayweather is the captain and the songs she sings are the ships that travel and carry freedom song messages in and out of space. Monáe would also explain how Cindi is like "the mediator between the mind and the hand . . . haves and have-not's, the oppressed and the oppressor. . . . She's like the Archangel in the Bible, and what Neo represents to the Matrix . . . together Janelle Monáe and Cindi become a bridge for saving humanity" (Andrews 2010). The versatility of her musical weapons and her alter-ego allows her to step outside the box that places her into a specific genre. According to Paste Magazine (2008) [as taken from a 2008 press release], rap superstar and mogul Sean "Diddy" Combs would describe Monáe as "a true visionary, with an original sound and a mesmerizing presence." Thus she does more than sing, dance, and perform; she tells a relatable story that recovers that past and elevates us to the future. Cindi Mayweather serves as a re-invention of who Janelle Monáe wants the world to know in hopes that listeners will tap into their own super powers and embrace the voice of change . . . within themselves and their own communities.

## AFROFUTURISM AND JANELLE MONÁE

Future and space are no longer a foreign concept, but a way of life. Women and little girls become empowered in their own skin not having to feel guilty about being different and unique. Everyone has dreams, it is what you do with them to make them a part of your reality. Thus, Monáe becomes a living example of this and what it means to be human. Monáe demands your attention with her abstract and at times controversial lyrics and video images. Her songs are meant to be taken at face value. She embodies what mentor Big Boi of Outkast would call this "psychedelic dance punk troupe" type vibe in which she confronts racism, sexism, classism, heterosexism, and a critique of systems of oppression in the U.S. as well as conflict in the black and feminist movements. Monáe deals with those "gray" areas such as black identity, black sexuality, black family, and community that often get ignored or swept under the political and media rug. Therefore, it is important to examine how Monáe negotiates the intersections of race and gender, nationalism, sexuality, and classism while extending a dialogue about Afrofuturism and its role in social justice.

As Mark Dery (1994) points out, "African American voices have other stories to tell about culture, technology, and things to come" (184). Society has evolved into this industrial revolution, in which music culture plays a significant role. And with everything becoming digital, some musical artists cannot keep up or cannot move fast enough. This is where Monáe shines through. She is living proof that art is life and art is a medium and/or pathway to self-actualization. Monáe truly captures what it means to be Afrofuturistic. She does not simply just address the what-ifs, but enthusiastically tries to prepare us for what is to come. It is more than just being eclectic and using digital technology, referring to yourself as an alien, droid, cyber-human, etc. As Monáe portrays through her personality and music, it is about blending cutting edge, futuristic production machines (non-human) and the observance to the likes of James Brown and Jimi Hendrix (human) linking the future and the past in this "call and response" style all riding on the "mothership."

As many within the black community criticize the lack of positive images in popular culture, the lack of power to influence the corporate capitalist responsible for such imagery, Afrofuturism as a genre with the help of artists like Janelle Monáe rearticulates this power by providing critical dialogues and interventions to liberate black minds from these tropes and stereotypes. One particular influence for Monáe becoming a transformative artist was the novels by Octavia Butler, she explains:

> Her work was first of all brilliantly written, and Wild Seed was the book that inspired me. I loved the characters, and the morphing. [Anyanwu] was just such a transformative character, and I look at myself as a transformative artist. Just the fact that [Butler] defied race and gender . . . You appreciated her work for being a human being. (as told in a 2010 interview to IO9-Andrews)

Monáe's willingness to venture into another musical dimension is particularly valuable as she allows her listeners and fans access to journey with her into the present-future as she gives voice to those silenced. As an Afrofuturistic musical artist, Monáe uses her music and performance to theorize and prescribe a revolutionary agenda that affirms the entire black community. She achieves this through methods that target self-definition, female empowerment, embracing alternate black aesthetics, defending women's sexual agency, and confronting oppression on all levels. As you will see, Monáe's music speaks to this idea of transforming to another level. She disrupts this notion that Afrofuturist artist and scholar, Ytasha Womack speaks to in her 2013 text *Afrofuturism: The World of Black Sci-Fi and Fantasy Culture* that "fatalism is equated to blackness." Her amazing talent of song (via her lyrics) provides a message of hope, empowerment, and femininity through an Afro-futuristic lens. As she tells us, "we believe songs are space ships. We believe music is the weapon of the future. We believe books are stars" (Wondaland Arts Society 2011). Additionally, Monáe through out her career always en-courages and embraces this idea of "it's ok if you don't fit in." She writes her own story while simultaneously becoming a social change agent.

In these next few pages we will examine how three songs ("Many Moons," "Cold War," and "Q.U.E.E.N.") from three different albums (*Me-tropolis: Suite I [The Chase]*, *The ArchAndroid*, and *The Electric Lady*) reflect the potent mixture of female empowerment, resistance, and self-iden-tity struggles through this Afrofuturistic lens.

## THE YEAR IS 2007 . . . WELCOME TO METROPOLIS . . .

*Metropolis: Suite I (The Chase)* is the 2007 debut EP from Janelle Monáe and would establish the first installment of Monae's seven part Metropolis conceptual series which follows this fictional tale of android Cindi May-weather. The album would comprise a mixture of pop, funk, dance-punk, and futuristic soul. Omar Burgess (2008) from *Hip-Hop DX* magazine would describe the album "as having references and notions of forbidden robot love and having a production style that takes its cues from something made in the past, as well as the future. The drums hit hard, and when combined with the synth keys, strings and the occasional electric guitar, they make for an oddly enjoyable mix." *Metropolis: Suite I (The Chase)* is an album that can be likened to having a Marxist metaphor as a narrative foundation. What is unique about this album and the song is how Monáe makes a conscious effort to bring restoration to an Afrofuturist cosmology and places it in the fore-front of contemporary urban music. This album along with the second single "Many Moons" (2008) offers a "therapy-by-fantasy" remedy into the world's issues and problems.

Immediately Monáe begins to focus on the situations at hand, which she simply just wants to have peace of mind, feverishly dance above ground, and ultimately be free. Despite operating underground, metaphorically they are dancing with shackles on their feet. She goes on further to explain how even though they can dance there still remain these notions of being held captive, oppressed, marginalized, underrepresented, or worse made to be invisible. Monáe also alludes to this longing for freedom from the matrix, or Metropolis,[3] where everything they want to say is not erased as if it never existed. As a result they live day to day in a state of confusion.

After she provides the listener with the lyrical lesson, she further breaks it down for us in a cybernetic chantdown or spoken word catalog that address various (damaging and harmful) stereotypes and tropes along with references to sociopolitical ills. Immediately, Monáe addresses such terms as "weirdo," "stepchild," and "freakshow" and how these terms, created by society, place people into boxes just because they do not fit into a particular norm. She goes on further to equate how being treated like a stepchild is the equivalent to being a part of a freak show. Additionally, Monáe also brings attention to specific phenotypes regarding black girls having "nappy hair" and broad, wide-set noses making these features seem as though they are not accepted as ideal beauty standards, thus only worthy of a "cold stare."

As the cybernetic chantdown continues Monáe offers us an additional set of choice words that address language such as "race songs," hunger, social-economic status (SES), and disease. Here one might pose the question, is Monáe speaking to this idea of how mindless words are often used in race songs; or could this be a play-on-words whereas "race songs" could be viewed as "e-rased songs"? And if it is a race song, it holds the risk of being an erased song, much like school boards and education committees are trying to erase true history, hence the use of foolish words or the lack thereof. Monáe also makes mention of this domino effect of such items attached to hunger and SES status as spoiled milk and stale bread, which ultimately refers to old unhealthy foods that are generally more affordable for people on welfare. Since these foods are not sustainable enough to actually survive on, people who are on welfare or in impoverished areas tend to die in large numbers much like they did during the Bubonic plague.

By reminding us of all these various ongoing issues and diseases still floating around in the universe/world, Monáe provides us with this warning that this could easily happen to anyone even today and potentially in the future. Thus, it is important to remain vigilant and quickly make moves for an escape from evil forces, in the case of Monáe/Cindi Mayweather the Android Monitoring Army/Police of Metropolis, while there is still a chance. Furthermore, it is in one's best interest to remedy these situations while there is still a fighting chance. As the song comes to an end, Monáe lulls us into a closing lullaby "Shan, shan shan shan-gri la" reminding listeners that after society and the world have beaten you up mentally and physically to always prepare to make your way back home. In those closing lines Monáe suggests this idea of when the world is not being fair to you, there will come a time when one can go to a better place. This is possibly another world, another realm, a higher place where no luggage is needed. The final line is possibly in reference to Shangri-La, a fictional, fantasy place described in the 1933 novel *Lost Horizon* by British author James Hilton.[4] Monáe uses this because

Shangri-La has become synonymous with any earthly paradise, it is seen as a permanently happy land, isolated from the outside world. This is the utopian refuge that Cindi Mayweather desires to escape from Metropolis.

In addition to the poignant lyrics the video is just as electric. The video, which Monáe promoted as a short film, takes place at the Annual Android Auction in the fictional city of Metropolis. Just picture it: a droid sale, part fashion show, part slave auction, in which dozens of riding-gear-clad Cindi Mayweather clones strut for an audience including fanged "tech dandy" Chung Knox, Neon Valley crimelord Mousey, jealous Metropolis police commander 6ix Savage, and "punk prophets" Deep Cotton (psychedelic punk musicians from the present and Monáe's collaborators). All this is taking place while Monáe's alter-ego Cindi Mayweather performs for the crowd during the auction. At the close of the song Cindi (Monáe) is so engulfed into her superhuman energized performance that she is elevated from the stage and shorts out, and soon after she is taken away by the Master of the ShowDroids (another alter-ego) and the Lady Maestra. As the video comes to a close Cindi (Monáe) leaves us with this thought-provoking quote that evokes a spirit of the Underground Railroad: "I imagined many moons in the sky, lighting the way to freedom."

## THE YEAR IS 2010 . . . THE YEAR OF THE ARCHANDROID

*The ArchAndroid* is the second studio album from Janelle Monáe, which would be released on Wondaland Arts Society and Bad Boy Records. The album comprises the second and third parts to Monáe's Metropolis concept series. With clear conceptual elements of Afrofuturism and science fiction, before we even listen to the album these elements are presented on the album cover. The Egyptian headdress that she dons on the 2010 cover *Archandroid* album can be viewed as her paying homage to free-thinking jazz pioneer artist Sun Ra in his 1974 "Space is the Place" film cover. *The ArchAndroid* resumes the series' fictional tale of a messianic android and features lyrical themes of love, identity, and self-realization. Monáe has stated in an interview with the *Chicago Tribune* (2010) that the album signifies "breaking the chains that enslave minorities of all types." Each of the songs on this album tells a musical story that fuses technology and traditional orchestra instruments to create songs from the "Palace of Dogs."[5] However one song in particular that stands out is the second single from the album, "Cold War" (2010). The Cold War (which actually takes place from 1945–1989) is used as a metaphor and framework of contemporary conditions of existence and is also a metaphor for the pervasive messages and power structures that tell people/groups there is something wrong with them (class/culture/race conflicts that exist within the U.S.). Using "Cold War" as the title of the song serves as a symbolic reference which is significant in that it generates a discussion and even a relationship between the past and present. Monáe's lyrics also confront and remind us listeners of past and present colonial, imperial, and oppressive forces.

The opening lines of the song are meant to speak with listeners and ask them to engage in the idea of being alone; but, simultaneously maintaining a level of sanity in today's current society filled with oppression. This is a two-fold situation that poses a question and makes a proclamation. The question she asks "So you think I'm alone?" is meant to be rhetorical because in the next line Monáe provides an answer. She clarifies that in our world there is nothing wrong with being alone, because the question is not merely about loneliness, but rather individuality. As a whole, the verse speaks of survival when one has to choose between loneliness and sanity. Monáe goes on further to explain how individuality is often criticized in society particularly because of gender narratives, which create notions that one must accept being alone because it is "the only way to be." Overall being alone and "underground" is a way to embrace differences and acceptance of oneself, much like how Afrofuturism revises and re-examines historical events of the past.

Next, the chorus is what gives the song clear purpose and destination (life): "This is a cold war, You better know what you're fighting for." In this brief line, Monáe directly references the stand off between the United States and the former USSR. The Cold War was filled with conflicts between people put in opposition with each other by the USSR and the U.S. These proxy wars allowed the global powers to battle over the direction the world would be heading in without ever putting their own people at risk. Furthermore with this song Monáe is proposing that those fighting (on any side of a conflict) be certain that their own interests are really what they're fighting for. Otherwise, you might be subjected to being someone else's pawn.

Finally, in the second verse Monáe is addressing further steps that must be taken in order to gain some type of liberation: "If you want to be free, Below the ground's the only place to be." Monáe portrays this emotional vulnerability while addressing the underground artist. Essentially, she speaks to this idea that underground artists have greater control of their music due to the fact they do not have the label pressuring them to conform to popular music standards in order to turn a profit. Now in the context of her alter ego Cindi Mayweather story, her role as this Android savior, with Androids representing an oppressed people, presents this idea where androids are viewed as second class thus going underground, in essence a revolution even if silent is where freedom lies.

The song is intensely personal and eclectic as she exudes this sense of passion and honesty. In many ways, "Cold War" speaks, indirectly, to this black woman's resistance and the struggle to self-identify. "Cold War" demonstrates how one can step outside the mainstream realm and allow for the expression of one's true creativity. Overall, this track emphasizes the importance of being true to one's self and not compromising one's vision or artistic integrity, which is analogous to the Cold War—a war about standing firm to one's ideals. Essentially when you rebel against the "programmed schedule" label as strange/rebel/dysfunctional you truly have to decide what side are you fighting for? In 2011 she would perform this song at the Nobel Peace Prize concert with a specific purpose to empower women and girls regardless of race to be who you are . . . as she says "trying to find my peace." Monáe wants to make it very clear that as an individual one must protect their mind from degradation, create new concepts, not allow anyone to oppress you, and promote self-love. The overall message of the song is essentially to embrace what makes you unique, even if it makes others uncomfortable.

## THE YEAR IS 2013 . . . INTRODUCING THE ELECTRIC LADY

In the final song we are brought to the present year 2013 and the newest album from Monáe, *The Electric Lady.* This album serves as the fourth and fifth installments of her seven-part *Metropolis concept series. The Electric Lady,* thematically, resumes the dystopic cyborg concepts of its predecessors, while offering itself in a more plainspoken, personal territory in addition to experimenting with other genres beyond conventional funk and soul music genres such as jazz ("Dorothy Dandridge Eyes"), pop/punk ("Dance Apocalyptic"), and gospel ("Victory"), as well as unsteady and sensual ("Primetime") vocal ballads. In this album, as well as can be seen in the previous two, Monáe seems to be following in the Afrofuturist, funkadelic footsteps of George Clinton, Bootsy Collins, and Sun-Ra in creating an allegory tale of Cindi Mayweather (aka The Electric Lady) while highlighting her own personal struggle/the current struggle with self/societal-acceptance that she and her brothers/sisters of the struggle face.

The groundbreaking first single would be "Q.U.E.E.N." featuring Monáe's fellow Afrofuturistic sista Erykah Badu. Immediately after its release, the single quickly becomes a fan favorite and a black feminist anthem particularly for black women. As cultural critic Joan Morgan (1999) states there is a method to making sure black feminism is productive and effective, it must "explore who we are as women-not victims" (56). Lyrically, both Monáe and Badu explore that productivity by using this song as a way of reclaiming agency and individuality as black women. It explores the inner psyches and the intricacies of being a black woman in today's society that often frequently marginalizes and omits the perspectives of black women. Both artists challenge the current identity politics while simultaneously negotiating gender and sexual binaries.

From the first line, Monáe is instantly caught off-guard as she is trying to comprehend the attacks from her critics.[6] She is trying to understand why individuals have so much animosity and as a result call her names and accuse her of wrong doing. Yet, despite the discomfort that others may get from her she still holds fast to embracing her true self. Monáe also speaks to this brand of breaking and creating their rules along with following their own script. Thus she and the Wondaland crew march to the beat of their own drum, as they identify as free-thinking, sex positive, independent women (and men), which fundamentally breaks all the norms of "traditional" society.

Since Monáe refers to herself as an android, she makes a stance to address her own sexual preference and its relationship to religion. Monáe speaks to this idea of asking for the acceptance and equality of one's sexuality and personal religious choices. She directly asks very specific and straightforward questions regarding approval and what her potential fate in the after-life may be. In her line of questions regarding whether or not she is "good enough for your heaven, or whether she is a freak for admiring another woman," Monáe could be making the implication that everyone has a different opinion, perception, and understanding of what God and Heaven is. Will God accept her for who she is, using the "in my black and white" as a metaphor for her personal character. Should she remain her own individual and be different from society (a rogue droid) or should she reprogram herself and have artificial happiness in the mainstream system and their beliefs?

In a brief hook, Monáe continues this idea of self-love despite how comfortable or uncomfortable others may be, enough that warrants her repeating the thought to make sure listeners understand. Basically, Monáe is standing firm on her beliefs and personality and will not change for anyone but herself . . . in essence she is saying , "Do you!"

The track takes an interesting detour with fellow futuristic sista Erykah Badu's interlude reaffirming the lessons and messages that Monáe has laid out in the beginning of the song.

Instantly, Badu informs us to listen for the drums as this is a sign that freedom is very much in sight. Furthermore she lets us know that these Electric Ladies are too strong to let themselves be oppressed by those who would try to destroy them and their movement. So when Badu lets us know how the melody will show us another way, she is informing the listener, just in case they were not already aware, how this particular track will introduce you to a more enlightened way of thinking. Badu here also refers to herself in the song as a droid (or android) and that as such we must continue to be true to that identification. As she closes out her part Badu's final testimony/ expression: "But you gotta testify because the booty don't lie" is evocative of the sentiment expressed in Parliament-Funkadelic's classic album "Free Your Mind and Your Ass Will Follow." Moreover, "the booty don't lie" is a reference to the idea that your body will move of its own volition when a song is good, and that your body is therefore trustworthy even when your mind is confused.

In the final moments of the song Monáe switches gears from being a songstress to a "flipping it" on you android rap style to make sure you understand what she is trying to convey. In typical battle rap style, Monáe lyrically grabs her opponent and lets them know, "I don't think they under-stand what I'm trying to say . . ." this punch line is all to reminiscent of how rappers start a typical battle rap. Then she jumps into what is meant to be a rhetorical question in asking are the people part of a lost generation of our people. The term "Lost Generation" refers to the group of artists who left America in the 1920s and found success abroad; this included such artists as F. Scott Fitzgerald, T. S. Eliot, Isadora Duncan, as well as others.[7] Likewise, Monáe's Wondaland team have felt exiled, but fortunately have found suc-cess worldwide. This line could also be referring to this widespread percep-tion of young African-Americans who are often referred to as being a "lost generation" due to involvement in various social ills.

Not only does she reference the "lost generation" but she continues to address the inequalities that continue to resurface from the past. Now, al-though the slaves were supposed to legally be free after the Emancipation Proclamation and the Civil Rights movement fought for the inclusion, accep-tance, and respect of black people in America, it would be assumed that they were added to the equation of the sociopolitical and economic American playing field. However, this did not mean that they were made equal. Monáe continues to throw musical jabs as she addresses figurative rights and proper-ties, specifically with regards to intellectual property (such as a film). It is without question that the royalties of the originator belong to that person, and as a result of its use one is paid for that and the derivations of it (i.e., sequels),[8] however this does not always end that way. Furthermore in this line of thinking, Monáe may also be referring to how we as individuals are responsible for our own lives, hence owning the script (how their life plays out) and the sequel (their future). This could also be a commentary on the fight over women's reproductive rights in the U.S. and around the world, and just in general the patriarchy's attempt to control women rather than women controlling their own lives and receiving the same freedoms as men in every facet of society.

Monáe's rap also provides us with a brief history lesson, where she pays personal homage to the "weight" of Queen Nefertiti's crown, to demanding reclamation of the Egyptian pyramids, to even acknowledging her hometown of Kansas City. First she brings to the table Queen Nefertiti, who was an Egyptian queen during the mid to late 1300 BC period, and was valued for her beauty, and would adorn a large crown. This could possibly speak to why Monáe makes this comparison to herself, as her hairstyles are often reminis-cent of a beautiful crown. And with Nefertiti's headdress/crown being considerably great in size, there is no doubt it was very heavy to wear on top of her head. The metaphor of the heavy physical burden of the crown represents the enormous burden of responsibility that comes with being a queen. Much like being an icon and role model within today's culture and society. Leadership has many consequences and responsibilities. Next she addresses one of the great wonders of the world. As it is told the Great Pyramids of Egypt were built by enslaved Africans; although recently many have called this into question, Monáe is metaphorically demanding the "fruits of labor" be given back to those who should rightfully possess it, which could also be likened to her hometown of Kansas City. Monáe is reiterating this sentiment by essentially trying to free her own community, further implying that the change must start from the inside.

The rap lyrical history lesson continues as she acknowledges such mix masterminds as Bernie Grundman and freedom trailblazers as Harriet Tubman. By directly referencing the influence of these two great giants, Bernie Grundman who has mastered thirty-seven Grammy-award winning albums and Harriet Tubman who would be known as freeing slaves through the Underground Railroad, we see the musical freedom connection unfold. Now Monáe serves as this generation's mix master and conductor by using her musical influence to free people's minds from the political and social issues of today and further leading them into a futuristic liberation. Monáe makes it very clear that nothing can stop her from using music as a tool, and she will continue to poke and prod in any way, which will help to promote her message. And although she may be tired of trying to figure what is going on with the world, much like Marvin Gaye and his song "What's Going On" the journey still continues. This allusion to the legendary singer-songwriter and musician is not exclaiming how she is literally tired of Marvin asking the question, but more so talking about the base message of "What's Going On," which promotes awareness and resistance to social problems, and for Monáe she even pushes this further with a more assertive approach of resistance.

Even still today, it remains nearly impossible to place Monáe in a box like other mainstream artists. Despite being categorized and labeled, she refuses to conform and subscribe to others' standards of who she is as a musician and artist. Although she is signed to Sean "Diddy" Combs Bad Boy Entertainment (which is primarily an urban/rap label), her music is an amalgam of funk, indie rock, RandB, dance-punk, techno, and much more . . . so how does one categorize that? It is also worth mentioning how this line speaks to how she defies expectations of femininity despite people questioning her sexuality, and thus it is hard to categorize in terms of gender and sexuality. This second part of these two lines has more of a racial overtone. Her meaning is with all of the history of racism and suffering by African Americans in the past, there will be some growing pains to suffer. Not discussing race has been a short-term solution to the American problem of racism. Ironically, not dealing with race seems to be the same thing that has kept African-Americans in a stagnant period of non-solution. Monáe also toys with this idea by wondering if this will be her "final act" of if she will be censored.

Much like how "Many Moons" ends, Monáe leaves us with some deep, penetrating questions: "Will you be electric sheep? Electric ladies, will you sleep? Or will you preach?" These final lines make reference to Phillip K. Dick's *Do Androids Dream of Electric Sheep.*[9] In addition this sentiment is reminiscent of her earlier work where she asks the question, *Are we really living, or just walking dead now?* So then the question is do you sit idly or take action? Overall, Q.U.E.E.N. as a song presents itself as a brand of activism that is not exclusive to any one group or individual.

## FUTURISTIC FREEDOM FIGHTER

All in all, contemporary work from artists such as Monáe have extended the boundaries that plainly embrace Afrofuturism imagining different times and places, in which they not only address issues of race, ethnicity, and color, but also examining issues of gender, politics, and technology. Janelle Monáe is one of the few current artists who use space and future as commentary to speak about humanity, racial equality, and female/girl power. According to Monáe's *Ten Droid Commandments (2010)*[10] in Commandment #9:

> By shows end you must transform. This includes, but is not limited to eye colour, perspective, mood, or height. So one must not leave the way the came, or else.

As we already know, Afrofuturism continues to serve as this intersection between imagination, technology, the future, and liberation (Womack 2013). As a genre it not only allows, but encourages individuals to unashamedly experiment, reimagine identities, and activate this sense of liberation (LaFleur 2011). And Janelle Monáe has done just that by pressing the reset button on music and busting through the musical seams.

She offers this alternative reality that does not follow a specific or assigned script; Monáe simply works off her own vision and destiny. Jez Collins (2013) of PopMatters further acknowledges this vision and destiny as he offer a positive review by adding, "Monáe is acutely aware of her history, and it's a history to be understood, respected, re-appropriated and re-purposed." But this is never merely pastiche, Monáe takes her history and updates it, makes it relevant and vital for today. This is smart, thought-provoking music. She continues to be an agent of change that imports her own personal thoughts and experiences, and then infuses them into a way in which they become life lessons. Her numerous messages are quite refreshing in that she is one of the few artists who strategically uses space and the future as commentary to speak about humanity, racial equality, and female power. An artist cannot go wrong when he/she combines a grassroots, feminist approach with a futuristic flair. Janelle Monáe with the help of android Cindi Mayweather, aka Alpha Platinum 9000, is more than just a one-trick pony, her rare gender-bending, genre-bending, Afrofuturist, cyber vibe is sure to keep you thinking, reflecting, and dancing all wrapped in one. Power Up . . . Power Up!

## NOTES

1. As quoted in Trey Ellis's 1989 article in *Callaloo*, "The New Black Aesthetic," pg. 238.

2. A droid/android in some cyber circles is defined as robots who look like humans. Robots are often regarded as "lifeless" or "mechanical" with no soul, much like how African Americans and those of the diaspora have been and continue to be treated as less than human.

3. The Metropolis concept draws inspiration from a wide range of musical, cinematic, and other sources, ranging from Alfred Hitchcock to Debussy to Phillip K. Dick.

4. Hilton describes Shangri-La as this mystical, harmonious valley.

5. A possible reference to the House of Annubis the jackal-headed god that is associated with mummification and the afterlife in ancient Egyptian religion.

6. This could also be a nod to musical godfather Prince as he starts out his song "Controversy" the same way, "I just can't believe / all the things people say."

7. The Lost Generation was considered the generation that came of age during World War I, but specifically a group of U.S. writers who came of age during the war and established their literary reputations in the 1920s. They would critique American culture by incorporating themes of self-exile, indulgence, and spiritual alienation. These individuals would also reject American post WWI values and oftentimes leave/escape the U.S. in hopes of a care-free lifestyle.

8. This could also be a reference to Sophia Stewart and the copyright lawsuit regarding The Matrix series.

9. A science fiction novel that Monáe has mentioned before on her EP *Metropolis: Suite I (The Chase)*.

10. A statement that is often handed out at her concerts, which encourages her audience members to embrace the idea of individuality.

## REFERENCES

Andrews, Gillian Gus. 2010, July 21. Janelle Monae turns rhythm and blues into science fiction. Retrieved September 2013, from http://io9.com/5592174/janelle-monae-turns-rhythm-and-blues-into-science-fiction.

Bristow, Tegan. 2012. We want the funk: What is Afrofuturism to the situation of digital arts in Africa? *Technoetic Arts: A Journal of Speculative Research*, 10 (1), 25–32.

Burgess, Omar. 2008, September 25. *Janelle Monae-Metropolis: The Chase Suite*. Retrieved October 2013, from http://www.hiphopdx.com/index/album-reviews/id.1015/title.janelle-monae-metropolis-the-chase-suite.

Calvert, John. 2010, September 2. *The Quietus | Opinion | Black Sky Thinking | Janelle Monáe: A New Pioneer of Afrofuturism*. Retrieved July 2013, from http://thequietus.com/articles/04889-janelle-mon-e-the-archandroid-afrofuturism.

Collins, Jez. 2013, September 9. *"Janelle Monáe: The Electric Lady" | PopMatters*. Retrieved September 2013, from http://www.popmatters.com/review/175178-janelle-monae-the-electric-lady/.

Dery, Mark. 1994. "Black to the Future." In Flame wars: The discourse of cyberculture. Durham, NC: Duke University Press.

Eglash, Ron and Bleecker, Julian. 2001. The race for cyberspace: Information technology in the black diaspora. *Science as Culture*, 10 (3), 353–74.

Ellis, Trey. (1989, Winter). The new black aesthetic. *Callaloo*, 38, 233–43.

English, Daylanne K. and Kim, Alvin. 2013. Now We Want Our Funk Cut: Janelle Monáe's Neo-Afrofuturism. *American Studies*, 52 (4), 217–30.

Haraway, Donna J. 1991. Simians, cyborgs, and women: The reinvention of nature . New York: Routledge.

King, Nikki. 2008, April 1. "P. Diddy signs Janelle Monáe to Bad Boy Records." *Paste Magazine*. Retrieved October 2013 from http://www.pastemagazine.com/articles/2008/04/p-diddy-signs-janelle-monae-to-bad-boy-records.html.

Kot, Greg. 2010, May 26. "Turn It Up: Janelle Monae, the interview: 'I identify with androids'." *Chicago Tribune [online archive]*. [Chicago]. Retrieved October 2013 from http://archive.today/QnTCl#selection-477.1-477.57.

LaFleur, Ingrid, 25, September 2011. "Visual Aesthetics of Afrofuturism," TEDx Fort Greene Salon, *YouTube*.

Mayer, Ruth. 2000. Africa as an Alien Future: The Middle Passage, Afrofuturism, and Postcolonial Waterworlds. *American Studies*, 45 (4), 555–66.

Monáe, Janelle 2008. "Many Moons." *Metropolis: Suite I (The Chase)*. [2007].

———. 2010. "Cold War." *The ArchAndroid*. [2010].

———. 2013. "Q.U.E.E.N." *The Electric Lady*. [2013].

Morgan, Joan. 1999. When Chickenheads Come Home to Roost: My Life as a Hip-Hop Feminist. New York: Simon and Schuster.

MTV UK. 2010, May 13. "*Janelle Monae Talks to Our Urban Blog | Janelle Monae | News | MTV UK*." Retrieved September 2013, from www.mtv.co.uk/news/janelle-monae/221762-janelle-monae-speaks-to-our-urban-blog.

Nelson, Alondra and Miller, Paul D. 2006, June 28. "About Afrofuturism": Afrofuturism. Retrieved from http://www.afrofuturism.net/text/about.html.

Nyong'o, Tavia. 2005. Punk'd Theory. *Social Text*, 84/85, 19–34.

"The Ten Droid Commandments" (n.d.). Holly Gocrunkly - The Ten Droid Commandments . Retrieved September 2013, from http://hollygocrunkly.tumblr.com/post/746007554/the-ten-droid-commandments.

Womack, Ytasha L. 2013. Afrofuturism: The World of Black Sci-Fi and Fantasy Culture. Chicago: Lawrence Hill Books.

Wondaland Arts Society. 2011. About | Wondaland Arts Society. Retrieved October 2013, from http://www.wondaland.com/about/.

*Chapter Six*

# Hip Hop Holograms

*Tupac Shakur, Technological
Immortality, and Time Travel*

## Ken McLeod

Whether it is the synthetic upgrading of voices with vocoders, autotune or in a proclivity for sampling and repurposing outdated technology juxtaposed against the latest digital recording and playback technologies, hip hop often refuses notions of "real time." In hip hop, time is always something provisional, something constructed in order to disappear again and thus enable a form of technological immortality. Over the past decade numerous scholars have discussed the general topic of Afrofuturism in popular music (Eshun 1998; Weheliye 2002; David 2007; Zuberi 2007; Rollefson 2008; Lewis 2008). Time travel and related notions of immortality, in particular, are recurring themes in the music of Sun Ra (*We Travel the Spaceways*, 1961; *The Futuristic Sounds of Sun Ra*, 1961), George Clinton (*Mothership Connection*, 1975), Outkast (*ATLiens*, 1996), and Janelle Monáe (*Metropolis Suite [The Chase]*, 2007; *The ArchAndroid*, 2010), among many other artists evincing Afrofuturistic ideals. While overt themes of time travel and/or futurism are not expressly present in the music and lyrics of Tupac Shakur, notions of immortality and future co-presence are nonetheless prominent in his posthumous legacy.

Our experience of music, and of the world in general, is increasingly becoming a hybridized mixed reality experience, a complex blend of the physical "real" and the digital. Whether through iPods, cell phones, automobiles, television, or online communities, machines increasingly mediate and/ or facilitate our musical experiences. Essentially, digital culture has witnessed a shift from a virtual reality paradigm to a mixed reality paradigm.

Virtual reality, a paradigm highly promoted in and associated with the 1990s, existed as a world parallel to the real world in which practitioners could lose themselves in a variety of exotic experiences. In the twenty-first century, while virtual reality still maintains a significant place in the popular imaginary, the separation between virtual environments and the physical world has been significantly eroded. This erosion is most pronounced in the advent of a number of "live" holographic performances by artists such as Gorillaz, Mariah Carey, Beyoncé, and by Japanese vocaloids such as Hatsune Miku. No holographic performance has engendered more comment and attention than Tupac Shakur's three-dimensional resurrection at the 2012 Coachella Valley Music and Arts Festival. This chapter will address how these types of such performances challenge our assumptions of reality and physical transcendence that often evoke forms of technological spirituality and immortality.[1]

Undoubtedly, the mere act of committing one's voice or performance to a recording already ensures a form of technological immortality. Furthermore, there are many examples of posthumous releases; Jimi Hendrix, for example, has "released" numerous posthumous albums. As a result of the untimely deaths and accompanying professional rivalry between The Notorious B.I.G. and Tupac, posthumous releases have been particularly prevalent in the world of hip hop. As manifest in the titles of The Notorious B.I.G.'s top selling posthumous albums *Life After Death* (1997) and *Born Again* (1999), the concepts of immortality and spiritual, if not physical, resurrection form a strong undercurrent in hip hop.

## HOLOGRAPHIC TUPAC: THE RESURRECTION

The holographic Tupac performance, sponsored by Dr. Dre and Snoop Dogg at the 2012 Coachella Festival seems to take the notion of technological immortality to a different level. Characteristic of more recent holographic performances the appearance was underscored by a sense of spiritual co-presence that mediated the reality of the moment with the virtual presence of the late rapper. Indeed, since his death in 1996 Tupac has become a sort of ethereal, digitally preserved, Jedi-god in the rap realm, where his virtual vocal "presence" is used to lend weight to innumerable posthumous releases. His resurrection in holographic form at the Coachella festival, however, stunned audiences who both reveled in Tupac's "presence" and simultaneously marveled at the technology that made his "presence" possible. When the vision of Tupac evaporated, witnesses described it as a "ghostly," "unbelievable," and a "mind blowing vision" that "left the crowd sighing" (Osterhout 2012).

Underscoring this quasi-religious ethereal "second coming," the holographic displaying Tupac's first song was appropriately his 1996 hit "Hail

Mary." Replete with a church bell ominously intoning throughout, the song is rife with religious imagery. Topically the work is in itself a reflection on reincarnation and revenge. Sung in the voice of Tupac's alter ego Makaveli, a reincarnated gangsta soldier, the lyrics directly evoke the notion of an afterlife as Makaveli proclaims "When they turn out the lights, I'll be down in the dark Thuggin eternal through my heart." Released just months before he was shot, some fans have even read the song as Tupac's pre-sentiment of his death. From the very beginning of the spoken introduction, Tupac presents himself as a Jesus figure, complete with biblical allusions to the Book of John and its message of eternal life. The allusion reads, "Whoever eats My flesh and drinks My blood has eternal life, and I will raise him up at the last day"; Tupac's introduction to "Hail Mary" reads:

> And God said he should send his one begotten son
> to lead the wild into the ways of the man
> Follow me; eat my flesh, flesh of my flesh

The "flesh of my flesh" lyric from "Hail Mary" takes on a particular irony, of course, when sung by a hologram. Perhaps even more unnervingly, the ghostly holographic Tupac started his mini-set, which included a duet with the live Snoop Dogg, by shouting and evoking the name of the festival that only began in 1999, some three years after the rapper's death in 1996. It is important to emphasize that this was not recycled concert footage but a new vocal and visual performance that was entirely the result of both a vocal and visual digital computer simulation of the late artist.

The performance became a global media sensation with over twenty-two million YouTube views and thousands of print, online, and broadcast reports. Perhaps as expected—the commercial benefits were substantial. In the following weeks, Tupac's album sales increased over five hundred percent. His 1998 *Greatest Hits* album regained the Billboard top 200 after a twelve-year absence and weekly downloads of "Hail Mary" increased by one thousand percent. The benefits also extended to the various technology companies involved in creating the event. The stock price of Digital Domain, the company responsible for generating the image of Tupac, for example, rose over sixty-percent.[2] While it is not the primary focus of this chapter, such financial returns raise questions about the ethics of profiting from the dead. In this instance Tupac's mother, Afeni Shakur, gave her blessing to the event after Dr. Dre requested permission to use her son's image and made a donation to one of Shakur's charities.[3] The questionable ethics of profiting from the dead aside, amongst other issues, the holographically digitized Tupac ties into Afrofuturist ideals. Freed from the shackles of his mortal body, the holographic Tupac essentially represents a utopian manifestation, or at least a vision, of eternal freedom and technological immortality. The performance also reflected on Dr. Dre's ability, both financially and through his creative control of advanced technology, to essentially play God and virtually resurrect his late friend.

The presence of and fascination with holographic performers, whether alive, dead, or animated, may for some conjure up fears of a dystopic posthuman future where human corporality has, literally and figuratively, ceased to matter. Of course notions of posthumanism in music have been used by various scholars in the construction of alternative representation and constructions of gender and race (Loza 2001; Dickenson 2001; Weheliye 2002; David 2007). As some would have it, in a post-human universe, governed by binary code, the body ceases to matter, thereby fracturing and ultimately dissolving ties to racialized, gendered, and locational subjectivity, positionality, and "self." The disembodied holographic representation of Tupac does little to challenge cultural stereotypes. Holographic Tupac was presented with a naked upper torso revealing his intimidating "Thug Life" tattoos and muscular abs. This in combination with the aggressive and profane "Coachella" shout out can be read as a continuation of ongoing stereotypes of threatening black hyper-masculinity.

## OTHER AFRICAN-AMERICAN HOLOGRAPHIC PERFORMERS

The Tupac hologram, it turns out, has inspired the creation of several other holographic performances by deceased rappers. In September 2013 the Rock the Bells hip hop music festival, employing the same technology company responsible for the Tupac performance, also used holographic technology to resurrect two more deceased rap giants. The founding member of the Wu-Tang Clan, Old Dirty Bastard, who died in 2004 of a drug overdose, and Eazy-E founder of N.W.A., who died in 1995 from AIDS complications, were reunited with surviving members of their respective groups to open and close the festival. The performances introduced these revered artists to a new generation of rap fans as younger concertgoers stood next to the older brothers and fathers who introduced them to the genre.

As the lights dimmed midway through Cleveland rap posse Bone Thugs-N-Harmony's set, a lighting rig lowered onto the stage and, to the tune of 1988's "We Want Eazy," the rap legend was beamed onto a well-hidden screen set up on an elevated platform in the middle of the stage. Clad in his signature Dickies and Compton hat, Eazy shuffled through his hits "Straight Outta Compton" and "Boyz in Da Hood" and was joined by Bone Thugs for "Foe Tha Love of $." "What's up, my thugs," Eazy asked, albeit much more profanely, as the audience was aglow with thousands of smart phones documenting the moment.[4] Similar to the reaction to the Tupac Coachella performance, as the *L.A. Times* reported, many people appeared awestruck at the "ghost" that sauntered slowly across stage, often stopping to address the audience with prerecorded banter.[5]

While Tupac's Coachella appearance remains the most high profile instance of the employment of holographic performance technology to date, other living African American artists have also used the technology. Beyoncé's recent 2013 Superbowl Halftime show, for example, featured a holographic performance. Following a sultry, horn-inflected "End of Time," from her most recent album, *4* (2013), Beyoncé stood before an electronic screen projecting multiple holographic images of herself as she sang her 2003 hit "Baby Boy." In similar fashion to Tupac, the holographic images of the 2003 version of Beyoncé, and underscoring the "End of Time" theme, seemingly brought to life in 2013, again suggested a notion of time travel or at least created a hyper-aware sense of time shifting.

Mariah Carey has also engaged in holographic performance. Predating Tupac's Coachella hologram by some five months, on November 17, 2011, Carey simultaneously appeared before audiences in Germany, Croatia, Macedonia, Montenegro, and Poland in the form of a hologram—interacting with real dancers and live audiences in each location. The performance was, somewhat ironically, in service of creating a "life is for sharing moment" promotion for the German telecommunications company Deutsche Telekom advertising campaign.[6] Appearing to the audience as if she was live in concert for the first ten minutes of the show, her holographic form then disintegrated into thousands of video fragments which burst into the sky, revealing the surprise to the live audience—many of whom (as manifest in reactions in the television commercial that was made from the event), had thought it was a "live" appearance. Her image subsequently reformed as it led all the countries in a moving rendition of the traditional carol "Silent Night," before finishing with "All I Want for Christmas Is You." The multi-media spectacular was witnessed in person by thousands of people around Europe and was streamed live globally through the lifeisforsharing.tv channel. Again the holographic technology facilitated a seeming distortion of time and place. While in this instance, unlike Tupac or Beyoncé, there was no attempt to reference or resurrect an artist's past, Carey was, nonetheless, given the appearance of being omnipotently "present" in multiple locations at the same time.[7]

## HIP HOP IMMORTALITY AND TIME TRAVEL

Holographic performances are by no means the only way by which hip hop artists engage in notions of time travel. As mentioned at the beginning of this chapter, the use of technology in hip hop often refuses notions of real time, place, and space. Both sampling and multi-tracking allow for a type of aural time travel through the simultaneous representation and experience of past and present. With sampling technology artists are able to juxtapose decades old speeches by Martin Luther King or loops from James Brown against contemporary hip hop tracks. Thus, such technology allowed artists to inter-textually signify a collective notion of African American historical memory. In a somewhat similar fashion the ingestion of drugs, often thought of as merely another form of technology brought to bear on popular music (Gilbert and Pearson 1999), also promotes a form of dislocation of time and space. Such effects are, of course, often amplified and/or complemented through the sensory overload associated with extreme dynamic levels and often flashing lights in concerts, nightclubs, cars, and other places of consumption.

The Afro-futuristic notion of flight and literal escape from earth can be understood as reaching as far back as nineteenth-century Negro spirituals. Many spirituals reflect a desire to reject Earth and the hardship and suffering it contains. "Swing Low, Sweet Chariot," "All God's Chillun Got Wings," and "This World Is Not My Home" are all thematically based on rejecting and taking flight from the material world. Equating these spiritual journeys to extraterrestrial travel and analogous themes of escaping Earth through super-human flight is not difficult. Indeed, the parallels can be glimpsed in films such as *Hancock* (2008), starring Will Smith, in which an African American is endowed with superhuman powers including supersonic flight, invulner-ability, and immortality. To some extent we might even look to the hip hop's association with basketball as a metaphoric parallel of the desire to achieve immortality and metaphorically fly through superhuman strength. In films such as *Above the Rim* (1994), which featured Tupac Shakur, or the cartoon gangsta-alien fantasy of *Space Jam* (1996) basketball is explicitly linked to rap music as a co-signifier of transcendence through struggle, creativity, and extraordinary ability for both the African American and white communities. As such hip hop and basketball combine to produce utopian visions of im-mortality and freedom in contemporary urban society. In their visual reincar-nations we may look on the presence of holographic rappers as, ironically, reinforcing a form of exceptionalist black hyper-humanity promoted in the body-centered politics of sports and entertainment.

In many ways the hyper-humanity of the Tupac hologram has many his-torical precedents in the history of music. To be sure we can understand the virtualization of the human body to have occurred at least since the advent of recording technologies. As noted earlier, the recorded voices of Notorious B.I.G. or Tupac heard in posthumous releases already project a sense of an uncanny ephemeral haunting. This disavowal of the embodied body is prob-ably an effect of a hegemonic phonographic (and media) history that empha-sizes the disembodiment that has accompanied recording and mediation of music performances ever since the late nineteenth century. However, sound amplification technology in concerts or on the dance floor, or indeed in personal listening devices, simultaneously remind us that music is also felt in the body as much as it is "heard" in the mind. Through powerful sound systems and headphones music becomes an experience that is literally felt by the body—a transference of vibration and energy from the machine to the body. The use of holographic technology to project at least the visual image of a body, ironically, goes some way to reverse the de-emphasis on human corporeal presence common in recent popular music. [8]

## THEORETICAL PERSPECTIVES AND HIP HOP SPIRITUALITY

Hip hop is thus commonly linked with notions of escape and related concepts of fame and immortality. However, rap and hip hop can also be understood in terms of Afrocentric concepts such as nommo—essentially a manifestation of the mystical power of words. As playwright and theorist Paul Carter Harrison describes it in relation to African American cultural life, nommo is a "force which manipulates all forms of raw life and conjures images that not only represent his biological place in Time and Space, but his spiritual existence as well" (1972, xiv). We might see the holographic rapper as representing a new form of digital nommo, one which underlines a form of what Ronald Jackson has discussed as an Afro-circular flow between the tangible words and spirituality (in opposition to a "Eurolinear perspective"), between the material and immaterial, between mortality and immortality, between liberation and enslavement (Jackson 2003, 122).

Hip hop has also often evinced more overt religious or spiritual associations. Distinct from the overt proselytizing associated with church based genres such as Holy hip hop or Gospel Rap, mainstream hip hop, as with many African American based music, has commonly revealed an element of spirituality. Indeed, the perceived commonalities between the rhetoric (typically revolving around notions of "spitting truth" or "tellin' it like it is") and the dramatic oratorical style employed by black preachers and rappers, and the participatory responses from their respective audiences have often been observed. Cornel West (2004) identified the importance of encouraging what he considers the more desirable "prophetic" hip hop, characterized by political overtones and a culture of protest and social commentary. Artists that have been identified with the prophetic hip hop movement include Lauryn Hill, Nas, Talib Kweli, Mos Def, Common, and Dead Prez (Lauricella and Alexander 2012).

While politics and culture play a part in prophetic hip hop, another defining element in this genre is spirituality. Sorett (2010) traces the trajectory of spirituality in rap back to MC Hammer's gospel track "Son of the King" on his 1987 debut album *Let's Get it Started*. In 1996 Nas paid homage to the divine by titling his 1996 album *It Is Written* and his 2001 release *God's Son*. References to God have even been made by 50 Cent in his tracks "Many

Men" and "Gotta Make It to Heaven." Perhaps most overtly, in 2004, Kanye West released "Jesus Walks," the third single from his debut album *The College Dropout*. Despite its nonconformity with typical mainstream hip hop at the time in its open embrace of religion and spirituality, "Jesus Walks" reached #11 on the Billboard 100.

Holographic performances, however, manifest a new form of disembodied yet physically present pop star. Tupac has essentially become an immortal, hyper-real pop star—his image is forever frozen in an idealized form. He will never age or cause any new controversies due to personal opinions or actions. His voice will never falter. In that sense he is even better than his real life contemporaries. Nonetheless, as with real pop stars—his resurrected fame will likely rise and fall, not with the novelty of his sound and style but rather as the novelty (and/or refinement) of his holographic and digital technology on which he is dependent, waxes and wanes.[9]

Understanding the recent popularity of holographic performers is at least in part to understand them as entities that can evoke quasi-spiritual experiences. They present an ethereal three-dimensional vision that often, particularly in the case of Tupac's Coachella appearance, represents a transcendence of death and that inspires utter beatitude on behalf of the witnesses. They are human memes that through a process of hyperstition are essentially bringing about their own reality. As evident in his album sales following his Coachella appearance the holographic Tupac is now as "real" as any other traditionally constructed pop star (indeed, how real is Justin Bieber or Lady Gaga?). Both religion and capitalist economics often work in a hyperstitional mode. As Cybernetic philosopher Nick Land explains: "capitalism incarnates hyperstitional dynamics . . . turning mundane economic 'speculation' into an effective world-historical force" (Carstens 2009). .Similarly the (fictional) idea of Cyberspace contributed to the influx of investment that rapidly converted it into a techno-social reality. Hyperstition is able to transmute immaterial beliefs into truths. Tupac's hologram has essentially become a "real" pop star with a "real" base of followers who continue to create its reality. Indeed, further blurring the line between the virtual and the real, the Tupac hologram has its own Twitter account with over 23,000 followers.

While fans perhaps intellectually understand holograms to be nothing more than a soul-less optical illusion, to some extent we can and do understand holographic performers and performances as, nonetheless, being invested with some form of actual human co-presence. Their ethereal existence and actions, human in form and behavior, are typically the result of a collection of creative human programmers responsible for the illusion of a physical presence. Thus, rather than decrying a loss of human agency, holographic performances can be viewed as serving to reflect the agency of collective human consciousness. As Katherine Hayles has observed: "our bodies are no less actively involved in the construction of virtuality than in the construction of real life" (Hayles 1996, 1).

There is, however, also a sense in which these essentially machinic, human creations take on a life of their own. For Karl Marx machines "are organs of the human brain, created by the human hand; the power of knowledge, objectified" (Marx 1857, 602). Philosopher Gerald Raunig, channeling Marx, has even claimed that machines and technology take on a virtuosic component separate from the human content that creates it. According to Raunig, "the machine emerges as a virtuoso, *having a soul of their own* (taken from workers), whose virtuosic handling of their implements and whose labour on and in machines merges into an activity that is a mere abstraction that is determined and regulated by the movement and parts of the very machine itself. The machine appears as a virtuoso, the activity of the worker is abstract" (Raunig 2010, 113—italics mine). In this manner, holographic performers can be said to transcend the limitations of their apparent inanimate construction and actively inherit the "souls" or spirits of their creators.

In some ways holographic performers represent a modern triumph of the *Deus ex machina.* The *Deus ex machina* in Greek theatre combined both notions of a theatrical artistic plot device, the intervention of the gods, and the physical device that allowed the effect to take place on stage. In some sense this represents both a conflation of the man-machine binary and an extension of it, as in any interpretation the plot is resolved by an immortal God—essentially an alien machine-God. The obvious artificiality of the plot device is mirrored in the seeming artificiality of the machine, aided by more machines that essentially speed up and smooth scenery and plot transitions, creating an illusion of seamlessness. The holographic Tupac fundamentally creates a similar seamless illusion between reality and the virtual, between the human and the machine.

Holographic musical performers epitomize a twenty-first-century fascination with the techno sublime—a techno spiritualism for lack of a better expression, which celebrates and fetishizes advances in technological magic. They also represent an increased emphasis on mediating performance and a related tendency to grant machines and technology a greater role in constructing human subjectivity. Both music and holograms exist in liminal ethereal states—neither is able to be physically touched but both evoke a powerful form of felt co-presence in audiences that is only enhanced when they are brought together. As evident in the viral reaction to the Tupac hologram, holographic performers are often worshipped as literal spirits—manifesting a virtual co-presence with and a visual and aural trace of a larger creative power. It is precisely in this that the quality of the machine beyond humanist, mechanistic, and cybernetic interpretations exists. To quote Raunig, it is "in the insistence of a dissonant power, a monstrous potency and enjoyment . . . an a-harmonious composition without a composer" (Raunig 2010, 119). Blurring the line between the real and the virtual holographic performers ironically embodies and inspires a variety of spiritual characteristics and ultimately forces us to ask what it means to be human.

In *Simulacra and Simulations* Baudrillard opines that holograms are "in some sense the end of the aesthetic and the triumph of the medium . . . which, at its most sophisticated limits, neatly puts an end to the charm and the intelligence of music" (Baudrillard 2007, 106). Baudrillard suggests that the hologram is merely an extension of the hyper-real experience of music that has been the result of electronic recording and music reproduction practices over the past century. Holographic musical performances, as such, are simply one more extension of the abstraction of the human self: "The hologram, [is a] perfect image and an end of the imaginary . . . an abstract light of simulation . . . the hologram is now part of this 'subliminal comfort' that is our destiny . . . (The social . . . is now nothing but a special effect, obtained by the design of participating networks converging in emptiness under the spectral image of collective happiness.)" (Baudrillard 2007, 107).

In many ways the search for cultural and personal meaning central to Afrocentrism can be linked to Baudrillard's ecstasy of the sign that obscures distinctions between the real and unreal, the simulated and the dissimulated. The ideal Africa articulated in Afrocentric signs is one in which, to paraphrase Baudrillard, nostalgia is energized, in which "there is a proliferation of myths of origin and signs of reality" (Baudrillard 1983, 14). In Afrocentrism, African values and ideas have their origin in both the distant past and recent living history. The digitized Tupac then can be viewed as a manifestation of both recent nostalgia and of mythic origin.

To be sure the ecstatically enthusiastic audience participation, typically using cell phone video capture to record the moment of resurrection, at holographic hip hop concerts seems to reinforce and underscore the concept of collective or communal happiness. We, perhaps ironically, find ourselves celebrating our collective humanity through the seemingly artificial—an ephemeral, intangible, and ultimately mechanical image of ourselves. In some ways it entails and represents a pataphysical understanding of the reality of existence. In a pataphysical conception, holographic performers are another empty illusion, a false transcendence that don't have to exist to exist. The archiving of 1000s of Tupac's return could all in the words of Baudrillard's essay on Pataphysics signify that we "have arrived at the end of . . . live historical time, and that one needs to arm oneself with all forms of artificial memory, with all the signs of the past in order to confront the absence of the future . . . ?" (Baudrillard 2007).

While I would argue that the absence of a future seems untenable for all practical purposes, it is certainly a future that is being impacted and shaped by contemporary dislocations of time and space of holographic performances and their archiving on social media sites. Pataphysical reality in theories concerning the potential multiple dimensionality of the universe is increasingly being recognized in the sciences. Indeed, though it is outside the purview of the current inquiry, recent influential work on String Theory and Quantum Mechanics such as Michael Talbot's *Holographic Universe* (1991) and Leonard Susskind's influential 1994 essay "The World as a Hologram" have looked to holographic theory, specifically the "holographic principle" (essentially the concept that what we experience as three-dimensional reality actually takes place on a very thin plane) to explain the possibility of hidden physical dimensions in the universe—questioning our perception of reality itself.

## HAUNTOLOGY AND HOLOGRAPHIC PERFORMANCES

Derrida's concept of hauntology is instructive to understand the recent fascination with holographic performances by African American artists. For Derrida, hauntology was a challenge to ontology that conceives of being as a self-identical presence (Fischer 2012, 19). Ghosts and holograms are ephemeral entities that play with and distort distinctions between past and present. They both essentially disrupt and problematize the concept of linear or "real" time. Both the ghost and the holographic (human) performer exist as spectral traces of a body that once was materially present. Derrida writes that fundamentally "the specter is the future, it is always to come, it presents itself only as that which could come, or come back" (as quoted in Zuberi 2007, 284). In this sense concepts surrounding hauntology can usefully be applied to Afrofuturism and its associations with ancient Egypt and the dislocations of time and space associated with the ghosts of slavery and the African diaspora. For example, the racial slur "spook," though its precise origins are unclear, was applied to black people by whites because their dark skin was thought to blend into the night, thus giving them a ghost-like quality.[10] Pursuing this line of thought we might think of enslaved Africans in North America as always having been regarded as holographic specters—though their material physical bodies were valued as commodities for labor, slave owners regarded them as essentially immaterial beings.

Hauntology in music is often tied to notions of retrofuturism or technonostalgia whereby artists evoke the past typically by employing the spectral sounds of old music technologies. In the words of Jamie Sexton, writing about the Ghost Box record label, hauntology refers to "a number of contemporary music artists [where] there is a marked tendency to reflect on how contemporary music culture is saturated by artifacts from previous eras" (Sexton 2012, 562). Sexton identifies a sense in which current digital technologies can be considered as being haunted by their analogue counterparts.

Haunted in the sense that there exist a number of hidden uncanny sonic traces whose presence is felt but often unacknowledged. Hip hop often employs a similar aesthetic in their deliberate muddying of contemporary sounds by the use of old or outdated technology and by incorporating old samples and recordings. In essence we might look on the grainy sound from needles playing old LPs, the leaks from drum tracks, the squelches of old Roland 808 dram machines as evoking the sonic ghosts of past performances. As Simon Reynolds describes, the very practice of sampling involves recycling otherwise dead energy to create a form of undead zombie, taking the once "embodied energy of drummers, horn players or singers," looping and thus "transform[ing] these vivisected portions of human passion into treadmills of posthumous productivity" (Reynolds 2006, 31).

Derridian hauntology associated with recordings can also be linked to an Afrocentric connectedness to ancestral spirits. It might be likened to a form of nommo—a digitally created form of the spiritual power of the word. To some extent we might look on the hauntological reincarnation of Tupac as a technological appropriation and posthumous exploitation of the labor produced by the living black body. Essentially, it becomes a representation of techno liberation, a disruption of the racialized "digital divide" (Hobson 2012, 109) on the one hand but also potentially a form of digital enslavement on the other. As Mark Dery suggests, white masculine technology has already "engineered our collective fantasies [and they] already have a lock on that unreal estate" (Dery 1994, 109). In the midst of the proliferation of recent digital culture, the presence of holographic rappers could merely reinforce the opinion, voiced by cultural theorist Janell Hobson that "the black male subject has been refigured and realigned with white masculine technological power" (Hobson 2012, 93). Such a view is mitigated, of course, by the fact that it is in turn largely black male subjects (in the form of Dr. Dre and others) who are primarily responsible for funding and initiating the construction of these appearances.

## CONCLUSION

In relationship to the recent prevalence of holographic performances by African American artists, whether living or dead, it seems there is a clear continuation and extension of sonic explorations of a technological future. Nabeel Zuberi observes: "Black music culture seems an appropriate portal through which to examine the emerging media architecture of remembrance and to investigate perceptions of (technological) change. Musicians have been at the forefront of the interface between the analog and digital in the last twenty years, excavating the audio rubble of the past as they sound the future into being" (Zuberi 2007, 286). As such holographic performances by both dead and living African American artists ties into the notion of the construction of the future based on a reference to the past—an image, albeit ephemeral and intangible, of a past future.

The future is always experienced as a form of haunting: as a virtuality that already impinges on the present, conditioning expectations and motivating cultural production. The virtual or simulated revivication of dead celebrities has become common in both corporate advertising campaigns (i.e., Fred Astaire dancing with a Dirt Devil vacuum cleaner) and popular music (i.e., Natalie Cole's duet "Unforgettable" with her deceased father from 1991).[11] To a large degree the newly emerging use of holographic performances merely builds on this tradition though with the notable difference of extending the simulation into returning the deceased for "live" performances. In referring to posthumous duets, primarily that of "Unforgettable," Jason Stanyek and Benjamin Piekut opine that "[posthumous] Collaborations . . . are built upon the restricted, yet still effective, motile emplacements of dead and living humans within mundanities teeming with all kinds of active non-humans"(Stanyek and Piekut 2010, 33).

Similarly, the holographic Tupac is the product of multiple past-recorded performances (which go into the synthesis of his voice), and associated labor and technologies associated with recording and producing those performances. It is simultaneously the product of contemporary labor and technologies responsible for the digital programming and construction of the hologram itself. The Tupac hologram underscores the hauntological unseen presence of sounds, voices, labor of past producers, performers, and technologies. Furthermore, in the plethora of video and sound recordings of the "live" holographic performance from Coachella itself these past sonic traces ultimately project themselves into a circulation of multiple presents and futures that disrupt and dislocate any sense of absolute temporal flow.

Such a recognition of the spectral presence of past, present, and future underscores the idea that individual human agency, Tupac's or anyone else, is, perhaps ironically, the product of infinitely complex interactions that cut across notions of materiality, corporality, and traditional distinctions between human and non-human. If we regard our own individual agency as the product of an intricate nexus of past and present labor and technologies, the distinction between the seemingly virtual, immaterial, non-organic hologram and our corporeal human presence, as we have traditionally understood it, becomes blurry at best. With allusions to the currently popular hip hop crew, it is an "Odd Future" that calls attention to a type of intentionally ironic hyper modern referencing of past and future.[12]

Moreover, as outlined earlier, the prevalent use of holographic musical performances in the African American community resonates with an ongoing Afrocentric spiritual discourse. They represent a new technologized re-imagining of the liberatory freedom originally invoked by Christianity, in some sense a digital decolonizing and decentering of linearity associated with the Judeo-Christian narrative. They thus provide new images of both utopian and dystopian pasts as well as functioning as digitally resurrected prophets of an as yet to be determined future.

## NOTES

1. Contrary to popular belief neither the Tupac hologram nor any of the other recent instances of performing holograms are in fact true holograms. A traditional hologram is a three-dimensional view of an object recreated by shining laser light on a recorded interference pattern. Such holograms are actually flat but the term has also come to mean a kind of volume-filling projection for the same purpose. The Tupac hologram (as well as those of Gorillaz, Beyoncé, Mariah Carey, Hatsune Miku, and others) uses an old stage magician's trick known as Pepper's ghost. A projector above the stage casts a moving image onto a reflective surface on the stage floor. The reflection then bounces onto a mylar sheet angled overhead. To an audience, the projected image appears to be standing onstage in three-dimensional space. The technology was developed by Musion Systems Limited of London. To quote from Musion's website and alluding to their forthcoming Elvis project, "With Musion's groundbreaking digital resurrection, you can bring musical legends back on stage for an encore. Elvis has just re-entered the building." For a description of the technology and its uses in both various advertising and musical events, http://www.eyeliner3d.com/ (accessed May 12, 2012).

2. Figures according to data provided on Musion Eyeliner's website: http://www.musion.co.uk/ (accessed June 6, 2013).

3. "Tupac Shakur's mom reportedly 'thrilled' with hologram of dead son" *NBCNEWS Entertainment* April 17, 2012, http://www.nbcnews.com/entertainment/tupac-shakurs-mom-reportedly-thrilled-hologram-dead-son-720487 (Accessed June 20, 2013). The ethics of releasing recordings with deceased artists, such as Natalie Cole's collaboration with her deceased father on a duet of "Unforgettable" (1991), is discussed at length in Jason Stanyek and Benjamin Piekut, "Deadness: Technologies of the Intermundane," *The Drama Review* 54/1 (Spring) 2010.

4. The increasingly common archiving of "the moment" on cell phones or other digital devices and the subsequent posting to YouTube, Twitter, or other social media sites provides another technological manifestation of the quest for immortality.

5. According to the *Times* report, the posthumous appearances were approved by Eazy-E's widow Tomica Wright and ODB's mother Cherry Jones.

6. The commercial can be accessed on YouTube: http://www.youtube.com/watch?v=nH2dBHZ47uU.

7. It is worth noting that in almost every case of holographic performance "real" musicians provide live/real time backing to the preprogrammed hologram, often enacting an onstage interaction with them. This interaction underscores the blurring of the real and virtual as outlined at the beginning of the chapter but also highlights the fact that the corporeal human performers are forced to play and perform more or less metronomically, perhaps even somewhat robotically, in synch with their virtual partners. Perhaps somewhat ironically in the case of African American performers, we might interpret this, at least in part, as a new form of human enslavement where live performers are forced to rhythmically obey the mechanically intransigent lead of the virtual master.

8. The prevalent use of MP3 files and players has, for example, removed much of the visual aspect of popular music consumption previously manifest in album and CD covers.

9. Holographic musical performances, at this moment in time at least, ultimately draw attention to the technology and the holographic light medium itself. In some sense, though it might seem to distract from the musical content of the moment, they also foreground technology that has always been inherent in musical performance, creation, and dissemination.

10. Well known African American electronic and hip hop turntablist, producer, and academic DJ Spooky (a.k.a. Paul Miller) notably reclaims the term in his stage name.

11. Jason Stanyek and Benjamin Piekut provide an extensive analysis of this phenomenon and associated case studies in their article "Deadness: Technologies of the Intermundane," *The Drama Review*, 54/1 (Spring 2010): 14–38.

12. The Odd Future crew and its sub-projects such as "Sweaty Martians" and "Jet Age of Tomorrow" by their names alone highlight a continued fascination with hip hop Afrofuturism, albeit often predicated on thematic irony and kitsch rather than with an overt fetishization of technology.

# REFERENCES

Baudrillard, G. 2007. Pataphysics of Year 2000, trans. Drew Burk, *CTheory.net*, January http://www.ctheory.net/articles.aspx?id=569. Accessed June 18, 2013.
———. 1994. *Simulacra and simulation*. Ann Arbor: University of Michigan Press.
Carstens, Delphi. 2009. Hyperstition an introduction: Delphi Carstens interviews Nick Land. http://merliquify.com/blog/articles/hyperstition-an-introduction/#.UkgkfLwi_2A. Accessed July 17, 2013.
David, Marlo. Afrofuturism and post-soul possibility in black popular music. *African American Review* 41, no. 4 (2007): 695–707.
Derrida, Jacques. 2006. *Spectres of Marx: The state of the debt, the work of mourning and the new international*. London and New York: Routledge.
Dery, Mark. 1994. *Flame wars: The discourse of cyberculture*. Durham: Duke University Press.
Dickinson, Kay. "Believe"? Vocoders, digitised female identity and camp. *Popular Music* 20 (2001): 333–47.
Eshun, Kodwo. 1998. *More brilliant than the sun: Adventures in sonic fiction*. London: Quartet Books.
Fischer, Mark. What is hauntology? *Film Quarterly* 66, no. 1 (2012): 16–24.
Gilbert, Jeremy and Pearson, Ewan. 1999. *Discographies: Dance music, culture and the politics of sound*. London: Routledge.
Harrison, Paul Carter. 1972. *The drama of nommo*. New York: Grove.
Hayles, N. Katherine. 1996. Embodied virtuality: Or how to put bodies back into the picture. In *Immersed in technology: Art and virtual environments*, eds. Mary Anne Moser and Douglas MacLeod. Boston: MIT Press.
Hobson, Janelle. 2012. *Body as evidence: Mediating race, globalizing gender*. Albany: State University of New York Press.
Jackson, Ronald L., II. 2003. Afrocentricity as metatheory: A dialogic exploration of its principles. In *Understanding African American rhetoric: Classical origins to contemporary innovations*, eds. Ronald L. Jackson II and Elaine Richardson, 115–29. New York: Routledge.
Lauricella, Sharon and Alexander, Matthew. 2012. Voice from Rikers: Spirituality in hip hop artist Lil' Wayne's "Prison Blog." *Journal of Religion and Popular Culture* 24, no. 1: 15–28.
Lewis, George, E. 2008. Foreword: After afrofuturism. *Journal of the Society for American Music* 2, no. 2: 139–53.
Loza, Susana. 2001. Sampling (hetero)sexuality: Diva-ness and discipline in electronic dance music. *Popular Music*: 349–57.
Marx, Karl. 2005. Fragment über Maschinen. *Grundrisse der Kritik der politischen Ökonomie*, MEW 42, Berlin, 590–609. http://www.marxists.org/archive/marx/works/1857/grundrisse/ch14.htm#p706. Accessed September 29, 2013.
Osterhout, Jacob. 2012, April 16. Rapper Tupac Shakur hits the stage at Coachella with help of 3-D technology. *New York Daily News*.
Raunig, Gerald. 2010. *A thousand machines: A concise philosophy of the machine as social movement*, trans. Aileen Derieg. Los Angeles: Semiotext(e).
Reynolds, Simon. 2006. Society of the spectral. *The Wire* 273: 26–33.
Rollefson, Griffith. 2008. The "Robot Voodoo Power" thesis: Afrofuturism and anti-anti-essentialism from Sun Ra to Kool Keith. *Black Music Research Journal* 28, no. 1: 83–109.

Sexton, Jamie. 2012. Weird Britain in exile: Ghost box, hauntology, and alternative heritage. *Popular Music and Society* 35, no. 2: 561–84.

Sorett, Josef. 2010. Hip-hop religion and spiritual sampling in a "Post-Racial" age. *Religion Dispatches,* March 24. http://www.religiondispatches.org/books/culture/2281/hip_hop_religion_and_spiritual_sampling_in_a__post_racial__age/. Accessed Sept. 8, 2013.

Stanyek, Jason, and Benjamin Piekut. 2010. Deadness: Technologies of the intermundane. *The Drama Review* 54, no. 1: 14–38.

Susskind, Leonard. 1994. The world as a hologram. *Journal of Mathematics Physics* 36: 6377–96.

Talbot, Michael. 1991. *Holographic universe: The revolutionary theory of reality.* London, England: Grafton.

Tupac Shakur's mom reportedly "thrilled" with hologram of dead son. *NBCNEWS Entertainment,* April 17, 2012. http://www.nbcnews.com/entertainment/tupac-shakurs-mom-reportedly-thrilled-hologram-dead-son-720487. Accessed June 20, 2013.

Weheliye, Alexander G. 2002. "Feenin": Posthuman voices in contemporary black popular music. *Social Text* 20, no. 2: 21–47.

West, Cornel. 2004. *Democracy matters: Winning the fight against imperialism.* New York: Penguin Press.

Zuberi, Nabeel. 2007. Is this the future? Black music and technology discourse. *Science Fiction Studies* 34: 283–300.

*Part III*


# Forecasting Dark Bodies, Africology, and the Narrative Imagination

## Chapter Seven

# Afrofuturism and Our Old Ship of Zion

## The Black Church in Post-Modernity

## Andrew Rollins

The emergence of Afrofuturist theory and praxis is relevant to religion and the effect of Post-Modernity on the Black Church. This topic gives bearing to the direction and destiny of African American people. It forecasts the outcome of black people in America and furthermore, presages the destiny of America itself. More specifically, Afrofuturism equips the Black Church to face the challenges of Post-Modernity, Transhumanism, Time-Space Compression, and the New Jim Crow, and revises its theology to meet the demands of a new age.

What is presently called *Afrofuturism* was initially a philosophical techno-cultural vernacular perspective that was engaged in a heterodox form of cultural production originating in socio-spatial temporal practices of black urban dwellers in North America after World War II.[1] However, the term *Afrofuturism* was coined in 1994 by Mark Dery in an article entitled *Black to the Future*.[2] Dery defined Afrofuturism as "speculative fiction that treats African-American themes and addresses African-American concerns in the context of twentieth century technoculture—and more generally, African American signification that appropriates images of technology and prosthetically enhanced future." Yet, Afrofuturism has outgrown this original formulation. Previously, Afrofuturism was considered a philosophy of aesthetics expressing and analyzing art, literature, and music, as well as a way of critiquing the impact of technology on African American life. However, Afrofuturism has matured and expanded. *Afrofuturism encompasses metaphysics, ethics, digital hermeneutics, geopolitics, and several other dimen-*

*sions of the humanities and sciences.*[3] Afrocentric metatheory, Africology, and the contemporary study of Africanity emerged in the latter twentieth century during the current western existential crisis. First, Afrocentricity is a theory of social change, and seeks agency and action, furthermore; the Afrocentric idea metatheory examins the structure and power of the rhetorical condition in relation to societal norms and analytically focuses on the "frame of mind, scope of context, structure of code, and delivery of message" (Asante 1980, 47, 48).[4] Moreover, "Africology is the trans-generational and transcontinental study of African phenomenon." Finally, Africanity is focused on the "customs, traditions, and traits of the people of Africa and its diaspora" (Asante 1998, 19).[5] Therefore, in relation to the aforementioned frameworks, in the twenty-first century, Afrofuturism is an *Africological* system of metaphysics, aesthetics, and social thought, used to analyze and interpret Africanity and Africanist art, literature, music, science, technology, and society from a perspective which informs the trans-generational study of the past, present, and future of African peoples.

Currently, the world is going through a cosmological revolution which is further reaching than the Copernican Revolution. The nature and structure of the universe is being re-interpreted. It is understood that when someone's cosmological perspective is altered, their theology is affected. The Copernican Revolution, which fundamentally changed Western cosmology, was the Eurocentric basis of debate between the Roman Catholic Church and the scientific community in the European Renaissance. For example, Eurocentrism is not a social or scientific theory that incorporates several different conceptual elements into a universal "coherent vision of society and history." Rather, it is an active "prejudice that distorts social theories; it draws from its storehouse of components, retaining one or rejecting another according to the ideological needs of the moment" (Amin 1989, 90). Eurocentrism is comprised of an archeologically annexed form of Hellenism that removes Greece from its geographical and historical relationship to the Near East or Levant and Northeastern Africa, particularly during the Romantic period of the nineteenth century, developing a racism necessary for European cultural unity, and reinterprets a Near East and African imported version of Christianity to maintain cultural unity, and constructs "a vision . . . on the same racist foundation, again employing an immutable vision of religion."[6] Moreover, the publication of Nicolaus Copernicus's groundbreaking treaties, *On the Revolution of the Heavenly Bodies* in 1543, ushered in the Eurocentric *modern* way of viewing the universe. The Copernican Revolution was a paradigm shift from a geocentric model, with the earth at the center of the planetary order, to a heliocentric model with the sun at the center of the planetary order. For 1,500 years the Catholic Church's doctrine was based upon a geocentric order of the universe. The idea of the planetary order being heliocentric challenged the church's theology. The church taught that geocentricism was the accurate depiction of our planetary system and used scriptures to support this concept. For centuries the church wrestled with heliocentrism until it finally found a way to accept it as true and blend it into its belief system.

Human beings are living in a time of birth of new knowledge and technologies comparable to what took place during the European Renaissance. For example, cosmological models have radically changed. Scientists have a new theoretical model of the composition of the universe. Normal matter, which is observable with technical instruments, makes up 5 percent of the universe. However, the majority of the universe comprises 68 percent dark energy and 27 percent dark matter.[7] There is also a greatly enlarged concept of the cosmos. It is estimated "that there are 100 to 200 billion galaxies in the Universe" and each galaxy "has hundreds of billions of stars."[8] Therefore, the cosmology of the Post-Modern Era is very different from that of the Modern Era. Thus, theoretical perspectives such as Afrofuturism empower African people to grasp counterintuitive revelations such as a universe that is immensely vaster than it was believed to have been in the past. Similarly the Post-Modern transformation of cosmology is a major source of debate today between the church and the scientific community.

In light of the new ideas and methodologies being formulated and implemented, the Black Church needs a revised theoretical framework. Pursuing this further, Afrofuturism is a necessary theoretical approach, due to the fact that it is informed by the new knowledge sciences that are essential ingredients which should be incorporated into the theology and practical ministry of the Black Church.

Also, Afrofuturism addresses the questions at hand for today's clergy person. How does the minister effectively preach the Gospel of Jesus Christ in an era informed by a world view comprising a larger universe, Dark Matter, Dark Energy, String Theory, and Spiritual Machines? Furthermore, how does a pastor tend to parishioners in a world in which people are suffering from Time-Space Compression and scientists are working in laboratories to bring the homunculus into existence? Ultimately, to be progressive, the perspective of the Black Church has to be Afrofuturistic, which means it is multi-dimensional, intergalactic, and informed by Afrofuturist metaphysics and the new science, especially in the areas of physics, astronomy, biomedical-technology, nanotechnology, information systems, and agriculture. Afrofuturism represents an overarching theoretical approach which can help African Americans find their way in these demanding times. Afrofuturism interprets the meaning of history, the purpose of life, and the individual's relationship with the cosmos. The Afrofuturist world view is based upon an Africological philosophy of history with additional intergalactic and multidimensional elements. Furthermore, Afrofuturism delineates the relationship of African Americans as family, race, and as members of the Diaspora from a

Pan-African perspective. Finally Afrofuturism speaks on the nature of black people's relationship to and within the cosmos. It addresses the metaphysical questions of the structure and constitution of reality, including the nature and relation of being and the nature and grounds of knowledge.

Afrofuturism also has a redemptive quality. Exposure to the Afrofuturist perspective can psychologically free black youth who are trapped in the disabling mindset of urban dystopian milieu. Far too many vibrant and intelligent African Americans in the prime of life are being caught up in the subculture of gangs, violence, and drugs. Afrofuturism begins the existential reorientation of African American youth from the nihilism of a hyper capitalistic consumer society. Moreover, Afrofuturism opens new vistas of alternatives, opportunities, and possibilities, as well as a metaphysical view which includes the vastness of the universe, thereby expanding their imagination beyond the confining perimeter of a race obsessed America.

Sexism and homophobia are also implicated in these systems and institutional structures; however, in the interest of brevity the essay will look at the interplay of race in relationship to futurological studies. Specifically, the focus of discussion will be on the Black Church in America, as it relates to the historical dimension of white supremacy and its possible future. Covering all the various branches of the Black Church throughout the world is beyond the scope of this essay. Also, for the purpose at hand when referring to the Black Church, Protestant Christianity will be referenced. There are other spiritual practices among black Americans; however, Black Protestantism as the representative model is appropriate in that it has been the largest faith tradition practiced within the African American community in North America.

Historically, the Black Church has played a central role in black America spiritually, culturally, politically, and socially. Currently there is much debate on the role the Black Church can play in the present and future. During slavery times, the Black Church was involved in the Abolitionist Movement's fight to end slavery. The Black Church also participated in the early Pan-African Movement. Dr. Martin Delaney and Bishop Henry McNeal Turner were champions of the nineteenth century Pan-African Movement. Three great slave revolts were led by Christian ministers: Gabriel Prosser, Demark Vesey, and Nat Turner. Reverend Ransom was one of the founders of the NAACP in the early twentieth century and was an advocate of the Social Gospel. He also served as a Bishop in the African Methodist Episcopal Church. In the middle of the twentieth century, the Black Church played a pivotal role in launching the Civil Rights Movement under the leadership of clergyman Dr. Martin Luther King Jr. Overall, throughout its history, the Black Church sponsored educational institutions, charitable societies, economic development, and self-help programs in very adverse circumstances.

The history of the Black Church is worthy of respect and honor. It is a noble history and there are valuable lessons to be learned from it. Certainly, the great achievements of the past should be recognized. Nonetheless, many people are saying; "That *was then this is now.*" Therefore, the pertinent question is "What is the role of the Black Church today?" Some people believe that the day of the Black Church has passed. They argue that our society is too diverse and/or too secular for the Black Church to play an effective role. More specifically, society has transitioned from an old historical era, *Modernity*, into a new historical era, *Post-Modernity.* It is the shift in historical eras that requires the Black Church to thoroughly examine itself. The forces of the Post-Modern Era are making a powerful impact on the Black Church.

It would be profitable to ask two important questions due to the powerful impact of Post-Modernity: When did the Modern Era end and the Post-Modern Era begin? What is Post-Modernity? Many believe the Modern Era died at Auschwitz and Hiroshima. According to Paul Connelly, the Modern Era of history began in 1620 and ended in 1945 when World War II was ended in 30 years by the use of an atomic bomb. In Connelly's time line, the Post-Modern Era begins in 1948. 1948 was a red letter year. In 1948, Shannon developed Information Theory, Weiner published Cybernetics, television became a mass market phenomenon, and Orwell completed his novel 1984. Subsequently, Gordon Moore, a co-founder of Intel, published a paper in 1965 that described an observable technological shift which accelerated change every 18–24 months in society. His paper was later referred to as Moore's Law and established the intellectual groundwork for the Post-Modern Era. Although the Post-Modern Era began in the late 1940s, it was not until the late 1980s, with the availability of desk top computers, that the historical shift had full effect on American society. From then on, social change has been going at an increased pace. This change has been accelerated by the Internet and other digital innovations.

Daniel J. Adams, a Presbyterian theologian, says that "The Post Modern era can best be understood in terms of four major characteristics: the decline of the West, the legitimation crisis, the intellectual marketplace, and the process of deconstruction." Adams believes the world no longer functions on a Eurocentric axis. Furthermore, the theory of the *"West is best"* and that all other cultures in the world are inferior to Western culture, is an unacceptable way to think in a society in which many members have embraced multiculturalism. Metanarratives have lost their authority fostering a *legitimization crisis*. Even the Judeo-Christian metanarratives are being called into question in a society with a *plurality of values*. Cultural value and religious knowledge are no longer controlled by intellectual and political elites. Deconstruction is being applied to all discourse in the Post-Modern Era. All texts, including sacred texts, are being subjected to this process. Adams believes "deconstruction has profound implications for theology." Adams concludes: "This means that sacred texts, such as the Bible, do not have a single ultimate meaning nor are such texts necessarily authoritative"(5). Consequently the morals, values, customs, and behavior patterns in Post-Modernity are not governed by Biblical scriptures because Biblical scriptures in this era are not regarded as unconditional and absolute.

Post-modernism with its values, world view, technology, communication systems, philosophy, culture, and art have affected the Black Church to its core. Never before has the Black Church had to deal with such fundamental change in the society in which it functions. The Black Church was founded in the modern world and the majority of its history has been in the Modern Era. The changes in society the Black Church faced before were primarily the result of generational changes. Therefore, as an institution, the Black Church has never had to navigate through the waters of historical era change.

The last time the Western world went through this kind of mega shift culturally was around 1500 to the early 1600s, transitioning from the Middle Ages to the Modern Era. Human beings are going through an equivalent magnitude of change as they transition from the Modern Era into the Post-Modern Era. Generational change is hard to handle, but historical era change is a great deal more difficult to manage. Historical era change entails major alterations of culture and methodologies that often shatter societies. The impact of the generation gap pales in comparison to the challenge of transitioning from one historical era to another historical era. Perhaps the Black Church can look outside of itself for approaches on how to face the challenge before it.

Without a doubt, the church in the Western world with the most experience in adapting to the change of the historical era proportion is the Roman Catholic Church. It has gone through the Ancient era, the medieval era, and the Modern Era and now is dealing with the Post-Modern Era. What the Catholic Church did was reinvent itself in every era. When the Catholic Church was assaulted by the Reformation, it responded with the Counter Reformation. In contemporary times, in an effort to be relevant, the Catholic Church has been a proponent of the Ecumenical movement. The Catholic Church discovered a way to make the necessary changes so that it could live on in new eras. The challenge for the Black Church is whether or not it can make the qualitative reforms necessary to effectively minister in the twenty-first century. The Catholic Church's leadership analyzed the problems that faced them, then developed strategies and methods to address what was confronting them in each new historical era. The Black Church must take a sober look at what is confronting it, then analyze it and develop a strategy to survive and function in this new era. An important determiner of winning a battle is realizing the nature of the opposition. Therefore, the Black Church must recognize that the social forces bombarding it are gigantic and paradigm shifting. It is only in that realization that the Black Church will be capable of developing the kind of strategies necessary to survive and establish relevancy.

There are elements in this new historical era that only pertain to black people. Post-Modernity is an outer circle of change affecting America at large. However, there is an inner circle of change specifically surrounding black people. African Americans are struggling to find their way in the Post-Civil Rights American society. This phenomenon has created another set of problems for African Americans. These problems are social, political, economic, and psychological. The psychological problems in the past that impacted blacks as individuals, or as a group, are being exacerbated by the speed and effect of Post-Modern society.

The question of identity has been a pervasive and vitiating problem within the black community. African Americans, who have been struggling with an identity problem since emancipation from slavery, adapting to Jim Crow society, and engaging in a hyper capitalist society, now have the extremely difficult task of re-negotiating their sense of self and state of being, in a legally desegregated Post-Civil Rights period which remains racist. This inner conflict over identity keeps the black community off balance and in a state of crisis. The basis of this theory has psycho-historical elements. During slavery, Africans were transformed from free African people into dehumanized slaves. In the twentieth century, black people in America referred to their changing identity as colored, Negro, black, Afro-American, and African-American and on the verge of a twenty-first century Astro-Blackness perspective, pursuing the quest of an intergalactic identity.

An anthology titled *The New Negro,* published in 1925 by Alain Locke, characterized this process. It delineates the evolution of black people from one state of consciousness to a new state of consciousness. Locke believed that the *Souls of Black Folk*, also the name of a book written by W. E. B. Du Bois in 1903, had been transformed after slavery. Locke believed that, "Negro life is not only establishing new contacts and founding new centers, it is finding a new soul." The *Old Negro* was the *Plantation Negro*. This *"Being"* was forged in slavery. However, sixty years after the end of slavery, things had changed. Locke declared that there was a new Black Man and Black Woman who never experienced slavery. Increasingly, there were African Americans in the 1920s that were urban, cosmopolitan, and internationally oriented. This *"New Being"* had race pride and appreciated his or her own black culture. The days of accommodation politics were brought to an end. The new Black Man and Black Woman would demand civil rights and respect as human beings. In short, the *"Old Plantation Negro"* was dead.[9]

Contemporary Black America has made a similar social/historical leap. Young African Americans have never experienced legal segregation and suffered under a Jim Crow society. Jim Crow was a set of anti-black laws

asserting white dominance by denying African Americans basic social, economic, and civil rights.[10] Further, it was a racial caste system imposing legal
segregation, operating between 1877 and the mid 1960s. Culturally, Jim
Crow was more than a set of laws. Jim Crow actually fashioned the total
fabric of society. It was a way of life that degraded and dehumanized black
people. This new generation only has a historical knowledge of Jim Crow.
They were born after the passage of the Civil Rights Act of 1964. Therefore,
they do not have memories of the *Civil Rights Movement* or the *Black Revolution*. Subsequently, their values and outlook on life are substantially different from those who had to live behind what W. E. B. Du Bois characterized
as the *veil*. These young African Americans have metamorphosed into the
Post-Modern Black Man and Black Woman. Finally, just as the days of the
*Plantation Negro* have passed, so have the days of the *Jim Crow Negro.*

To have a future, the Black Church has to come to terms with the reality
that the theology, music, worship style, and ministry approach of the past is
not suitable for this era. The theology of the Jim Crow period and the Church
of the Jim Crow period cannot adequately serve the people of today. What is
needed is a Black Church informed by an Afrofuturistic perspective. This is
especially true because this generation of blacks has to also handle the effects
of the dark side of Post-Modernity as they deal with the pernicious and
debilitating race problem in America. Though Jim Crow has passed off the
scene, racism has evolved into a dreadful Post-Modern form. This form is
subtle, sophisticated and more lethal than its predecessors. African
Americans are being hit by a two pronged attack of racism and the social
pressures of Post-Modernity.

A phenomenon from the darker side of Post-Modernity that is having a
devastating effect is Time-Space Compression. Time-Space Compression is
a conceptual formulation that characterizes a process that accelerates the
experience of time and reduces the significance of distance.[11] Technology is
now able to elide spatial and temporal distances due to such technologies as
the telephone, the fax machine, and the Internet in communication, as well as
cars, trains, and jets in travel. Humans have entered a geographic space,
known as speed-space, by faster means of transportation and communication.
Experiences upon entering this space can be disorienting. In some cases the
individual mind is not able to process the compressed group of experiences
fast enough to understand what is happening or to make good decisions.
Time-Space Compression has caused people to be rootless and to lose their
bearings. Many feel even more alienated than people did during the Modern
Era. In the Post-Modern Era, large numbers of people do not have a sense of
community and are living with a painful feeling of disconnectedness as society acquires unprecedented amounts of new knowledge. Therefore, it must be
noted that, though the acquisition of new knowledge is having positive results, lamentably it is also having negative results.

Another example of a field that is having both positive and negative effects on society is Human Enhancement. Human Enhancement, also known as Singularity and popularly called Transhumanism, is a field which its advocates promote as a means to alleviate human suffering by augmenting human capacities. Supporters of Transhumanism envision many benefits in its implementation, namely longer life spans, prevention of diseases, and the development of methods to repair and rebuild damaged nerves, tissues, limbs, and organs. There is no question that Transhumanism has positive attributes. Yet, to fully grasp the meaning of Transhumanism, it has to be viewed comprehensively. It should be analyzed within a context that also includes the harmful components of this movement.

Transhumanism is a movement that uses genetics, robotics, artificial intelligence, and nanotechnology as tools to redesign human minds, memories, and physiology. The goal of Transhumanism is to rewrite human DNA by combining humans with beast and technology. The plan is to integrate human, animal, and machines to re-engineer humanity.[12] Furthermore, Transhumanism could provide a well-educated and wealthy elite group with the means to impose absolute control over the majority of humanity. Joseph P. Farrell and Scott D. de Hart speak of "the high degree to which genetic engineering is also social engineering and therefore, is also the alchemical transformation of human consciousness and society."[13]

Due to the increasingly apparent growth of the interface between machines and humans, pastors in the near future will find themselves in the position of having to counsel enhanced human beings. This challenge demands asking ourselves these questions and seeking answers to them: How will enhancement affect the cognitive process and ethical perspective of the enhanced? Are enhanced people human? Is there a point where a human has been artificially altered to such a degree that they are no longer human? The social, moral, and political implications of this subject have important ramifications. According to author and Canadian University Professor Amarnath Amarasingam, "the changes taking place in technology will radically alter human nature in the near future."[14] Amarasingam is referring to "humanity being completely transformed by the unprecedented progress anticipated" due to "Singularity/Transhumanism." Amarasingam further states, "Such metaphysical speculation leads a scholar of religion to wonder what role traditional forms of religion might play in the world, if these technologies are indeed perfected." He sees these changes in genetics, robotics, information technology, and nanotechnology as having the potential to be the basis for a new religion. To illustrate that point, he sites futurologist Ray Kurzweil's thinking of *Singularity* as a kind of technological *Rapture*.[15] Currently, the church has to compete in the marketplace of ideas with techno-spirit religions in a time when the media are churning out widely marketed, mind-altering books, films, and music with transhumanism themes and fantasy role-playing computer games. Society is permeated with new age thought. Therefore, for many people, Christian religious principles no longer determine the ideas guiding the thinking and behavior of many citizens, as society has increasingly promoted science and the occult as the standards for its worldview.

Regrettably, there are people who do not believe the Black Church should be retooled and refitted, but should be discarded. These people want to decommission the *Old Ship of Zion*. They have fallen under the delusional influence of an idea floating in the atmosphere these days that there no longer is a need for the Black Church because America has entered a pristine period of Post-Blackness. Yet, the brutal murder of Trayvon Martin in 2012 is a poignant example of how racist America is 60 years after the murder of Emmett Till. Reynaldo Anderson, Humanities Professor at Harris Stowe State University, noted recently: "Post Blackness was a Post-Modern form of Double Consciousness." Paralleling Du Bois's notion of Double Consciousness, a psychologically disorienting condition experienced by some African Americans at the height of Modernity, Anderson believes that Post-Blackness is characterized by African Americans examining themselves through the Post-Modern prism of other people's culture. Consequently, they are defining themselves through the lenses of the *other* and evaluating who they are on the standards and customs of the oppressor. Post-Blackness declares explicitly in the use of the prefix "*post*," therefore implying that black people must deny their blackness by going beyond being black in order to be human and acceptable.[16]

It is an act of self-delusion to believe America is post-racial. That type of thinking is bad faith (self-deception and misrepresentation of what it is to be for self). It is also false consciousness (the inability to understand the true nature of the situation and accurately interpret the means of oppression). Racial discrimination and racial inequality are still happening even though an African American has been elected President of the United States. African Americans have gone from being victimized by Jim Crow to being victimized by the New Jim Crow. The New Jim Crow is a Post-Modern racist system of oppression and exploitation.

Michelle Alexander, in her book *The New Jim Crow: Mass Incarceration in the Age of Colorblindness*, states in the introduction: "Denying African Americans citizenship was deemed essential to the formation of the original union. Hundreds of years later, America is still not an egalitarian democracy."[17] According to Alexander, just as the Jim Crow laws replaced slavery as a form of racial control, the New Jim Crow system has replaced the original Jim Crow system in the Post-Civil Rights Era, as a form of racial control. The criminal justice system in the United States is currently functioning as an instrument to label large numbers of black men as felons, thereby trapping them in permanent "second class status." Large numbers of black men have been marginalized, disenfranchised, and denied employment because they have been criminalized. Alexander emphatically states that, "No other country in the world imprisons so many of its racial or ethnic minorities." Illustrating this point, she goes on to say, "More African American adults are under correctional control today—in prison or jail, on probation or parole—than were enslaved in 1850, a decade before the Civil War began." Furthermore, she exposes a heart-wrenching travesty of justice, disclosing that, "More black men are imprisoned today than at any other moment in our nation's history. More are disenfranchised today than in 1870, the year the Fifteenth Amendment was ratified prohibiting laws that explicitly deny the right to vote on the basis of race." The New Jim Crow is a pernicious system brutally assaulting black men and women, the black family, and the entire black community psychologically, politically, and economically. It dehumanizes, disenfranchises, and demoralizes. According to the U.S. Bureau of Justice Statistics in 2009, 34.4 percent of the U.S. prison population was black. In addition, according to the 2010 census of the U.S. Census Bureau, 13.6 percent of the U.S. population was black. This is a sad commentary of appalling injustice. Just think. This is but *one* example of the perpetuation of racism in contemporary America. There are more areas in which racism is having a devastating effect. To name some: there is racial discrimination in employment which contributes to staggering unemployment, fostering a permanent black underclass; there is racial discrimination in the educational system limiting opportunity and quality of life; and there is race based police harassment and brutality exemplified by the cold blooded murder of Michael Brown in Ferguson, Missouri.

With all these social forces arrayed against the African American people, it is evident that there is still work for the Black Church. However the Black Church will have to go through a major reform to be effective in the Post-Modern Era. First of all, the thinking in the Black Church has to be revolutionized. World view and theology are two areas in which the Black Church needs to reform in order to be up for the challenges of our times. The Black Church would be able to see clearer with an Afrofuturist world view. And a theology with a blend of Neo-Pentecostalism and Black Liberation Theology would serve the Black Church well as a guide in the twenty-first century.

Having reviewed some of the challenges facing the Black Church, the question must be raised "What is to be done?" As was stated earlier, the type of theology needed to inform, guide, and empower the Black Church in the Post-Modern Era is a blend of Neo-Pentecostalism and Black Liberation Theology. This mixture of Neo-Pentecostalism and Black Liberation Theology offers a critique, a source of refuge, and a template for resistance. As a critique, it is a system to spiritually, politically, and culturally analyze society and the impact society is having on the individual, the family, and the community; as a source of refuge it is an instrument to heal persons spiritually and emotionally wounded by the negative aspects of Post-Modernity; and finally, as a template for resistance, it empowers the spirit and mind of those who have been victimized and presents ways to challenge and overcome the powers that want to continue to exploit and oppress.

First, a major component is the Neo-Pentecostal portion of the theological formula. Neo-Pentecostalism contains the requisites to minster to people in the Post-Modern Era. It has the ingredients and spiritual power to combat the negative factors in this age. The origin of the Neo-Pentecostal Movement (which includes the Charismatic Movement and Full Gospel Movement) is in the Pentecostal Movement. The Pentecostal Movement began in the early twentieth century. The Neo-Pentecostal Movement began in the later twentieth century as an outgrowth of the earlier movement. Whereas Pentecostalism was confined to Pentecostal denominations, Neo-Pentecostalism is operative in both traditional denominational and newly formed non-denominational churches.

The Pentecostal Movement was birthed out of the Asuza Street Revival in Los Angeles, California (1906–1909). This great revival was led by William Joseph Seymour, the son of a former slave. Seymour was born May 2, 1870 in Centerville, Louisiana, five years after the end of the Civil War. Overcoming great odds, Seymour grew into an outstanding preacher, teacher, and episcopate. Yale University has recognized him as one of the ten most influential leaders in American religious history.[18] Seymour was a spiritual and social prophet and came of age during what the historian, Rayford Logan, characterized as the *nadir of American race relations* when overt racism was at its worst. In response, drawing upon Africanist perspectives, Seymour delved deep into the realm of the supernatural. Seymour also challenged the American color line by holding racially integrated worship services during the Jim Crow period. In recognition of his contribution and achievements, Seymour deserves to be a hero in the Afrofuturist pantheon. He is an Afrofuturist precursor and his life and ministry was an announcement of things to come. Seymour was a harbinger of a new age.

William Seymour's ministry and the Asuza Street Revival, which were the origins of Pentecostalism, were expressions of Africanism. By Africanism, I mean something that is characteristic of African culture and tradition. Africanism was the seed of Afrofuturism and was also the seed of Pentecostalism. Afrofuturism and Pentecostalism stem from the same Africanist influences. In fact, Pentecostalism is an Afrofuturist form of spirituality. Therefore, William Seymour can be characterized as a forerunner of the Afrofuturist Movement. Similar to the jazz musician and philosopher, Sun Ra, Seymour came out of an African heritage seeking a future in a color conscious, hostile country. Seymour's quests lead him beyond the terrestrial sphere to the supernatural realm. On his spiritual quest, Seymour formulated a theology and spiritual practice out of his African heritage tailored to help blacks suffering from racism, urban alienation, and the evil in the world.

The renowned scholar, Dr. W. E. B. Du Bois, wrote about the African roots of the Black Preacher over a hundred years ago in his classic work *The Souls of Black Folk*. He goes in depth in a chapter titled "Of the Faith of the Fathers." There, he demonstrates that there was a historical and cultural connection between the African Priest-Medicine Man and the American Black Preacher, attesting to the age-old universal human need for a spiritual guide in a bewildering, strife ridden, and terrifying world. Du Bois argues "that the social history of the Negro did not start in America. He was brought from a definite social environment." Du Bois further states that, "the plantation organization replaced the clan and tribe" and "the old ties of blood relationship and kinship disappeared." Having said all that, Du Bois chronicles a preternatural course of development of the African in America. In the New World, we were transformed into a new people in the crucible of slavery. Our original African culture and customs were assaulted and eradicated by brutal systematic methods. However, there were African cultural residuals in spite of the efforts of the slave masters. Some forms of our original African culture were transposed in the new environment. Du Bois goes on explicitly stating, "Yet some traces were retained of the former group life and the chief remaining institution was the Priest-Medicine Man. Early on he appeared on the plantation and found his function as the healer of the sick, the interpreter of the Unknown, the comforter of the sorrowing, the supernatural avenger of the wronged and the one who rudely but picturesquely expressed longing, disappointment and resentment of a stolen and oppressed people." As American society evolved, the Black Preacher emerged replacing the function of the Priest-Medicine Man. [19]

William Seymour operated out of a tradition that originated in Africa, characterized by the role of the Priest-Medicine Man or Shaman. Ness Mountain asserts, "Traditionally, a Shaman is a tribal healer who journeys into alternative states of consciousness—into the underworld and the overworld—and returns safely with the treasures found there. They can also show others the way. Shamans are found in tribal societies worldwide, and practice in an incredible variety of forms." [20] Understanding can be gained by comparing Seymour's spiritual life to Mountain's descriptive statement about the Shaman. As the comparison is made, the similarity of the Priest Medicine Man and the Black Preacher can be clearly seen.

Seymour was a mystic, seer, prophet, and healer and had an intense hunger for God. Thus he lived a life of fasting and prayer. The great healing evangelist, John G. Lake, recalled a testimony by Seymour which shows how dedicated Seymour was in his spiritual pursuits. Here it is in Seymour's own words: "Prior to my meeting with Parham, the Lord had sanctified me from sin and had led me into a deep life of prayer, assigning 5 hours out of the 24 every day for prayer. This prayer life I continued for three and a half years, when one day as I prayed, the Holy Ghost said to me, 'there are better things to be had in the spiritual life, but they must be sought out with faith and prayer.' This so quickened my soul that I increased my hours of prayer to 7 out of 24 and continued to pray on for 2 years longer until the baptism fell on us."[21] This testimony vividly describes how Seymour lived on a high spiritual plane. Though Seymour was physically on earth, he spiritually lived in the realm of the supernatural. In Seymour's testimony we hear how he faithfully petitioned heaven for years, until fire from heaven came down at Asuza Street. Furthermore, scholars are aware from historical records that Seymour used the revelations and power he received from his spiritual journey to be a blessing to others. Seymour's mission was to lead others into a deeper relationship with God and into the realm of the supernatural. He endeavored to *"show others the way."*

Historian Leonard Lovett says that "Seymour emerged from the womb of black slave religion with roots in African soil" and that "Seymour was indeed the fruit of black slave religion, which has its roots anchored deep in African . . . religion." Estrada T. Alexander, in her seminal work *Black Fire: One Hundred Years of African American Pentecostalism*, highlights several points of African spirituality believed in and lived by members of the Asuza Street Mission. They believed in one Supreme God and that God was a part of every aspect of their lives. They believed they were surrounded by spiritual realities. Here we have a striking similarity with the African all pervasive cosmic view of God and Spirit. They believed the Spirit was everywhere and the Spirit of God and angels and Satan and demons were moving in their midst. Honoring their forbears was an important part of their spiritual system. This was an obvious retention of the African custom of venerating their ancestors. Communal solidarity was emphasized, a retention of the strong family and tribal bonds in African culture. Rhythmic music was a significant part of their worship experience. It would be the Asuza shaped theology; worship, and music style that would be the model for all future Pentecostal, as well as Neo-Pentecostal communities. Alexander turns to the work of political scientist James Tinney, "The Blackness of Pentecostalism" to support her theory. Alexander argues that Tinney believes the nature of Pentecostalism is "truly African." For Tinney, this "is visible in worship style, philosophy of faith, practices and an organizational structure."

It would be this form of religion that would minister to the masses of African Americans who migrated from the rural south to the urban centers in the first half of the twentieth century. These migrants came from a rural southern environment looking for opportunity. Fleeing southern racism, they ran head long into a new form of racism in northern cities. Furthermore, in this new environment, they were also assaulted by the alienation and disorientation of urban life. To make matters worse, these hard-pressed people were being forced to deal with all that while they still were healing from the wounds of slavery. It was spirit-filled religion which helped many to survive and make it in harsh and debilitating circumstances. It was a religion of Christian Africanism which sustained them.

A similar type of religious experience and practice is needed for African Americans to overcome the trauma, disorientation, alienation, anxiety, hopelessness, and fear generated by the negative aspects of Post-Modernity, the emerging Transhumanist challenge, and the New Jim Crow. African Americans need a spiritual discipline that can minister to them in the Post-Modern environment and interface with them in a manner appropriate for these times. The social and psychological pressure that was on African Americans in the Modern Era has intensified in the Post-Modern Era. Fortunately, there is a positive side of the Post-Modern quest which presents an opening to do ministry. The cyber-anthropologist, Steven Mizrach, asserts that Post-Modernism "wants to recover the religious sensibility" from the pre-modern world.[22] Reason was the corner stone of Modernity. However, intuition will be an essential attribute of this new stage of history. It is intuition that hones the human sensibilities so a person is able to have a religious experience. In the Postmodern world view, reason and intuition are not in conflict but work as partners. During the Modern Era, intuition was devalued, looked down upon as primitive, anti-intellectual, and unscientific. In that era, which spawned "The Age of Reason," intuition was not regarded as a sound way to create, to make leaps in knowledge, or even to connect with the Spirit. Reason was believed to be the pathway to travel in order to acquire fulfillment in all of these areas. However, appreciation of intuition has always been an integral part of Black Folk Culture and the Neo-Pentecostal Movement. Flowing in the Spirit has been a guiding principle in black life. The scripture "Not by might, nor by power, but by My Spirit says the Lord of host" (Zachariah 4:6) has been an undergirding text for Black Christian Spirituality and Neo-Pentecostalism. In fact, Neo-Pentecostalism is a Post-Modern spiritual expression that does not limit truth to the rational dimension. The apostolic experience of the Holy Spirit that values the intuitive is intrinsic to Neo-Pentecostalism. In fact, Neo-Pentecostalism is a Post-Modern form of spirituality due to its value of the intuitive which is essential in the Post-Modern world view.

The tools of Neo-Pentecostal spirituality are indispensable for the welfare of humanity in the Post-Modern Era. Far too many people, particularly people of color and the poor, are living crippled lives because of evil social, psychological, and spiritual forces. These hurting and desperate people need healing and deliverance. They need access to a way in which the Spirit breaks "into the objective world with power and purpose" to redefine their reality.[23] Neo-Pentecostalism operates in the redemptive power of the Holy Spirit and the gifts of the Spirit, such as prophecy, healing, deliverance, and miracles. There is belief in the reality and availability of the charismata. The charismata are extraordinary power gifts given to Christians by the Holy Spirit. These gifts will be used to perform exorcism—expelling evil spirits from a person or a place. They have the power to generate a catharsis—the process of releasing—providing relief from negative emotional, physical, and spiritual ailments. Neo-Pentecostalism teaches that these gifts are endowments given by the Holy Spirit that the church must operate in to fulfill its mission and that these gifts are available to heal, deliver, and comfort people suffering from the negative effects of Post-Modernity. Descriptions of these gifts are found in the New Testament, specifically in Romans 12, I Corinthians 12, and Ephesians 4.

Although there are those skeptics who are concerned about Neo-Pentecostalism being a form of escapism, a response to those who feel this way is that Neo-Pentecostalism does not require the Black Church to give up its historic commitment for social justice as it goes deeper in the spiritual realm. The Gospel of Jesus Christ that is preached should have spiritual salvation and social justice components. It should be balanced and holistic. Estrelda Y. Alexander points to the combination of deep spirituality emphasizing the Holy Spirit and activism in the community as the winning formula to do ministry in the twenty-first century. In her book *Black Fire: One Hundred Years of African American Pentecostalism* Alexander quotes Bishop John Bryant of the African Methodist Episcopal Church, who she regards as the father of African American Neo-Pentecostalism, to refute any claim that Neo-Pentecostalism is a medium of escapism. Bishop Bryant said, "The meat of the Holy Spirit is for our empowerment. It is for liberation and development. It is for our strength as a people."

Turning to the other aspect of a revised theological approach for the Post-Modern era, Black Liberation Theology will give a description of what can be characterized as the social justice component for the future. Spiritually, it can be explained as "identifying the Spirit as the liberator who could empower the African American community." Black Liberation Theology seeks to liberate black people from political, social, economic, and religious oppression and exploitation. It grew out of the Civil Rights and Black Power Movements of the 1960s. James Cone, author of *Black Theology and Black Power*, published in 1969, was the first systematic presenter of Black Liberation Theology. Black Liberation Theology is a compass, pointing the way for the Black Church, as it continues to minister in the Spirit of God and fight for freedom and justice.

Definitely there is a need for a church informed by Black Liberation Theology in a racist society. African Americans are still being subjected to abusive and demeaning treatment because of their race. There is still race-based social, economic, and political discrimination in American society. Therefore the struggle for freedom and justice has to continue. To that end, the Afrofuturist world view for the Post-Modern Black Church must have a Black Liberation Theology element, if it is to be true and strong. Black Liberation Theology is the backbone of the Black Church, and without a backbone the church will not be able to stand up to fight for justice and righteousness. Moreover, it will not be able to minister and nurture in Post-Modernity, as it ministered in the depths of slavery and Jim Crow. Without a Black Liberation element, the Black Church will not be able to be faithful to the ancestors, the mothers and fathers, who fought the good fight in slavery and segregation. Finally, without a Black Liberation Theology element, the Black Church will not have the fortitude and ethical substance to be faithful to Jesus who proclaimed:

> The Spirit of the Lord is upon Me,
> Because He has anointed Me
> To preach the Gospel to the poor;
> He has sent Me to heal the broken hearted,
> To proclaim liberty to the captives,
> And recovering of sight to the blind,
> To set at Liberty those who are oppressed;
> To proclaim the acceptable year of the Lord. (Luke 4:18–19)

In order to aid in attaining a fuller understanding of the meaning, value, and purpose of Black Liberation Theology, we are going to examine the ideas of theologian J. Deotist Roberts. In his book, *The Prophethood of Black Believers: An African American Political Theology for Ministry*, Roberts beckons the Black Church to form itself after the holistic ministry model of Jesus. The Church is to minister to the total person: spiritually, physically, psychologically, and socially. He says that this is the legacy of the Black Church, which for more than two centuries, "Has been involved in healing the scars of the oppressed and embattled in vigorous protest against oppression based upon race."[24] The mission has not been easy. Often, it has been tragic. Roberts gives voice to that experience when he declares, "Ministry in the black churches has been a ministry to an oppressed community. Black people have been caught up in a bid for survival during their entire sojourn in the United States." In spite of phenomenal difficulties, the Black Church has been faithful. It has continued to seek out the lost and minister to the down-trodden and dispossessed. There is a unique call by God on the Black Church. It was called to be a bridge over troubled water for the slaves and later for the victims of Jim Crow. At this point in time, the Black Church is being called to be a beacon of light for the victims of Post-Modern high-tech racism. According to Roberts, "The black church was born in protest against racism. It first had to confront the brutal system of chattel slavery. Since discrimination based on race has continued, the protest character of black religion/ theology persists." Historically the Black Church has been a prophetic voice challenging the powerful who oppress and exploit the powerless and a voice of hope to the hopeless teaching them how to "hope against hope" and "make a way out of no way."

The prophetic voice of the Black Church is needed now as much as it was needed during the Slavery Period and the Jim Crow period. America, at this juncture, is not headed toward a more perfect union. Rather, the future of America, if it keeps traveling down the path it is on, will look more like the dystopia constructed upon racial and economic social stratification depicted in Walter Mosley's literary work *Futureland*. In *Futureland*, through a series of science fiction short stories, Mosley describes a very morbid future for America. It is a future in which a ruthless technocrat owns a company with sovereignty status that he uses to exploit and abuse the citizens and workers with impunity. It is a world that has a cruel prison system, epitomized by Angel's Inland, the world's largest privately own prison. In this prison, inmates are controlled through drugs and the administration of shock waves to their bodies by a technical device, to modify their behavior and even their thoughts. Society in *Futureland* is in the absolute control of an elite group who utilize finance, technology, science, and force to maintain their position.[25] These stories paint a picture of a future where racism and classism run rampant. Enhanced with the aid of new scientific and technical advances, it will be a society where it seems like racism and classism are on steroids. The necessity for action, along with thought and prayer, is indisputable in these apocalyptic times. Leaders are needed with the courage of a Harriet Tubman or a Denmark Vesey and with the prophetic voice of a David Walker or a Henry McNeal Turner. Scripture teaches that faith without works is dead (James 2:17).

In an essay written before The Prophethood of Black Believers, J. Deotis Roberts states, "Consciousness is not adequate by itself to liberate a people; it must be empowered."[26] This statement makes it clear that Black Liberation Theology is hinged on action. Ideas by themselves will not liberate the oppressed. Education is not the only objective of Black Liberation Theology. Ideas must be accompanied by action to bring about change. A cardinal principle of Black Liberation Theology is to inspire and lead people to take the necessary steps to improve their lives.

There is a lesson to be learned from the science fiction movie *Matrix*. It is from the famous scene in the film about the red pill and the blue pill. In that scene, Morpheus explains to Neo that he is living an illusion and really is a slave to the Matrix. That's when Neo's moment of decision comes. Morpheus gives Neo the choice between taking a blue pill or a red pill. If Neo takes the blue pill he will be content in the illusion and passively remain a slave. If he takes the red pill, reality will be revealed to him and he will begin the journey down the rabbit hole. Neo chooses the red pill, the life of resistance to being enslaved by the Matrix. In reality, African Americans also are enslaved in a Matrix. At this critical moment the Black Church should not be passing out blue pills. To do so would be a travesty. Jesus said, "The truth shall make you free." (John 8:32). The Black Church has been called by God to spread the liberating Gospel of Jesus Christ and to set the captives free.

In conclusion, the African American people have been on a long, excruciating march travelling to slave castles, to slave ships, to plantations, to ghettos, and to prisons. On this demanding journey, African Americans have proven to be a valiant, strong, and resilient people. Though black people have fought and won many battles, the war is not over. Black people have not yet overcome. Marcus Garvey spoke of this many years ago. After traveling to different countries, Garvey said everywhere he went, black people were on the bottom of the socio-economic ladder. A century later, this continues to be the state of black people in the world. In this day, black people still do not have the power to determine their own destiny. Even Africa, the Mother Land, is teetering between a Pan-African Renaissance and being recolonized in a twenty-first century *Scramble for Africa*.

Although there are more battles to be fought before total victory, the Black Church must continue to nourish the hope and belief that one day, black people will completely overcome. It is there that the faith will emerge among the masses of the people that a new generation of young Africans, with an Afrofuturist vision and an Astro-Black consciousness, will emerge to carry on the mission. These visionaries will proclaim a message of liberation, healing, deliverance, hope, and reconciliation, in a world that has acquired more knowledge and power than it apparently has the rectitude to use in a fair way. This new generation of freedom fighters will not be afraid of being branded *Enemies of the State*. Undaunted by the might of the *Power Elite* or the *Deep State,* they will have the courage, strength, and knowledge to take the necessary action. It is my hope that the twenty-first century reformed Black Church will play a major role in this mission, thus living out its divine call from God.

## NOTES

1. R. S. Anderson 2013.
2. Dery 1994.
3. Anderson and Jennings 2014.
4. Asante 1980.
5. Asante 1998.
6. Amin 1989.
7. Connelly 2008.
8. Adams 1997.
9. Locke 1925.
10. Chegg.com n.d.
11. Pilgrim 2012.
12. Harvey 1992.
13. Farrell and de Hart 2012.
14. Amarasingam 2008.

15. Horn and Horn 2010.
16. R. S. Anderson, Personal Communication 2014.
17. M. Alexander 2012.
18. E. Alexander 2011.
19. Du Bois 1903, 132.
20. Mountain Fall 1997.
21. Lovett 2014.
22. Mizrach n.d.
23. MacDonald 2006.
24. Roberts 1994.
25. Mosley 2013.
26. Roberts 1993.

# BIBLIOGRAPHY

Adams, Daniel J. "Toward a Theological Understanding of Postmodernism." *Cross Currents* 47 no.4, 1997: 518–30.

Alexander, Estrelda. *Black Fire: One Hundred Years of African American Pentecostalism.* Downers Grove: InterVarsity Press, 2011.

Alexander, Michelle. *The New Jim Crow: Mass Incarceration in the Age of Colorblindness.* New York: The New Press, 2012.

Amarasingam, Amarnath. "Transcending Technology: Looking at Futurology as a New Religious Movement." *Journal of Contemporary Religion* 23, no.1, 2008: 1–16.

Amin, Samir. *Eurocentrism.* Translated by Russell Moore. New York: Monthly Reveiw, 1989.

Anderson , Reynaldo S., and John Jennings. "Afrofuturism: The Digital Turn and the Visual Art of Kanye West." In *The Cultural Impact of Kanye West*, ed. Julius Bailey, Chapter 3. New York: Palgrave MacMillan, 2014.

Anderson, Reynaldo S. "Fabulous: Sylvester James, Black Queer Afrofuturism, and the Black Fantastic." *Dancecult: Journal of Electronic Dance Music Culture* 5, no.2, 2013.

———. "Personal Communication." March 10, 2014.

Asante, Molefi Kete. *Afrocentricity: The Theory of Social Change.* Buffalo: Amulefi Publishing Company, 1980.

———. *The Afrocentric Idea* (rev. ed.). Philadelphia: Temple UP, 1998.

Chegg.com. *Definition of Jim Crow Laws.* n.d. http://www.chegg.com/homework-help/defini tions/jim-crow-laws-43 (accessed 2014).

Connelly, Paul. "Modernity in the Sequence of Historical Eras." 2008. www.darc.org/connelly/ religon5.html (accessed 2014).

Dery, Mark. "Black to the Future: Interviews with Samuel R. Delany, Greg Tate, and Tricia Rose." *Flame wars: The discourse of cyberculture* (1994): 179–222.

Du Bois, William Edward Burghardt. *The Souls of Black Folk.* Oxford University Press, 1903.

Farrell, Joseph P., and Scott D. de Hart. *Transhumanism: A Grimoire of Alchemical Agenda.* Feral House, 2012.

Harvey, David. *The Condition of Postmodernity: An Enquiry into the Orgins of Cultural Change.* Wiley, 1992.

Horn, Thomas, and Nita Horn. *Forbidden Gates: How Genetics, Robotics, Artificial Intelligence, Synthetic Biology, Nanotechnology, and Human Enhancement Herald the Dawn of Techno-dimensional Spiritual Warfare.* Defender, 2010.

Locke, Alain L. *The New Negro.* New York: Simon and Schuster, 1925.

Lovett, Leonard. "William J. Seymour: Peril and Possibilities for a New Era." *Enrichment Journal.* 2014. http://enrichmentjournal.ag.org/200602/200602_046_Seymour.cfm.

MacDonald, Ronald A. *A Pentecostal- Charismatic Hermeneutic Model in a Postmodern Context.* PhD Dissertation, Open University, 2006.

Mizrach, Steve. "Talking Pomo: An Analysis of the Postmodern Movement." *Academic Matter - Florida International University.* n.d. http://www2.fiu.edu/~mizrachs/pomo.html (accessed 2014).

Mosley, Walter. *Futureland: Nine Stories of an Imminent World*. Open Road Media, 2013.

Mountain, Ness. "Urban Shamanism: From the Old to the New." *Alternatives: Resources for Cultural Creativity*. Fall 1997. http://www.alternativesmagazine.com/03/mountain.html (accessed 2014).

Pilgrim, David. *What Was Jim Crow*. September 2012. http://www.ferris.edu/htmls/news/jim-crow/what.htm (accessed 2014).

Roberts, J. Deotis. "Contextual Theology: Liberation and Indigenization." *Christian Century*, 1993: 64–68.

*Chapter Eight*

# Playing a Minority Forecaster in Search of Afrofuturism

*Where Am I in This Future, Stewart Brand?*

Lonny Avi Brooks

I share a dream: to ensure that long oppressed racial minority and diverse voices can articulate themselves in the futures imagined in the practices of long-term thinking and in the professional areas of foresight.[1] Promises about the future in the strategic fields of long-term thinking and how they are portrayed in popular culture have quickened their pace in early twenty-first century digital culture about what we will do, think, and build. Mark Fisher (2000) calls this science fiction capital.[2] This elite field of work attempts to map out how our future society will look like for major corporations, government agencies, non-profit industries, and for the rest of us. As a witness and practitioner of the futures being shaped by forecasters, I see their radius of cultural boundaries as far too narrow and parochial with a few notable exceptions.

The mapping of the future still confronts the weighted language of colonial expansion, exclusion, conquest, and erasure for imagining the dilemmas of racial identity and intersecting identities as we race to the future. Intersecting identities take into account the fluid, complex, and contradictory nature of the social identities we inhabit and perform. The social identity categories of gender, race, class, age, ability, sexuality, as well as their full expression and currency in anticipatory visions require greater not less diligence. "But let justice roll down like waters" as we interrogate how science fiction capital operates and, more importantly, how we can expand its horizons for defining who partakes meaningfully in the future.

As Ronald Jackson states, the mainstay of an Afrocentric rhetorical view of the world underscores the "interconnectedness of all things" (2003, 120). In explaining the principles of an Afrocentric worldview, Jackson (2003) points to the confining Western view of binary interpretations of the dialectic state of opposed views. The Afrocentric view would shift this emphasis from opposition to juxtaposing dimensions where a range of truths can be held, that next digital feat where quantum computing can hold the 1 and 0 simultaneously. Where science fiction capital erases race and Afrocentric points of view especially in the professional industry of futures research, I aim to restore them and re-categorize future scenarios by noting absences of Afrocentric values. Re-imagining the future with the rhetorical tools found in Afrocentric and Africology worldviews confirms a multiverse of possible identity futures held at once and interconnected and now heralded in the exponential algorithms of quantum computing.

Through this exercise, three scenarios to critique science fiction capital and the futures industry emerge. First, the relentless promotion of *Futures, Inc. Unlimited*, as a capitalistic enterprise, projects a constant feeling of change that excludes not just others but ethnicities whose futures it cannot imagine or quite grasp. Google's mission is to organize the world's information while its hiring practices and embedded socioeconomic system reify an extremely segregated workforce where only 2 percent of its employees are African-American (Jacobson 2014). The emergence and promise of decentralized entrepreneurial startups affirm the new digital truth of segregated labor practices in Google's homeland.

The second foresight frame, *Futures, Inc. Performed/Performative*, views science fiction capital as a continual series of performances in various social texts in popular culture that offer future scenarios and shape the professional futures industry. The circulating artifacts of science fiction and corporate/government future scenarios carry moral and economic weight. Television shows and films in the last few years have experienced a renaissance of science fiction themes from the renewal of old franchises, such as "Star Trek" and "Battlestar Galactica" to new shows that persist in binary depictions of race such as "Continuum" and "The 100," each one exploring humanity in the next decades or hundreds of years complete with marauding darker Others. The primarily black and brown freedom seekers from 2077 in "Continuum" are depicted as violent terrorists. The brown hued "grounders" in the "The 100" represent the leftovers of a post-apocalyptic nuclear war on Earth plaguing the relatively squeaky clean and mostly white teenagers who arrive to reclaim the Earth from their rapidly decaying orbiting space station called the Ark. The first and second foresight frames interweave and cross their boundaries in the case histories and spaces of futures consultancy and culture I have performed as minority forecaster.

If the first two foresight frames continue to assault Afrocentric views of connectedness and spirituality, then *Queering Futures, Inc.* offers to create a language for queering the future in re-storying interpretations of unfolding futures. Queering the future challenges binaries and artificial polarities and confirms Alondra Nelson's insight that "an appraisal of identity . . . does not simply look to what is seemingly new about the self in the 'virtual age' but looks backward and forward in seeking to provide insights about identity, one that asks what was and what if" (Nelson 2002, 2). Afro-queering the future especially in re-interpreting the Afrocentric rhetorical perspective (Asante 1990; Jackson 2003; Turner 1991) emphasizes where the interconnectedness of all things, collective responsibility for all, and the oneness of mind, body, and spirit are missing. As Nelson describes, the science fiction lineage of African American authors like Ishmael Reed 1972 novel *Mumbo Jumbo*, "jes grew" is the sought after meme of African diasporic culture contesting the Atonists, supporters of the "Western civilization" mythology of world history" (2002, 5). The novel's plot centers on "competing efforts to encourage and restrain the itinerant cultural virus, 'jes grew'" (Nelson 2002, 5).

Reed borrows and augments this phrase from civil rights activist, and cultural and gay theorist James Weldon Johnson, who used it to describe the proliferation of ragtime songs, commenting that they "jes grew" (or just grew). Nelson explains how "jes grew" in Reed's novel refers to "African diasporic cultures that live and evolve in the forms of gesture, music, dance, visual culture, epistemology, and language, crossing geography and generations by moving from carrier to carrier and thus threatening the knowledge monopoly of the 'West'" (2002, 6). In this futuristic detective story "Jes Grew" as Nelson expresses "traversed the land in search of its Text: the lost liturgy seeking its litany. Its words, chants held in bondage by the mysterious Order" (2002, 6). Jes Grew are the missing alternative counterfutures that confirm the promising simultaneity of quantum code to include "the missing text, which originated in ancient Africa" encoding "African diasporic vernacular culture and create a tangible repository of black experience of past 0s and future 1s."

The fragility of an Afrocentric long-term vision and the diasporic rhythms of "jes grew" are telling in the case of the early *Star Trek* series when it launched with its first multiethnic crew. Consider the story of the 1960s TV series *Star Trek*'s Nichelle Nichols who portrayed the only African-American woman on the show, as the communications officer Lt. Uhuru, and who upon announcing her plans to leave from the series, was informed by Martin Luther King that her departure would remove any trace of African-American women from the future (Martin 2011; Nichols 1995).[3] Nichols explained to Gene Roddenberry, *Star Trek*'s original executive producer and creator in 1966 that she was ready to move on after the first season ended since tantalizing offers of a career on Broadway beckoned. Roddenberry, with shock, asked Nichols to consider the vision he was attempting to convey and to reconsider her decision over one weekend. While stunned by Roddenberry's reaction, Nichols attended an NAACP dinner during which she felt a tap on her shoulder by a staff member who informed her that she had a secret Trekkie admirer who wanted to say hello. Her devoted fan was none other than Martin Luther King Jr. As surprised as she was to see the civil rights leader, she thanked him for his compliments and related that this would be her last season on the show. His praise transformed into insistence that she remain on "Star Trek." "You don't understand, you are the only show Coretta and I allow our children to watch!" Dr. King informed her that her departure would remove any trace of African-American women from the future. I share in Dr. King's fear that the masking and erasure of racial identity in the future is still as pervasive and real as that moment in 1966. And that erasure persists in the scenarios created by professional forecasters and other producers of science fiction capital.

As Kodwo Eshun frames this field from his imagined African archeologists of the future, "it is commonplace that the future is a chronopolitical terrain, a terrain as hostile and as treacherous as the past" (2003, 288). The most comprehensive report to date on global forecasting confirms this erasure. The report is from the "Mapping Foresight" project (Popper 2009) of the European Foresight Monitoring Network (EFMN)—a Europe-wide network inspired and financed by the European Commission for the Foresight Knowledge Sharing Platform. This report is the first large international effort designed to understand the makeup of foresight practices in Europe and other world regions, including Latin America, North America, Asia, and Oceania. The report underscored that "the large number of foresight exercises mapped between 2004 and 2008 (over 2,000 initiatives) is clear evidence of the rising of the 'foresight wave.' This is mainly because foresight has become more than just a tool to support policy or strategy development in Science, Technology, and Innovation. (STI)" (Popper 2009, 8).

An often highlighted feature of foresight exercises is their potential to become a "space for opinion gathering and reflection among a wide-ranging group of stakeholders" (Popper 2009, 8). Expectations for the diversity and scale of participation are assumed to go beyond what is usually attainable in more standard agenda-setting arenas. Participation often contributes towards the value-added and shared ownership goals of foresight. EFMN admits a couple of difficulties with the mapping of this dimension: Africa remains underrepresented and was not even considered in the report's title and regional scope; participation in most of these exercises hovered from 50 to 200 participants, and diversity was difficult to assess. Therefore, while forecasting has now become a mainstream activity for elite policy makers, the upswing in foresight requires greater accountability. This groundbreaking report cycle bodes well for the pace of foresight activities and industry with the exception of creating the broad anticipatory public space outlined. The study's own self-reported omissions encourage a future world ill-prepared to embrace radical diversity and what Richard Iton has called the "Black Fantastic" (2008, 16).

Iton points to an alternative future he defines as the black fantastic that represents current political boundaries as "the minor-key sensibilities generated from the experiences of the underground . . . beyond the boundaries of the modern" (2008, 16). This quote represents a filter for me as I flash back over the last fifteen years of my journey as a minority forecaster and educator about long-term thinking. Still in 2013, despite the election of an African American—read multiracial—U.S. President who plays down his racial diversity, that the spaces to imagine racial identity and see minorities represented in the future have rarely made headway as a serious, sustained conversation within the realms of foresight think tanks and forecasting outfits.

Silicon Valley, home of the forecasting hubs I studied, remains an insular place where model minorities may thrive while those that have suffered the most repression continue to reside at the gates of the fringes of a society that glimpses their status with a shrug. Despite Silicon Valley philanthropic public relations campaigns, aspiring undergraduates from less than Ivy League universities are usually turned away for internships or entering positions, where even "Cal State Nowhere?" in reference to the California university state system has been uttered at alumni who have managed to break through that elite barrier.[4] Still the black tax[5] persists as minorities in order to be displayed in the future must show some exemplary quality that makes them either extraordinary or a major threat requiring containment. I want to empower minority communities by making the tools of futures thinking more accessible and visible in order to see themselves in the often closed-quarters of forecasting where elite visionaries hunker down and hack out the future. Even as forecasting think tanks such as the Institute for the Future proclaim an open source work day on their Facebook page: "IFTF co-working starts in 10 minutes. Join us if you're in Palo Alto!" their networked sentiment is aimed at a rather small elite audience.

The black fantastic unsettles "the conventional notions of the political, the public sphere, and civil society that depend on the exclusion of blacks and other nonwhites from meaningful participation" (Iton 2008, 17). Against this backdrop, I tell a story about foresight practices that could use an awakening to the possibilities of the black fantastic. Instead of the scary black swans, the wild card bad events that could happen in the future, why not propose black foresight frames and black fantastics? I argue for re-framing foresight practices to take into account racial and multiple forms of identity as a futures window for progressive change.

Too often, narratives of the future look towards a post-racial future as if race, gender, and class no longer matter when social science research confirms the near millennial effects of hundreds of years of the persistence of racial bias, discrimination, and socioeconomic echoes that will continue to reverberate and affect life chances in the near and long term future. As Wendy Chun contends, considering "race and/as technology" shifts "the focus from what is race to the how is race, from knowing race, to doing race by emphasizing the similarities between race and technology" (2012, 38). Imagining how race as a technology is constructed, denied, and projected into the future offers possibilities for the black fantastic. If we take race as a practice, something we do and project onto ourselves and others as a technique and technology "that one uses even as one is used by it—a carefully crafted, historically inflected system of tools, of mediation, or of 'enframing' that builds history and identity" (Chun 2012, 38), then we can use the tools of forecasting to intentionally map the contours to expand beyond token diversity to navigate racial identity and racism.

While Jason Tester of the Institute for the Future coined an all-embracing term for engagement with the future he refers to as "human-futures interaction," (Tester 2007; Pescovitz 2007, 1) a rigorous inquiry would explore its alternate and subversive meanings. I want to reframe and interrogate more deeply human-futures interaction as a set of tactics and literacy for understanding race as a technology and as racial identity futures interaction. Here, I am inspired by the work of Philip, Irani, and Dourish in "Postcolonial Computing: A Tacitical Survey" (2012), where race as technology is embraced as a tactical move to decenter privileged conceptions of ubiquitous computing. This move strives to understand the complexity of racism in its nuanced subtleties and abrupt shocks as a form of science fiction capital that accrues and rapidly circulates.

The professional work of forecasting and long-term thinking has too often been the provenance of think tanks whose existence depends on a complex mix of support from multinational corporations, nonprofit foundations, and government agencies. Together these entities already favor a specific set of elite interests in how the future becomes real, ordinary, and taken for granted. These stakeholders bid on the future and look to forecasting think tanks for navigating and negotiating anticipatory landscapes in parallel with normative and mirrored organizational interests. While glimmers of nonprofit outreach work to address the lack of minority and impoverished voices is underway in Silicon Valley and other contexts, the issue of strengthening anticipatory democracy continually requires advocacy.

Between 1995 through 2012, as a communication graduate student and scholar at UC San Diego and incoming professor at Cal State East Bay, I interned, work with, interviewed, and traveled through one new media incubator, Interval Research Corporation, and two major think tanks: 1) the Institute for the Future, and 2) the Global Business Network in the San Francisco Bay area. By gaining access to these major hubs for forecasting the future (i.e., in areas such as technology, business, and health), I was able to witness and unpack how decisions about technology and communication futures are shaped, enacted, and created by a set of powerful people working within a particular and peculiar context and with a deeply embedded and carefully massaged set of assumptions. My first stop circa 1995 was at Interval Research Corporation created in 1992. Although Interval became defunct by 2002 as part of its ten-year mandate, Interval was funded by Paul Allen, the co-founder of Microsoft and was an early player in incubating new digital industries. Interval alumni continue to shape the evolving digital landscape and culture.

The Institute for the Future, founded in 1968 by engineers at the RAND corporation, a well-known and pivotal civil defense policy think tank, grew within a specific context of forecasting the future of urban planning and cities in the late 1960s. The Global Business Network (GBN) began in 1985 by a number of forecasters who previously worked for Stanford Research International (SRI), Shell Oil, and the Whole Earth Review. Now acquired by Monitor and Deloitte and Touche, GBN and its crew morphed into the Long Now Foundation co-founded by Stewart Brand and Brian Eno. These continuing centers and former nodes continue their roles and influence in forecasting the future of digital culture. Their peer networks extend to popular culture and trade industry literature with frequent profiling of their exploits in magazines such as *Wired*, *Fast Company*, and *Boing Boing* to major consulting roles in notable films like Minority Report and more recently in serious gaming.

Even as some forecasting outfits address issues of poverty, conversations about the sheer weight of racial oppression and its past seem to vanish as the embedded computing algorithms of new imaginary future worlds favor the already powerful and privileged. Forecasting captures present moments and imagines their possibilities. These visions become templates for organizational thinking and for coding our anticipatory future behavior. The framing of these visions tends to squeeze out the messiness of cultural histories and the complexity of exclusion.

In retelling my journey as a minority forecaster, I critique how the future stories being shaped favor erasures of race where a post-racial other predominates in a post-racial digital culture. The practices of forecasting continue forms of racial exclusion and oppression anchored in the past to create new threads of digital bigotry in its wake. Despite progressive scholarship in forecasting, few academics have examined rituals of foresight as it is being produced as its practitioners create narrow and less diverse images of a tomorrow-land. We can do better in rethinking how forecasting works to imagine our futures while simultaneously visualizing black fantastics of radically empowering and queer diversity. Queer in this instance means to "queer the Infrastructure. . . . To queer: to challenge the basis on which categories are constructed" from science technology studies scholar Susan Leigh Star. I aim to queer the categories of forecasting, futures studies, and foresight as they are practiced and as they relate to communication and other social science disciplines. To engage in this analysis, Afrofuturism promises a useful framework for re-framing current practices in foresight.

Afrofuturism combines science fiction and fantasy to re-examine how the future is currently imagined and to re-construct futures thinking with deeper insight into the black experience, especially as slavery forced Africans to confront an alien world surrounded by colonial technologies (Dery 1994; Eshun 2003). Dery (1994) characterizes this genre as African-American cultural language that reinterprets images of technology and a "prosthetically enhanced future" to take on the white technologies that have, like aliens, enslaved and transported African people from one world to another one to erase their past and remake their future. Cut off from their original cultures, Africans in the colonial world endured that abrupt erasure by creating innovative cultural and scientific strategies to reassert novel identities. The social death of their origins transformed into shields of sonic vibration as music and the vernacular of oppression turned into daily micro-practices of artistic identity, renewal, and solace. From the perspective of Afrofuturism, race is a continual form of science fiction capital not completely biological or cultural but a mix of science, art, culture, and fantasy.

This struggle retells how stories of the future can move beyond the narrow confines of *Futures, Inc.*, a catch-all term I define as future imaginaries designed to protect the status quo of organizational power over science fiction capital. The forecasting I envision encompasses Afrofutures, stories with expanded insight to provoke conversations about racial identity. We continue to struggle with language for how Afrofutures can look. I grew up with *Star Trek* in the early 1970s, the first televised show to portray diversity in the future that still serves as a constrained benchmark for how to speak about racial and social justice as a major forecasting objective. Afrofuturism as a basic framework suggests promising directions for reinvigorating our language to speak about racial identity in the deep past and long-term future. Eshun declares that "[t]oday, however, power also functions through the envisioning, management, and delivery of reliable futures" (2003, 289). This power has roots in the ascendance of modern forecasting and in the founding of the Institute for the Future (IFTF) in 1968. At an IFTF dinner in 1998, a digital storytelling video premiered to celebrate its 30th anniversary as a forecasting think tank.

During the anniversary dinner of IFTF's 30th year, a videotape of IFTF's digital story presented the Institute's direct relationship to the research cultures at RAND and its think tank cousin SRI as well as to the counterculture shared by its present leadership and co-founders. The story acknowledged its influential forebear RAND and IFTF's intimate connection to the early forms of the Internet and the personal computer. The video unfurls a series of images to accentuate how the 1960s influenced IFTF. Along with a smiling image of Bob Dylan, the 1968 image of Olympic athletes appears of African American Olympians, fists clenched in a Black Power salute, thrust defiantly in the air. Former IFTF President Robert Johansen narrates the video and emphasizes: "And I went to the seminary that Dr. King went to. I was there at the time that he died. So right at that period, just as the Institute for the Future was being formed, Dr. King was being shot. And I think the combination, the juxtaposition of those events, had a lot to do with our image for the future of the group." With a nod, Johansen referenced MLK's death as an inspiration for building a progressive future. Historically, that memory symbolized the peak of instability and the arrival of inner city rebellion—events that prompted IFTF's mission to contain and manage the future of urban life although the dominance of African-American imagery hinted at a bleaker truth.

Their vision barely acknowledges the aspirations of the surrounding 1960s protest movements that were, instead, seen as challenges to national security from a Cold War world perspective. Paul Baran, the principal co-founder of IFTF and recognized designer of the early Internet, held a long-standing interest in urban defense at the RAND civil defense think tank prior to starting IFTF. Baran expressed how RAND's role in defending national security expanded from a focus on external threats to a focus on the internal challenges to societal order. By the mid 1960s the definition of "National Security" was changing. The Watts Riots, civil disobedience, and violent anti-war behavior growing in the campus were viewed as new threats to social stability.

As Eshun argues "[t]he powerful employ futurists and draw power from the futures they endorse, thereby condemning the disempowered to live in the past. The present moment is stretching, slipping for some into yesterday, reaching for others into tomorrow" (2003, 289). Baran's stance during this period displayed the imprint of RAND's siege mentality where the macrocosm of U.S. interests incorporated its citizens as strategic assets and potential adversaries in the larger Cold War struggle. Despite his desire to move to nonmilitary research, the persistence of an all-encompassing war footing would continue. Even as he tangled with corporate bureaucracy, Baran urged the expansion of the definition of National Security to encompass internal security issues. He worked to broaden the definition of RAND's National Security charter to include problems of social unrest and law and order issues.

At the beginning, IFTF's forecasting work paralleled this intense concern about repairing and reining in a fraying social order. Baran's goals, while laudable, portrayed the conservative tone of technological determinism. The War on Poverty and focused work on simulating urban futures incorporated the tenets of interdisciplinary war (Light 2003), the arsenal of cultural and scientific tools, that fed a campaign of pacification against the urban inner city riots at IFTF's founding and were written into IFTF's mission. IFTF's study of the future of cities, initiated in 1968, paralleled the Cold War obsession with extending and equating nuclear war strategy and urban ghettos. Tracy Augur, in 1946, gave a presentation to the New York chapter of the American Institute of Planners, arguing for new scientific planning approaches in urban areas. Urban blight was likened to atomic bombs. He called for studies of urban poverty that would equal our investment in nuclear weaponry. With a combination of liberal intent and conservative military rhetorical strategy, Augur argued that slums bred communism by creating people alienated from capitalism and, therefore, ghettos represented a grave security risk (Light 2003). As Baran would similarly comment a decade later, blight and bombs could be avoided by urban dispersion, which he understood as a necessary defense against internal enemies as equal in importance to an external attack. The rhetoric imagined predominately black ghettos as the internal Cold War enemy either to be rescued through disbanding, which hinted at forms of internal exile, or simply erased and demolished.

IFTF, born out of a well-intentioned effort to distance itself from military concerns, ironically extended RAND logic to securing the future internal order of urban spaces. Marginality in IFTF's story became a hip asset and a form of coolness for its client futurist audience. Countercultural symbolism became animated through icons of a hopeful idealism that sidestepped IFTF's military past. This story was not necessarily intended to deceive. Johansen's digital story was a reconstruction of a very personal, selective memory based on and categorized from the perspectives of a powerful elite group of managers of a forecasting network. Its logic sound, its practices credible for its audience, IFTF's *A Look into the Past* projected a different story, a story that celebrated the counterculture but disguised its fear of 1960s Black rebellion. Even as Nichelle valiantly stayed in her role on *Star Trek*, the framing of futures research sought to deny her future persona.

Unfortunately, during the post-*Star Trek* TV series years, many of the forecasts and the forecasting sages I have witnessed look absurdly ethnically homogeneous across this field, and in the future scenarios created by the foresight industry, even as our national and global societies become increasingly diverse. The question for all futures professionals, business trend makers, and communicators who are translating the latest technological and scientific studies for the rest of us is to wonder if we can avoid creating a future where we continue to pretend as if race does not belong in the future. Without a language for articulating and expanding racial and other identity futures interaction, we will fail to lift our collective prosperity.

The persistent and nagging question that kept looming during my visits to the futurist labs and think tanks was: where are all the folks like me, the multi-racial people of color, in these futures? Forecasters continue to celebrate the varied and largely homogenous cultures (i.e., China, Japan, and some European countries) and stories of trendy innovation while the discussion of racial minorities closer to home locally and nationally in the future appears to vanish. However, in those instances when they do appear, it is as a part of chaotic disruptions that have to be managed by some vague invisible hand of a corporate power. The continuing legacy of our ghettos, now and into the future, serves our system as centers for calculation where we can exclude and confine the Others to perpetual underemployment and outside the corridors of power.

As the future scenarios I witnessed continue to unfold and start to take actual shape in the present, the large absence of racial minorities and the neglected consideration of racial dilemmas in high level discussions of organizational long term thinking is depressing. The future racial divide and its troubling implications were vividly on rare display in a recent film to address the future of the poorer 99 percent. The year 2154 as depicted in the film *Elysium* starring Matt Damon shows a stark panoramic view of the earth as one large mega-shanty town wrecked and ravaged by global climate change and inhabited by a largely Spanish-speaking majority. In contrast and in high orbit around our planet, the elite eternally youthful French-speaking minority live in a luxurious earth-like space habitat. The film shows the attempts of the earth bound to penetrate this orbiting paradise and at least heal their damaged bodies with DNA repair via MRI-like machines.

Although the final scenes of the film show a startling reversal of fortune and we get our Hollywood Robin Hood ending, one is still left with the nagging sensation that, despite the sympathetic treatment of the earthbound poor, that the barbarians had come to power. As the Latino leader of the immigrant space smuggling ring now issued orders to the Androids that had enslaved him, I wondered if they would do any better than the elite they overthrew. The film still perpetuates the images of minorities who will simply continue the logic of inherited power they have decimated. As a glimpse into 2154, the forecasting industry of the long term thinking professional can rest assured that their services will still be used to protect the fortunes of entrenched and powerful interests over the next one hundred years.

As a participant-observer of IFTF from 1998 to 2001, I gained access to this futurist-making enterprise and was able to study it from a critical cultural perspective. With the procession of futures created for various clients, I longed to view a future that acknowledged my own blended ethnic and cultural diversity and sexual orientation within the range of normative scenarios outlined. I discovered in the historical archives of founding members of the Institute for the Future, the face of pervasive ethnic fear in their early rhetoric of the future for containing and circumscribing African-American urban anger as if it were an internal communist threat, a fear that existed during the early years of IFTF in 1968. In the last ten years of my journey through some of the most central forecasting think tanks in the world, I saw the continuing danger of elites managing a future in a cocoon to preserve their status quo against their own self-fulfilling prophecies of an increasingly balkanized, segregated, and divisive world.

In terms of measuring the future, I define forecasting as the attempt to map out how human society, and especially forms of communication, will evolve over the near and long term future: i.e., 10 to 50 and 100 years and even 10,000 years ahead in time. Current forecasting industry practices generally play it conservatively at 10 years ahead. More radical practices in the field have started to challenge this pace. Time horizons and longer trajectories from 5,000 to 10,000 years in the future have entered into wider public forums as organizations like the Long Now Foundation seek to create a cathedral-like 10,000-year clock monument. New educational efforts are establishing that time-range as a priority including the Long Term and Futures Thinking Project at Cal State East Bay. Most forecasting and futures think tanks do not look nearly that long into the future; usually it is under the 50-year time horizon. Our stories about the future are saturated with the near term future where issues of racial identity are often pushed aside in favor of an expanded and transcended identity beyond the human body. Matt Damon in 2154 embodied that fictional Christ-like cyborg who redeems our fate. Even in this transcendence, racial identity still gets read as a white crusader.

The venerable sage of futures wisdom at the Long Now Foundation, Stewart Brand and his executive staff, have started to make strides in supporting greater public outreach about the long term future. As partners with the Long Term and Futures thinking project at California State University, East Bay, they have offered their name and profile in highlighting efforts to reach more diverse audiences to engage in long term thinking exercises. This effort could begin a more sustained effort in offering counter-futures to the usual future scenarios that protect white privilege in their erasure of multicultural and ethnic diversity. While I acknowledge that this post-racial trend may be changing, the pace is slow and the counter-futures too few to serve as viable competing narratives.

With generous respect to the Long Now Foundation, I take issue with Stewart Brand's particular framing of long term thinking and forecasting that tends to favor a journalistic objectivity that ignores some recent advances in the social sciences and in qualitative research—the observance and study of culture and groups of people. Until the 1990s, the field of forecasting and foresight privileged technological and quantitative physical sciences at the expense of social sciences and the social study of science, of how human cultures adapt and repurpose technology. While humanism and the use of storytelling anthropological perspectives have entered into the jargon and methodologies of forecasting, the avoidance of addressing the messiness of racial assumptions has resulted in bland, underwhelming forecasts about technocultural futures of diversity. Brand has simultaneously forwarded the field while constraining more critical conversations about the persistence of "wicked problems" (Ramos, Mansfield, and Priday 2012, 72; Rittel and Webber 1973) by ignoring the future of race, class, and gender.

Brand writes in his foundational manifesto for the Long Now foundation, *The Clock of the Long Now*, that the difference between real futurists or forecasters and soothsayers or amateur, unprofessional forecasters involves their inability to distinguish desire from their "ruthless curiosity about the world and what is truly going on in it, not from their politics" (Brand 1999, 113). While I agree in principle with looking at the long term future with curiosity and boldness rather than imagining and longing for an elusive utopian world, what Brand states next troubles me as a social scientist in his labeling of forecasters with progressive agendas as "futurismo." Specifically, this is what he views as those held captive by ideology as if the state of forecasting is not already captivated and enthralled with capitalistic innovation branding.

Brand proclaims with sympathy, "Futurismists are not bad people, and certainly not fraudulent. If anything they are captive of their goodness. High-minded and earnest, they have meetings to determine 'the goals of humankind,' and to advance worthy causes such as feminism, multiculturalism, and a world free from hunger" (Brand 1999, 112). So if professional forecasters express interests and a stance in the social scientific pursuit of social justice, then they are immediately suspect as biased forecasters in his view?

Brand continues that "The distinguishing trait of futurismists is that they have an agenda: something they want to have happen or something they want to prevent from happening in the future, often based on a particular ideology, political bent, theory of history, or special interest" (Brand 1999, 113). He refers to the forecasters I have interviewed, Peter Schwartz, former head of the Global Business Network and Paul Saffo, former director at IFTF, as liberal and as ideal leaders in the field because they were able to hold their politics in check to exhibit a rigorous sophisticated curiosity. Great! I could accept that statement with greater ease if their visions were not already enmeshed in the elite worlds they have lived in themselves for some time personally and in the organizations they advise. Moreover, they are some of the most well-known and progressive futurists in the field! Although these fellows attracted me to futures studies in the first place, they, nevertheless, bring the ironic contradictions of white privilege with them too, what Peggy McIntosh (1988, 31) calls the "invisible weightless knapsack." David Mumby aptly describes this knapsack as "the set of privileges and practices white people carry around them that protect them from everyday injustices" (Mum-

by 2013, 239). Communication scholars and social studies of science researchers have revealed over the last thirty years the continuing fallibility and
bias inherent in maintaining objectivity that is itself a means of excluding
and including relevant facts and tacit, intangible experiences. What we frame
inevitably leaves something out of view and mind. Forecasting is no different
in this respect.

Brand places futurismists who advocate feminism and multiculturalism
on the same playing field as cult-like messianic futurist groups: "Some hive
off into sectlike groups, such as the Extropians-a 01990s California enclave
of bright and enthusiastic Singularity advocates who could hardly wait for
the techno-Rapture. They have a classic case of what Paul Saffo calls macro-
myopia: 'we overexpect dramatic developments early, and underexpect them
in the longer term'" (Brand 1999, 113). While I admire Stewart Brand and
his work in provoking us into dialogue about the long term especially in
making it a mainstream professional endeavor, he has mistakenly lagged
behind what social science has to offer to the forecasting world. While Futurismo may not be what we need, what we require are more social science
frameworks that take the future seriously.

I call these Cultural and Critical *Foresight Frames* inspired by efforts to
further the intellectual development of Afrofuturism. Forecasting and foresight have close similarities with communication fields such as advertising
and public relations. Imagining the future and its accruing science fiction
capital circulates as a powerful form of social currency in various genres of
media such as popular culture, advertisements, magazine articles, film,
books, and television about what the near term future promises. Worlds of
the near future abound while deeper long-term thinking lags behind and takes
up less space in this ecosystem of future stories. Forecasting professionals
and their audiences of managers, scientists, and engineers breathe in these
future visions, ones they have grown up with in forging our ubiquitous computing environment today.

By the 1990s, I felt uncanny recurrences of alien invasion as the Internet
became more accessible and the future scenarios of what it might do enacted
another form of enslavement by the exclusion and erasure of lower class,
non-model minorities in forecasts of undulating computer rhythms. Afrofuturism is the accompanying story of the countercultural memory to rewrite
and remind us of what the official future scenarios of think tank forecasting
often forget. Critical and Cultural Forecasting Frames based on my own
experiences in the forecasting industry and re-read from an Africological
perspective offer approaches for re-reading and re-mapping assumptions and
the self-fulfilling promises for how technology and communication futures
are shaped, enacted, created, and circulated. Forecasting as a practice and as
part of a set of assumptions in popular culture about how the future will take
place is increasingly being translated into digital algorithms for predicting

our behavior. Future oriented forecasts and scenarios about the future make promises for how that future might look by capturing moments and snapshots in our lives.

As these glimpses of the future are captured, they leave out too much on the cutting room floor and the messy discarded notions of culture that add to the sensuality of real life. Instead of erasing culture and race, what can we gain by celebrating the black fantastic? I borrow from the language and methods of future scenarios, usually told as a set of three narratives about the near term future. The logic of this method asserts that the actual future is bound to contain elements of all three. I flip this methodology around to hold forecasting and foresight up for scrutiny and transformative accountability.

## CONCLUSION

With each future story I encounter and experience, I reflect and deconstruct it with three lenses. First, Foresight Frame Scenario One—Futures, Inc. Unlimited, which entails the relentless promotion of Futures, Inc. projects a short-term future of a ubiquitous digital presence in the model of permanent capitalistic expansion. Stories about the near term future assemble a language of branding and mining resources vying to become normal aspects of our daily present as promises and sets of expectations (Berkhout 2006). I found myself restricted in this view of forecasting as well, that thinking about the next 100 years or 10,000 was too difficult to translate or envision for my students. My own conception of long-term thinking had become constrained by this currency of short-term future sells (read spreadsheet cells) of narrow slices of myopic possibilities.

In my analysis of the various sets of future visions and case studies, I view them as competing bids on the near to long term future, similar to advertising although distinct. I witnessed how as popular narratives they get produced, distributed, and adopted by various stakeholders. The future as a story is an easily distributed commodity, although how that vision is made and for what purposes, is not always transparent. The idyllic *Elysium* images of a space colony, a beautiful wheel shaped habitat revolving on its own axis with a gleaming artificial earth-like atmosphere captured my imagination as a metaphor for the race for the future where only a few will benefit from the few prognosticators who are given the power to shape temporal landscapes.

Second at play is the Foresight Frame and Scenario Two—Futures, Inc. Performed/Performative. This frame views Futures, Inc. as an evolving series of theater-like and performance spectacles that combine into a moral and economic force. Future visions project and act out economic and moral value. Jan English-Lueck (2006) indicates how communicating about the future as artifacts and tools of foresight provides knowledge workers with more tangible pathways to signify their processes of innovation. Foresight takes on special currency and power especially in a region where buildings are often nondescript and where digital work is not easily showcased in three-dimensional form. Foresight shapes digital culture by constantly projecting its future value. And the think tanks I studied avidly engaged performance genres for enacting the future for their clients. The future as a spectacle acted out future dilemmas on stage, in games, and on the walls as colorful displays of imagined organizational power taking shape.

Future imagined carries performative weight as well as we construct Futures, Inc. fantasies through our daily actions. While performance is about acting out parts in a play, performativity examines how we construct our identities through micropractices or daily rituals. Our smartphones afford opportunities to assimilate to our science fiction dreams while reducing our gazes into one form of human computer and human futures interaction. We tend to forget that computing is a culture open to re-editing as well and therein resides our loss of power in understanding what Tarleton Gillespie has called the relevance of algorithms. The force, power, or nommo (Jackson 2003; Woodyard 2003) of our laws becomes hidden from sight and embedded in our digital artifacts and in the circulating science fiction capital that promotes continual binaries of constrained future paths.

I played the role of minority forecaster and the Other non-white futurist. As a participant-observer assimilating to the professional culture of forecasting, I arrived with quiet access and muted voice. I expanded my role as a promise champion of the future and then realized how I was being seen and categorized as less than equal, as a minority seeking to be included. With the dot.com crash in 2001, I then channeled to my "appropriate place" as teacher reformer at a state university and even this relatively academic elite status is conveniently labeled to preserve racial distinctions and forms of power. Lisa Nakamura's conception of cybertypes reveals the tenacious grip of race categories in cyberspace. Similarly, Nakamura's label provides a useful path for tracing *Futuretypes* in forecasting as profiles of our imagined future selves, human beings and digital artifacts and what they represent socially and where they are situated in terms of status as desired, feared, and erased forms of humanity.

Foresight Frame and Scenario Three—*Queering Futures, Inc.* is the third lens in which current future visions project racial, segregated, and elite future landscapes. The demographics of forecasting, who forecasts the future and towards what ends, re-enforce beliefs of racial segregation and discrimination. Creating a language for queering the future involves retelling and critiquing the forecasts already being deployed and forecasts in the making. We can augment visions of anticipatory democracy as a vital social network for purposes of social justice and diversity in bringing forth Afrofuture frames and tactics. Africological theories see ntu, universal life rhythms and the holistic human being and "treat human behaviors as manifestions of the spirit/forces behind and between words, images, illusions and other signs" (Woodyard 2003, 21). I have arrived back from the future to retell a number of stories and for each story I discuss about my sojourn in the forecasting world, I examine how it reflects the promises of a *Futures, Inc. Unlimited* and a *Futures, Inc. Performed/Performativity* and how any good story of the future can be queered from an Afrofutures 2.0 perspective.

## NOTES

1. The field of strategic long-term thinking is known by a variety of names from futurism to forecasting to foresight, a term popular in Europe and gaining currency in the United States. For the purposes of this chapter, I refer to futures work and long-term thinking as forecasting or foresight.

2. Fisher, Mark. 2000. SF Capital. *Themepark magazine*.

3. NPR Interview January 17, 2011. Nichelle Nichols: "And his face got very, very serious. And he said, what are you talking about? And I said, well, I told Gene just yesterday that I'm going to leave the show after the first year because I've been offered - and he stopped me and said: You cannot do that. And I was stunned. He said, don't you understand what this man has achieved? For the first time, we are being seen the world over as we should be seen. He says, do you understand that this is the only show that my wife Coretta and I will allow our little children to stay up and watch. I was speechless."

4. One self-report from Rich Cline, an alumnus of Cal State East Bay based in Hayward, California, related his successful journey into public relations and his mayoral candidacy for Menlo Park, an upscale suburb of Silicon Valley. At a meeting to announce his first, now successful bid for mayor, he reported his educational credentials. A spectator sarcastically interjected "Cal State Nowhere?" (2010, alumnus visit and interview). And this incident occurred with a very successful white male in the PR business and founder of Voce Communications, acquired by Porter Novelli.

5. The "black tax" refers to the well referenced notion in African-American culture that black people must demonstrate their talents and exert twice as much effort to be recognized for their achievements compared to white people and other exemplary minorities.

## REFERENCES

Asante, M. K. 1992. Kemet, Afrocentricity and knowledge. Trenton, NJ: Africa World Press.

Baran, Paul. 1999. Oral history, conducted by David Hochfelder, IEEE History Center, New Brunswick, NJ.

Berkhout, Frans. 2006. Normative expectations in systems innovation. *Technology Analysis and Strategic Management* 18, no. 3-4: 299–311.

Brand, Stewart. 1999. *Clock of the long now: Time and responsibility*. New York: Basic Books.

Chun, Wendy. 2012. Race and/as technology. In *Race after the internet*, eds. L. Nakamura and P. Chow-White. New York, NY: Routledge.

Dery, Mark. 1994. *Flame wars: The discourse of cyberculture*. Durham, NC: Duke University Press.

English-Lueck, Jan A. Rites of production: Technopoles and the theater of work. *Anthropology of Work Review* 25, no. 1-2 (2004): 21–27.

Eshun, Kodwo. Further considerations on Afrofuturism. CR: The New Centennial Review 3, no. 2 (2003): 287–302.

Fisher, Mark. 2000. SF Capital. *Themepark magazine*.

Institute for the Future (IFTF). 1998. *A Look to the Past, a digital storytelling video celebrating IFTF's 30th anniversary*. IFTF: Palo Alto.

Iton, Richard. 2008. *In search of the black fantastic: Politics and popular culture in the post Civil Rights Era*. Oxford and New York: Oxford University Press.

Jackson, Ronald L. 2003. Afrocentricity as metatheory: A dialogic exploration of its principles. In *Understanding African American rhetoric: Classical origins to contemporary innovations*, eds. Ronald L. Jackson, II and Elaine Richardson, 115–29. New York, NY: Routledge.

Jacobson, Murrey. 2014. Google finally discloses its diversity record, and it's not good. http://www.pbs.org/newshour/updates/google-discloses-workforce-diversity-data-good/.

Light, Jennifer S. 2003. *From warfare to welfare: Defense intellectuals and urban problems in Cold War America*. Baltimore, MD: Johns Hopkins University Press.

Martin, Michel. 2011. Star Trek's Uhura Reflects on MLK Encounter. NPR Podcast. January 17. http://www.npr.org/2011/01/17/132942461/Star-Treks-Uhura-Reflects-On-MLK-Encounter.

McIntosh, Peggy. 1988. White privilege: Unpacking the invisible knapsack. *Independent School*, 49(2), 31–36.

Mumby, Dennis K. 2012. *Organizational communication: a critical approach*. Thousand Oaks, CA: Sage Publications.

Nelson, Alondra. 2002. Future texts. *Social Text* 20, no. 2: 1–15.

Nichols, Nichelle. 1995. *Beyond Uhura: Star Trek and other memories*. New York: Boulevard Books.

Pescovitz, David. 2007. Jason Tester: Case for human-future interaction. *Boing, Boing.* http://boingboing.net/2007/02/21/jason-tester-case-fo.html.

Philip, K., L. Irani, and Paul Dourish. 2012. Postcolonial computing: A tactical survey. *Science, Technology, and Human Values*. 37, no. 1: 3–29.

Popper, Rafael. 2009. Mapping foresight: Revealing how Europe and other world regions navigate into the future. Publications Office of the European Union, European Commission, EFMN, Luxembourg.

Ramos, Jose, Tim Mansfield, and Gareth Priday. 2012. Foresight in a network era: Peer-producing alternative futures. *Journal of Futures Studies* 17, no. 2.

Rittel, Horst and Melvin Webber. 1973. Dilemmas in a general theory of planning. *Policy Sciences* 4: 155–69.

Star, S. L. 2002. Infrastructure and ethnographic practice: Working on the fringes. *Scandinavian Journal of Information Systems*, 14(2), 6.

Tester, Jason. 2007. The case for human-future interaction. Institute for the Future. *Emerging technologies and their implications for the future*, February 16. http://future.iftf.org/2007/02/the_case_for_hu.html. Accessed October 17, 2010.

Turner, James. [1991] 2004. Afrocentrism: Affirming consciousness. In *Child welfare revisited: An Africentric perspective*, ed. Joyce Everett. New Brunswick, NJ: Rutgers University Press.

Woodyard, Jeffrey L. 2003. Africological theory and criticism: Reconceptualizing communication constructs. In *Understanding African American rhetoric: Classical origins to contemporary innovations*, eds. Ronald L. Jackson, II and Elaine Richardson, 133–54. New York, NY: Routledge.

*Chapter Nine*

# Rewriting the Narrative

*Communicology and the
Speculative Discourse of Afrofuturism*

## David DeIuliis and Jeff Lohr

The title of this volume, *Afrofuturism 2.0*, is a doubly dehumanizing concept. First, Afrofuturism responds to a society in which the black body is invisible and, second, Web 2.0 overlooks the human body in favor of the machines they sit behind. Resistances to either of these dominant cultural discourses reduce the black body to "disembodied different at a distance" (Catt 2001, 293), a handicap to Afrofuturist interpretation and inquiry. The human science of communicology combats these dehumanizing trends by first, approaching the speculative discourse of Afrofuturism as an embodied event that foregrounds the *experience* of invisibility and, second, inviting Afrofuturism into a methodologically-rigorous discourse that preserves—and privileges—its experiential roots.

This chapter proposes communicology as a theoretical and methodological framework for understanding Afrofuturism as speculative discourse within the context of Africology. With Richard Lanigan, this chapter defines communicology as a science of human communication that "refocuses attention on the performance and practice of persons communicating" (Lanigan 1992, 2). Communicology seeks to understand human discourse and interaction as embodied practices that situate people within their worlds. The act of expressing oneself reveals cultural codes (i.e., race, gender, and sexuality) which, in turn, shape and constitute the expressive body. Communicology's method of explicating "human consciousness and behavioral embodiment as *discourse* within global culture"[1] allows for the study of Afrofuturism as not only "the speculative fiction of the African diaspora" (Thomas 2000) but also the diasporic transmission of the *experience* of blackness.

Communicology shares with Africological theory its attention to the inventive power of language to define "what it means to be human in inhumane contexts" (Woodyard 2003, 133). For communicology, inhumane contexts reduce the experience of communication to information transmission. For Africology, inhumane contexts, like those described by Ellison in *Invisible Man*, exclude the black experience from the dominant and rational cultural discourse. Afrofuturism rewrites the discursive narratives of inhumane contexts through critical examination of cultural artifacts of the black experience.

All three frameworks are theoretically linked as not only areas of scholarly pursuit, but also ways of understanding our being-in-the-world. Africology begins with the ontological study of the "life and cultural experiences of African peoples" (Woodyard 2003, 133). Communicology begins with cultural experiences in order to understand the ontological nature of human communication. Afrofuturism begins with cultural artifacts of the black experience and rewrites the ontology of the narrative of the "whitewashed" West (Yaszek 2005, 297). Similarly, while Africology works from "Afrocentric tendencies in the exploration of human texts" (Woodyard 2003, 133), communicology begins by bracketing these tendencies in order to identify their ontological origins, and Afrofuturism provides critical yet constructive direction for reworking these tendencies.

Woodyard writes that Africology demonstrates that "viewing human activity from some constructed African vantage is a sensible, reliable option for reading human experiences" (Woodyard 2003, 135) where the "prevailing ideology . . . is centering in a configuration of African ideals and values" (Woodyard 2003, 143). Likewise, communicology concerns how constructed vantages come to infuse experiences with meaning. While Africology is grounded in a particular (in its attention to particular communities), yet collective (in its continental scope) vantage that it constructs through theory, communicology is grounded in a universal (in its attention to human experience), yet individual (in its attention to individual human conscious experience) method that brackets all vantage points to study pure conscious experience. As theoretical foundations for Afrofuturism, Africology and communicology provide new insights into relationships among race, gender, sexuality, and technology in *human* communication, where "Afrofuturism and thinking about the future will take on the local characteristics of an African population as it evolves in relation to technology" (Anderson and Jennings 2014, 36).

Communicology is thus theoretically and methodologically compatible with the call of Africological communication studies for a "conversation about humanizing tendencies" (Woodyard 2003, 135). Communicology, like Africology, assumes that human knowledge is a byproduct of human culture.

For Africology, culture is the "operative value in understanding human communication" and, for communicology, communication is the ground of culture and culture the ground of communication.

With this dialectic of expression—the literature of Afrofuturism—and culture—the transcendent, speculative transmission of its signs and codes—as a methodological starting point, this chapter proceeds with two major sections. First, we frame the intellectual origins of communicology as a liberating hermeneutic, and introduce the methodology of communicology as a way to engage Afrofuturist discourse. Second, we review the recent literature on Afrofuturism as a critical method and liberating hermeneutic that, with communicology as a theoretical and methodological framework, can rewrite the narrative of human experience through mainstream academic discourse.

## COMMUNICOLOGY AS LIBERATING HERMENEUTIC[2]

In the famous first and last paragraphs of *Invisible Man*, a seminal Afrofuturist novel (Yaszek 2005), Ralph Ellison refers to communication as an embodied human experience. In the first paragraph, Ellison writes, "I am an invisible man. No, I am not a spook like those who haunted Edgar Allen Poe; nor am I one of those Hollywood-movie ectoplasms. I am a man of substance, of flesh and bone, fiber and liquids—and I might even be *said* to possess a mind" (Ellison 1952, 3). In the last paragraph, he concludes, "Being invisible and without substance, a disembodied voice, as it were, what else could I do? What else but try to tell you what was really happening when your eyes were looking through? And it is this which frightens me: Who knows but that, on the lower frequencies, I *speak* for you?" (Ellison 1952, 581). In both cases, invisibility results from a "phenomenological slippage" (Yancey 2008, 76) between being black and cultural perceptions of the black body, from being not only invisible, but also divisible by and dispossessed from the rational discourse of a "whitewashed" society (Yaszek 2005, 297). Much like Ellison, communicologists place communication and culture at the bookends of human existence, and treat spooks, ectoplasms, and human bodies as not things, but *signs* of human experience. With this in mind, we now draw on the work of Richard Lanigan, Jacqueline Martinez, and Isaac Catt, among others, to explicate the a) intellectual origins and b) semiotic phenomenological method of communicology.

*Intellectual Origins of Communicology.*[3] The scope of communicology extends from mass communication and media studies to public relations and political economy—"whenever and wherever the signs and codes of culture impact on the perception of bodily expressive modes."[4] The term has since been applied in the context of family communication (Eicher-Catt 2005), female/feminine embodiment (Eicher-Catt 2001), and racial relations (Catt 2001). Communicology offers a human-centered approach to conscious experience that rivals social scientific and behavioralist approaches that reify culture (Klyukanov 2010) and reduce communication to message and mind to mechanism (Catt 2010). The origins of communicology emerged a century ago and reside in a large and disparate literature within the phenomenological human science tradition of William James (1842–1910) and Wilbur Marshall Urban (1873–1952) in America, and Ernst Cassirer (1874–1945), Roman Jakobson (1896–1982), Karl Jaspers (1883–1969), and Michel Foucault (1926–1984) in Europe. As a term for the study of the discourse of human communication, communicology emerged in the late 1950s alongside the social science of communication as a "product" of Continental phenomenology of Edmund Husserl (1859–1938) and Maurice Merleau-Ponty (1908–1961) and the American pragmatism of Charles Sanders Peirce (1839–1914) (Eicher-Catt and Catt 2010, 20) with the work of, among others, Franklin Knower and Elwood Huey Allen Murray, and later, with the publication of Joseph DeVito's *Communicology: An Introduction to the Study of Communication* in 1978 (Lanigan 1988, 209).

The primary contemporary theoretician of communicology is Richard Lanigan, whose works, *The Semiotic Phenomenology of Rhetoric* (1984), *The Phenomenology of Communication* (1988), and *The Human Science of Communicology* (1992), codified the study of communication into a human science of embodied discourse that "refocuses attention on the performace and practice of persons communicating" (Lanigan 1992, 2). Communicology achieved formal recognition as a discipline in 2000 with the founding of the International Communicology Institute by Richard Lanigan at Southern Illinois University. As defined by the International Communicology Institute, communicology is a human science of communication that, using the research methods of semiotics and phenomenology, investigates human conscious experience as constituted through embodied and culturally-embedded discursive practices.[5] This definition synthesizes the semiotics of Foucault and Peirce and the phenomenology of Husserl and Merleau-Ponty to account for the experience of human communication with methodological rigor.

From the perspective of communicology, then, Ellison's concept of invisibility is a product of the Web 2.0 world's reduction of culture to technological capacity. A *human* science of communication, communicology attempts to liberate "the existentially humane from obscurity in an Information Age (Catt 2011, 123) by focusing on not message transmission between disembodied automatons—or invisible men—but on the conscious experience of communicating with another person. Communicology presupposes that communication, whether face-to-face or technologically-mediated, 1.0 or 2.0, is not a mere transfer of information among machines, but a lived experience performed in and through the human body (Catt and Eicher-Catt 2010, 17).

Following the phenomenology of Merleau-Ponty, communicology presumes language as the origin of conscious experience. It approaches human communication as an embodied practice, an experience made meaningful or rendered meaningless by cultural signs and discursive codes. The human body relies on these signs and codes to express itself and, through expression, the body is shaped and changed by the signs and codes.

Communicology examines this "reversible, reciprocal, and reflexive nature of the 'expressive and perceptive body'" (Catt and Eicher-Catt 2010, 17) embedded in a culture that grounds communication (Catt, forthcoming). However, communication and expression are not reversible in conscious experience. Communication requires expression but, as Ellison shows, expression may not result in communication, especially if the speaker is outside the rational or mainstream discourse. Communication is a goal and possibility of expression, never an assumption or probability of ignorance. Because cultural signs and discursive codes are meaningless until embodied, the possibilities of communication depend on the human body expressive of signs and codes: "As an experience, communication is invisible. The constraints of discourse on communicative possibility are, then, the substantive objects" of communicology (Catt, forthcoming). The focus of communicology is not the invisible body, but an embodied sign of invisibility.

Another fundamental presupposition of communicology is that communication is intertwined with culture, and culture with consciousness: "Communication and culture are reversible in conscious experience" (Catt, forthcoming). Communication is the ground of culture and culture the ground of communication or, as Jacqueline Martinez writes, the synthesis of communication and culture is "what gives us our ever-evolving and dynamic sense of self as a person" (Martinez 2011, 117). To communicate is to embody certain signs and codes that are shared by another in culture. We make sense of perceptions in the lived world by reifying them into "concepts and, because concepts cannot speak for themselves" (Catt, forthcoming) they must be spoken to be communicated. Mere analysis of texts, objects, behaviors, and cultural artifacts overlooks this experience of communication (Catt, forthcoming).

Instead, communicology treats the act of communication as an event, the embodiment of signs in culture. For instance, Isaac Catt describes an initial encounter with a "stranger," the intercultural unknown, to illustrate the relationship of communication to culture. In asking whether an unfamiliar other thinks the way oneself does, one does so in the context of "normally anticipated reciprocities of consciousness" (Catt 2001, 293) where the other is familiar and known. One creates context for encountering the other through experience, not abstract rules that can never "be perfectly followed, even if unconsciously recognized" (Catt 2001, 298). In this case, communication is an experience of the other, a "stranger" embedded in culture. At the same time, every word we speak "is an encounter with an Other. . . . The stranger is already within" (Catt, forthcoming).

The communicological approach, as illustrated by Catt's explication of the "stranger" code, is of particular importance for the Afrofuturist project because it, first, liberates discourse from the handicap of the stranger code by beginning with the stranger in oneself and, second, it reflects a "felt need to reflect the common, cultural sense of things, rather than interrogating . . . a rationality of discourse" (Eicher-Catt and Catt 2008, 119) that "imposes its own version of consciousness upon experience by suggesting that equality exists" (Catt 2001, 311) where there is only invisibility. Afrofuturism, then, is an embodied meaning played out in personal experience and cultural discourse. The signs and codes that infuse experience with meaning often go unexamined in a taken-for-granted "natural attitude" (Martinez 2011, 117) that infuses cultural consciousness with commonsense. Communicology examines this relationship between the signs and codes that infuse culture with a shared common experience, and the ways those experiences are discursively expressed both individually and collectively.

This approach is particularly applicable to Web 2.0, where the speed and hypertextual nature of communicative technologies promote "present shock" (Rushkoff 2013), and intellectual superficiality (Carr 2011). To discuss how the presuppositions of communicology play out in Web 2.0, we outline four levels of discourse—intrapersonal (self), interpersonal (self-other), social (group-organizational), and intergroup (cultural)—that together form the background of communicology's experiential approach to communication and culture. Proposed in the 1950s by Jurgen Ruesch in his seminal work, *Communication: The Social Matrix of Psychiatry* (1951) and further explicated by Ruesch and Gregory Bateson in *Semiotic Approaches to Human Relations* (1972), the levels are a reaction to the Western tendency to reduce communication to technicalities of information transmission. They account for human social existence as a dependent hierarchy where each level presupposes the prior, and embodiment of signs at an intrapersonal, subjective level is a prerequisite for intersubjective understanding at the interpersonal, group, or cultural level (Catt and Eicher-Catt 2010).

The first domain, intrapersonal (self), begins within the body and concerns issues of subjectivity, consciousness, and identity formation (Catt and Eicher-Catt 2010, 20). The intrapersonal domain provides a foundation for increasingly complex human relationships. Within the self network of discourse, one engages in a dialogue within oneself in which subjectivity is inextricably intertwined with intersubjectivity, the self with other. The second domain, interpersonal (self-other) begins in this relationship of self and other, or "ratio" of individual embodiedness to shared cultural experience (Catt and Eicher-Catt 2010, 18). In the interpersonal level, communication becomes more complex as it meets other people and personal perception meets others' experience and behavior (Catt and Eicher-Catt 2010, 18).

The third domain, social (group-organizational), concerns how discursive practices within institutions and organizations are constituted through intra- and interpersonal networks (Catt and Eicher-Catt 2010, 18). The group level increases again in complexity. Although intrapersonal and dyadic interpersonal domains exist within the group, as the number of people increases, the human body becomes increasingly abstracted and subject to non-human forces. The fourth domain, intergroup, begins with culture and concerns how shared cultural experiences are intersubjectively constructed through discourse. In the intergroup level, the human body is further abstracted from its expressive capacities and categorized according to technological affordances.

Approaches to mass communication that focus on affordances often begin at the intergroup level and overlook the ways in which these technologies reorient human consciousness at the intrapersonal, interpersonal, and group levels of human experience (Catt 2010). The levels provide a framework for studying the relationship between communication and culture that adequately accounts for this complexity of human experience. Codes, contexts, and messages are synthesized in cultures, society, and self as embodied and experienced communication (Catt 2011, 128). In sum, these four levels ground communicology as a liberating hermeneutic that frees the *experience* of communication from quantification and reification in a Web 2.0 world. Before reviewing the complementary aspects of Afrofuturism as a liberating hermeneutic that frees the *experience* of blackness from Euro-centric visions of the past, we outline the semiotic phenomenological method to show what communicology looks like in practice.

*Communicology and the Semiotic Phenomenological Method.* Communicology's "paradigm exemplar" and method of inquiry is semiotic phenomenology (Catt and Eicher-Catt 2010, 20). For communicology, "the complexity of communication stems from the fact that its occurrence is both a semiotic-cultural process and a phenomenologically-embodied event in a social context" (Catt 2011, 133). Semiotic phenomenology synthesizes semiotics—the study of signs and sign-systems—and phenomenology—the study of human conscious experience—to examine how the signs that guide our experience of the social world come to be through embodied practices of communication. Using recordings of speech, written texts, and videos of behavior, semiotic phenomenological inquiry proceeds in three steps: Description, Reduction, and Interpretation.

The Description describes an experience, the Reduction reduces the Description to experience in consciousness, and the Interpretation interprets the meaning of the experience itself. Rather than beginning with potentially problematic presuppositions, semiotic phenomenological inquiry starts with conscious experience and works backward to identify the presuppositions that infuse experience with meaning. In the Description one brackets all presuppositions that may distort an accurate description of an experience. In the Reduction, one reduces the Description to its essential parts free of the subject's emotions. In the Interpretation, one identifies the presuppositions that were initially bracketed. We now discuss each of these three steps, beginning with the Description.

*Description.* Description, the first step in the semiotic phenomenological method, is an "initial account: or awareness of a lived-through experience, a 'depiction'" (Lanigan 1992, 36) of what a phenomenon is. It is the act of describing a lived-through and interpersonal experience of a phenomenon in which one recognizes meaning in oneself, in one's relations to others, and in the situation in which one is enrooted (Lanigan 1992, 36). The description focuses on experience (Lanigan 1988, 173) by asking "What am I experiencing?" or "What am I conscious of?" and answering the question by stating "To me, it is" (Lanigan 1992, 36). German philosopher Edmund Husserl called this step the *epoché*, the act of "unplugging" or "bracketing" perceptions to keep out extraneous presuppositions and preconceived notions.

*Reduction.* Reduction, the second step in the semiotic phenomenological method, reduces the description to a definition or essence of human communication (Lanigan 1992, 2). It is an awareness of an awareness of a lived-through experience that gives a "fundamental account" of how the initial account is meaningful. It focuses on experience in consciousness (Lanigan 1988, 173) by asking, "How am I experiencing, or "What would other people, who know me, say I am conscious of?" and answering the question with, "To me, myself, it is" (Lanigan 1992, 36). For instance, if the Description is the act of looking up a word in the dictionary, the Reduction is the act of looking up a *meaning* in an encyclopedia.

*Interpretation.* Interpretation, the third and final step in the phenomenological method, is the act of interpreting the reduced description. It focuses on experience itself (Lanigan 1988, 174) by asking, "Why am I experiencing?" or "What would I, who know myself, have said I am truly conscious of?" and answering the question by stating, "To me, myself, I judge it to be . . . " (Lanigan 1992, 37). In this step, one reinterprets the description to identify the presuppositions that made up the experience.

In her 2011 book, *Communicative Sexualities: A Communicology of Sexual Experience*, Jacqueline Martinez offers an applied example of the semiotic phenomenological method in a classroom setting. Working in groups, students first identify a phenomenon, or "anything experienced that becomes meaningful" (Martinez 2011, 114). In the context of human sexuality, phenomena may include the experience of sexual desire, power, regret, or fulfillment, or the "experience of being sexually objectified," or the "experience of having sexual desire that is at odds with social expectations" (Martinez 2011, 114). Having decided on a phenomenon, groups then divide into pairs. Each member of the pair interviews the other about a particular experience related to the phenomenon. Both the interviewer and interviewee write a narrative, or description, of the experience. While the narrative written by the interviewer is often more direct, descriptive, and free of justificatory language, the narrative of the interviewee, the person who experienced the phenomenon, often focuses more on a rationale for the behavior than the experience itself. By comparing the two narratives, students become aware of the extent to which their description of an experience is clouded by biases and preconceptions. Students have now entered the *epoché* and performed the first step of the semiotic phenomenological method.

After students wrote a description of the experience and entered the *epoché*, they then identify and list what Lanigan calls "revelatory phrases," the "words and phrases of the person, words that nominate what the discourse is about as a conscious experience" (Lanigan 1988, 147). The revelatory phrases reveal the meaning in the description. For instance, a narrative of the "experience of being wanted by the other more than wanting the other or the reverse" may result in a revelatory phrase such as, "I had planned it all to be very romantic but it was really just awkward" (Martinez 2011, 122). Students then interpret this revelatory phrase to locate the sign systems and normative conventions that make it meaningful. The experience of a sexual encounter as unromantic and awkward assumes a societal norm that sexual intercourse should result from romantic and chivalrous courtship. The students can then see what it means to embody culture through communication. An experience of an event is not only linked to, but also constituted by cultural codes and discursive conventions.

For another example, consider a phenomenon such as, "experience of sexual power" (Martinez 2011, 115). Students may describe this phenomenon with revelatory phrases such as, "I kept thinking about how I was going to be able to tell my friends" (Martinez 2011, 123). In this case, the anxiety from telling one's friends about a sexual encounter may be tied to a third real or imagined entity that constitutes the experience, such as a mutual friend or previous partner. The experience of the third is a disruption of the societal norm of the sexual dyad, a norm that is experientially unnoticed, and empirically meaningless without semiotic phenomenological inquiry that focuses on human conscious experience.

The world of Web 2.0 has opened up countless possibilities for new experiences, as well as new ways of documenting them. The semiotic phenomenological method shows that the revelatory in human communication exists not in a vacuum, but in a matrix of codes and conventions that allow us to make sense of this mediated world. To engage in semiotic phenomenology is to investigate the "becoming of the sign" (Catt 2011, 125) in discourse, how it was produced and developed through the interaction of communication and culture. In a postmodern moment characterized by narrative and virtue contention (Arnett 2005, 104), it is essential to liberate ourselves from the presuppositions of the dominant rational discourse and investigate the experience of communication. This perspective lends itself well to the discourse of Afrofuturism in the Africana Studies classroom as the study of the African experience, or to texts such as *Invisible Man*, itself a narrative of the experience of being invisible or, as Franz Fanon says, of being not only inferior, but also nonexistent. Together, communicology and semiotic phenomenology provide respective theoretical and methodological ground for Afrofuturism as a critical method and liberating hermeneutic.

## AFROFUTURIST SPECULATIVE DISCOURSE: A CRITICAL METHOD AND LIBERATING HERMENEUTIC

In this section, we draw on the work of, among others, Ytasha Womack, Mark Dery, George Yancy, and Reynaldo Anderson to explicate Afrofuturism as a critical method and liberating hermeneutic. In framing Afrofuturism as a liberating hermeneutic within the context of Web 2.0, this chapter follows the work of Anderson and Jennings (2014), who frame Afrofuturism as a digital hermeneutic that interprets the aesthetics of Afrofuturism as metaphysical manifestations of the black experience. Just as an Afrofuturist digital hermeneutic engages the ways in which peoples of the African diaspora transform and are transformed by a digital world, Afrofuturism as a liberating hermeneutic imagines a world where non-whites are not only free from the White Gaze (Yancy 2008), but also free to navigate the narrative and virtue contention of a postmodern world as human beings with visible bodies and respected voices.

Just as communicology resists approaches to human discourse that limit human communication to information transmission, Afrofuturism responds to and resists the experience of living in a world with "whiteness as the transcendental norm" (Yancey 2008, xxiii). In *Black Bodies, White Gazes,* Yancy points to the epistemic issues raised in the historic experience of black identity formation, "a shared history of Black people noting, critically discussing, suffering, and sharing with each other the traumatic experiential content and repeated acts of white racism" (Yancy 2008, 7). Consistent with communicology, Yancy's work details the "reversible, reciprocal, and reflexive" (Catt and Eicher-Catt 2010, 17) implications of racism in American culture, where the white gaze is a product of the historic embodiment of racism. For Yancy, a white woman afraid of and disgusted by the male black body that joins her on an elevator is a "prisoner of her own historically inherited imaginary and the habitual racist performances that have become invisible to her" (Yancey 2008, 19). He proposes positive resistance in the form of "decoding" (Yancey 2008, 110) as a "process of recoding Black embodied existence through processes of opposition and affirmation" (Yancey 2008, 112). By promoting a visible and necessary black presence in the future, Afrofuturism is one form of resistance that escapes tendencies to problematize or victimize blackness.

The loosely configured and organic (Jackson 2000, 49) methods and theories of Afrofuturism allow multiple spheres of values, beliefs, and attitudes. The term has expanded since its initial use describing the sci-fi reality of a bleakly "whitewashed" African future (Dery 1994) to encompass issues related to the experience and expression of blackness and technology. By providing interpretive ground for marginalized and disparate black experiences that rupture mainstream prescriptions of time, space, and narrative, Afrofuturism imagines positive futures that, through speculative discourse, sever the shackles of slavery's shadow.

Afrofuturism proper began not with cultural criticism, but with an open ended and self-reflexive question, "Why do so few African Americans write science fiction?" (Dery 1994, 179). This question does not cast stones or blame, but is an additive probe akin to the *epoché* that reflects on circumstances as they are. Dery suggests that the science fiction genre is suited for "strangers in a strange land"[6] that are in a "very real sense . . . the descendants of alien abductees" (Dery 1994, 180). With this line of inquiry, Dery opens three major currents of Afrofuturist thought: time, narrative, and technology. He blends the temporal experience of African abductees with that of present day African Americans who temporally and spatially "inhabit a sci-fi nightmare" still held captive by illusive "force fields of intolerance" (Dery 1994, 180). He also points to the invisibility of Diasporic Africans whose "past has been deliberately rubbed out" (Dery 1994, 180) and identifies technology as a site of struggle where "technology is too often brought to bear on black bodies" (Dery 1994, 180). Although not all Afrofuturists agree with Dery's views on the black experience in relation to technology, the intersection of race and technology emerges as a dominant theme in Afrofuturist inquiry.

Long before Dery coined the term, there existed a "legacy of Afrofuturist cultural production" (Rollefson 2008, 84). For example, Frederick Douglass challenged linear time, Ellison expressed the existential angst of blackness in a white world, and Jazz great Sun Ra rejected earthly citizenship. Though scholars from a variety of disciplines continue to expand and interpret its practices, Afrofuturism has become "a recognizable field of scholarly inquiry and artistic production" (Rollefson 2008, 83). As this volume demonstrates, there is a growing body of scholarship that articulates various themes and practices that coalesce under the term Afrofuturism (Womack 2013). Afrofuturists work in the margins of pop culture with texts as sites of resistance that reveal "models of expression that transform spaces of alienation into novel forms of creative potential" (Nelson 2002, 36). A common thread that unites most Afrofuturist work is that "it reclaims theorizing about the future" (Nelson 2002, 36) in ways that provide space for multiple possibilities. (Indeed, the purpose of this essay is to propose the theory of method of communicology as such a possibility.) However, we primarily attend to the additive aspects of Afrofutursim, not as a prescription for what Afrofuturism is or ought to be, but in order to examine the conversation on its own terms. This conversation leads to three distinct teleological spheres: to write a global history attentive to the African voice in global development, to create an a-historical/ a-global history unencumbered by the master/slave framework, and to introduce a horizon of future possibilities for a positive experience of blackness. We now frame Afrofuturism as a critical method that speculates on these spheres.

*Afrofuturism as Critical Method –(Re)writing the Narrative.* A key concern in the Afrofuturist conversation is the "representation of history" (Yaszek 2005, 298). Afrofuturists contend that traditional history objectifies blackness, perpetuates an image of the primitive African, and mitigates the role of Africa historically and moving forward. Lisa Yaszek contends that "whatever medium they work in" (Yaszek 2005, 298–99), Afrofuturists critique traditional accounts of history that minimize the "black Atlantic experience" (Yaszek 2005, 299) and, in response, "generate counter-histories that reweave connections between past, present and future" (Yaszek 2005, 299). She argues that the tendency to privilege written texts and prescribed methods over intuition and improvisation dismisses alternative methods of history. Afrofuturists must contend with a different set of realities than those privileged by traditional historians, contained in stories that involved *experiences* that words could not capture. This problem is particularly acute in narratives of the Middle Passage.

The narratives of the Middle Passage survived as oral texts in the form of improvised stories and songs. This element of improvisation is essential to Africana culture (Womack 2013, 37). For instance, in her article "'Africa as an Alien Future': The Middle Passage, Afrofuturism, and Postcolonial Waterworlds," Ruth Mayer explores revisionist moves in Afrofuturist speculative discourse. She identifies the problems with recovering the narratives of millions of Africans abducted and transported to the Caribbean, and surveys present-day attempts to recount these experiences as "fantasy spaces . . . that represent themselves as mixed-up, ambivalent, floating" signs (Mayer 2000, 556). Similarly, in his book *The Black Atlantic*, Paul Gilroy, a British proto-Afrofuturist, explains how music played an essential role in expressing the inarticulable values and emotions of millions of displaced blacks (Gilroy 1993). He draws attention to the "conspicuous problems with ethnocentrism and nationalism" (Gilroy 1993, 5) inherent in rhetorical construction of culture.

Gilroy's work shows that the contemporary experience of diasporic Africans does not fit neatly into a modernist paradigm delimited by national boundaries or localized ethnic distinctions. Also, descendants of the slave trade find themselves in a peculiar bind absent a direct experience of nationhood or African heritage. Gilroy's work foregrounds the racial and nationalistic biases inherent in the hegemonic European historical narrative of black intellectualism (Gilroy 1993, 5). In a variation of the semiotic phenomenological method, he uncovers the discursive construction of blackness and identity in the African Diasporic by problematizing the polemic of race. He writes, "cultural historians could take the Atlantic as one single, complex unit of analysis in their discussions of the modern world and use it to produce an explicitly transnational and intercultural perspective" (Gilroy 1993, 15). Much like communicology attempts to recover human experience from a dominant social scientific paradigm, Afrofuturist discourse proceeds outside the hegemonic paradigm. It accounts for the larger experience of the Black Atlantic by revealing a more expressive and constructive transnational identity. A first step, then, in re-visioning the narrative of blackness is to describe the experience of blackness and bracket any racial and nationalistic biases from the description.

As cultural critics, many Afrofuturists consider contemporary history a fiction. They suggest that we are the objects of an "imperial historicism" that imposes on culture the Western Euro-centric "protocols of institutional memory, historical citation, national origin, and territorial sovereignty" (Youngquist 2005, 183) without attending to the authenticity of the lived-experience. As Yancy writes, "the body is a site of contested meanings" which "*signifies* the historicity of its 'being' as lived and meant within the interstices of social semiotics, institutional forces, and various discursive frames of reference" (Yancey 2008, xxii). Within these institutional forces, the experience of history "assumes new forms and new antagonisms in different situations" (Gilroy 1991, 11) where racist cultural production both transforms and is transformed by history.

Afrofuturism is attentive to this phenomenological ambiguity that results, most notably, in the lived experience of slavery in which the experience of foreignness transcends history. Reynaldo Anderson among other scholars notes that Africans were "among the first alien abductees" (Anderson qtd. in Womack 2013, 34–35) and, for Womack, the common sci-fi trope of alien abduction is a quite literal description of transatlantic slave ships carrying (less than) human cargo "from another world" (Womack 2013, 30). She explains that the "alien motif" has emerged as a "framework to examine how those who are alienated adopt modes of resistance and transformation" (Womack 2013, 35) under the shadow of bondage.

This continuing legacy of bondage is a pervasive theme in Afrofuturist work. Ellison, for example, writes in *The Invisible Man,* that, "I am not ashamed of my grandparents for having been slaves. I am only ashamed of myself for having at one time been ashamed" (Ellison 1952, 16). The conversation surrounding the legacy of slavery interrupts linear time, another theme of Afrofuturist discourse, explicated by Womack in her work on the transtemporal experience of slavery. She writes that, "Slavery" is not an "ancient far removed past. The tragedy that split the nation into warring factions has effects that can be felt in the politics of the present" (Womack 2013, 156). This underscores the prevalence of "bending time" in Afrofuturist practice, of realizing the extent to which the experience of the present is constituted by the past, just as Martinez's students came to understand that their (anti-)climactic sexual experiences in the present were constituted by past presuppositions.

For Womack, the muted significance of Africa and Africans is a "gaping hole" (Womack 2013, 80) in mainstream accounts of historical progress. Afrofuturists attempt to color the past by refocusing on black "scientific inventors past and present," and incorporating them "into a larger conversation about technology, creativity and race" (Womack 2013, 46). As a theoretically and methodologically rigorous academic discourse, communicology can address the gaping hole and invite the discourse of Afrofuturism into the academic mainstream. However, as itself an approach on the margins of a dominant paradigm, communicology also privileges the playful and improvisational elements of the black experience as a liberating hermeneutic, a fellow traveler on the mission where no (black) man has gone before.

*Afrofuturism as Liberating Hermeneutic.* Afrofuturism is a liberating hermeneutic in the sense that its discourse reveals possibilities for envisioning a world untethered from the transcendental norm of whiteness, in which a contemporary Euro-American cannot write a personal future without mentioning Africa. While the conventional confines of history provide creative space for those of white European descent, there is no African future that is not in some way tethered to forced diaspora. Even stories of victory are written in a framework designed by the master. Like a red-shirted crew member on an away mission in the original *Star Trek* series, the depiction of black characters in future stories have a "dour fate" (Womack 2013, 7).

In her discussion of the development of narrative portrayals of black characters in science fiction, Womack writes that in the early years of television and film, blacks were simply excluded from the future. As roles began to emerge, the characters were minor, short-lived, and essentially irrelevant: "people of color weren't factors at all" (Womack 2013, 7). Growing up, she partially identified with leading white characters in science fiction, but the "quest to see myself or browner people in this space age, galactic epic was important to me" (Womack 2013, 5). The quest to brighten the muted and nullified experience of blackness in science fiction urges new imaginative possibilities for the future of nonwhite discourse.

Many of these emancipatory possibilities are found in art and music. In *Shadow and Act*, Ellison himself wrote that, "In those days, it was either live with music or die with noise, and we chose rather despertaely to live" (Ellison 1953, 187). Later, he echoes Lanigan, Catt and Martinez: "one of the chief values of living with music lies in its power to give us an orientation in time. In doing so, it gives significance to all those indefinable aspects of experience which nevertheless help to make us what we are" (Eliison 1953, 197). Kodwo Eshun further explores various Egyptian and futuristic themes used by black musicians, from Sun Ra and Miles Davis to George Clinton. An exemplar of the creative possibilities of Afrofuturist resistance, the music of Jazz legend Sun Ra is rife with Egyptian images and spirituality. Sun Ra challenges the Euro-centric historic narrative in a variety of ways: "For Ra, Enlightenment rationality, Western progress, and white supremacy are inseparable. They reflect only one narrow vision of the world and therefore could not possibly capture any real truth" (Rollefson 2008, 97). Sun Ra defined his own existence by rejecting his given name and earthly citizenship. He disrupted attempts to spatially own or temporally classify him, and resisted earthly limitations of racist cultural production. As his biographer John Szwed explains, "Sun Ra destroyed his past, and recast himself in a series of role in a drama he spent his life creating" (Szwed 1998, 143). In challenging traditional history through music, Sun Ra laid the groundwork for later time-bending Afrofuturist musicians and artists such as George Clinton, who also incorporated ancient Africana symbols into his art and music: "The pyramids become examples of ancient alien technology which the extraterrestrial brothers 'have returned to claim.' Funk becomes a secret Science, a forgotten technology that 'has been hidden until now'" (Eshun 1998, 143). This blending of past and future reverberates throughout much of Afrofuturist work, which represents not only a challenge to history, but also a history of the future.

Afrofuturism is a liberating hermeneutic that provides interpretive ground for future speculation not bound to a Euro-centric vision of the past, where slave ships did not sail. Afrofuturism is in many ways a response to this imagined reality, where a "culture of black sci-fi heads" write new stories, create new histories, and invent new futures "through the arts and critical theory" (Eshun 1998, 143). Reacting to a long legacy of intellectual lynching, Afrofuturists problematize future narratives that reify black marginal life in a white dominated world. Rather than follow these narratives to gallows where the African heritage is silenced, forgotten, and objectified, Afrofuturists challenge them by inventing a future not tied to a Euro-centric history of transatlantic voyage, a future in which a new subject emerges that is not "locate[ed] . . . in tradition; instead it dislocates you from origins" (Eshun 1998, 143). In short, both the Afrofuturist and communicologist experience the world as human beings looking toward a horizon of imaginative possibilities. Together, the discourse of Afrofuturism and theory and method of communicology can realize an imagined future, both in the pages of academic journals and in the lived-world.

## CONCLUSION

In this chapter, we first outlined the presuppositions, intellectual origins, and semiotic phenomenological method of communicology, then applied its theoretical foundations to Afrofuturism, a speculative discourse similarly "embroiled in the laborious process of defining itself" (Devito 1978, v). The human science of communicology seeks to understand human discourse and interaction as embodied practices that situate people within their worlds. In a historical moment in which communication is viewed primarily as a form of technique, skill, or tool (Catt 2010), communicology sheds light on how and why people use technology to interact through language. It focuses on the body as sign, not mere "flesh and bone, fiber and liquids" (Ellison 1952, 3). The human science of communicology—and its "paradigm exemplar," semiotic phenomenology—can serve as a complementary theoretical framework for approaching Afrofuturism, one that does not reify or categorize distance or the different, but attends to the background assumptions, the black words on a white page.

Afrofuturism and communicology share a common goal, to recapture the experience of communication. Afrofuturism responds to the transcendental norm of whiteness to recover the human experience of blackness. Paradoxically, forward-looking Web 2.0 technologies can preclude the very preservation of humanity that Afrofuturism promotes. By approaching the speculative discourse of Afrofuturism as embodied human communication, the human science of communicology accounts for an *experience* of being human that, through description, reduction, and interpretation, is measured in the past, made meaningful in the present and—at least on the lower frequencies—metastasized in perpetuity.

## NOTES

1. Richard L. Lanigan, "Communicology: Lexicon Definition" *International Communicology Institute,* 2007–2013, http://www.communicology.org/content/definition-communicology.

2. In his book, *We Have Been Believers: An African-American Systematic Theology* (Minneapolis: Augustberg Fortress, 1992), James H. Evans, Jr. defines a liberating hermeneutic as a perspective that "allows one to be grasped by the truth, in full consciousness of one's limitations and in deep awe and respect for the reality that is being revealed." We use the term in reference to communicology's focus on communication as revelatory of the human condition.

3. For an extensive review of the development of communicology and its cognates, see Richard L. Lanigan, "Communicology: Approaching the Discipline's Centennial," Special Issue: "Semiotica y Comunicologia," Razón y Palabra, No. 72 (Mayo-Julio), http://www.razonypalabra.org.mx/N/N72/Monotematico/8_Lanigan_72.pdf.

4. Richard L. Lanigan, Maureen Connolly, and Thomas D. Craig, "What is Communicology? Who is a Communicologist?" *International Communicology Institute,* 2005, http://www.communicology.org/content/definition-communicology.

5. Lanigan, Connolly, and Craig, "What is Communicology? Who is a Communicologist?"

6. The phrase "Strangers in a strange land" comes from Exodus 2:2 (KJV): "And she bore him a son, and he called his name Gershom: for he said, I have been a stranger in a strange land." The name Gershom in Hebrew can be translated as "a sojourner there." This allusion to ancient history forecasts the bending of time in Afrofuturism.

# REFERENCES

Anderson, Reynaldo, and John Jennings. 2014. Afrofuturism: The digital turn and the visual art of Kanye West. In *The Cultural Impact of Kanye West,* ed. Julius Bailey, 29-44. New York, NY: Palgrave Macmillan.

Arnett, Ronald C. 2005. *Dialogic confession: Bonhoeffer's rhetoric of responsibility.* Carbondale, IL: Southern Illinois University Press.

Carr, Nicholas. 2011. *The shallows: What the internet is doing to our brains.* New York: Norton.

Catt, Isaac E. 2001. Signs of disembodiment in racial profiling: Semiotic determinism versus Carlo Sini's phenomenological semiotics. *American Journal of Semiotics* 11, no. 4: 291–318.

———. 2010. Communication is not a skill: Critique of communication pedagogy as narcissistic expression. In *Communicology: The new science of embodied discourse,* eds. Deborah Eicher-Catt and Isaac E. Catt, 131–50. Madison, NJ: Fairleigh Dickinson University Press.

———. 2011. The signifying world between ineffability and intelligibility. *The Review of Communication* 11, no. 2: 122–44.

———. (forthcoming). Culture in the conscious experience of communication. *Listening: Journal of Communication Ethics, Religion and Culture* 48, no. 2.

Catt, Isaac E., and Deborah Eicher-Catt. 2010. Communicology: A reflexive human science. In *Communicology: The new science of embodied discourse,* eds. Deborah Eicher-Catt and Isaac E. Catt, 15-32. Madison, NJ: Fairleigh Dickinson University Press.

Dery, Mark. 1994. Black to the future: Interviews with Samuel R. Delany, Greg Tate, and Tricia Rose. In *Flame wars: The discourse of cyberculture,* ed. Mark Dery, 179-222. Durham, NC: Duke University Press.

DeVito, Joseph A. 1978. *Communicology: An introduction to the study of communication.* New York: Harper and Row.

Eicher-Catt, Deborah. 2001. A communicology of female/feminine embodiment: The case of non-custodial motherhood. *The American Journal of Semiotics* 17, no. 4: 93–130.

———. 2005. Advancing family commmunication scholarship: Toward a communicology of the family. *Journal of Family Communication* 5, no. 2: 103–21.

Eicher-Catt, Deborah, and Catt, Isaac. 2008. What can it mean to say that communication is "effective" (and for whom) in postmodernity? *The Atlantic Journal of Communication* 16, no. 3-4: 119–21.

Ellison, Ralph W. 1952. *Invisible man.* New York: Random House.

———. 1953. *Shadow and act.* New York: Signet.

Eshun, Kodwo. 1998. *More brilliant than the sun: Adventures in sonic fiction.* London: Quartet Books.

Evans, James H. 1992. *We have been believers: An African-American systematic theology.* Minneapolis: Augsburg Fortress.

Gilroy, Paul. 1991. *"There Ain't no Black in the Union Jack": The cultural politics of race and nation.* Chicago, IL: University of Chicago Press.

———. 1993. *The Black Atlantic: Modernity and double consciousness.* Cambridge, MA: Harvard University Press.

Jackson, R. L. 2000. Africalogical theory building: Positioning the discourse. *International and Intercultural Communication Annual*: 22, 31–41.

184 David DeIuliis and Jeff Lohr

Klyukanov, Igor. 2010. Culture in the context of communicology. In *Communicology: The new science of embodied discourse*, eds. Deborah Eicher-Catt and Isaac E. Catt, 183-199. Madison, NJ: Fairleigh Dickinson University Press.
Lanigan, Richard L. Communicology: Approaching the discipline's centennial. Special Issue: "Semiotica y Comunicologia." Razón y Palabra 72 (Mayo-Julio). http://www.razonypalabra.org.mx/N/N72/Monotematico/8_Lanigan_72.pdf .
———. Communicology: Lexicon Definition. International Communicology Institute, 2007-2013. http://www.communicology.org/content/definition-communicology.
———. 1984. *Semiotic phenomenology of rhetoric: Eidetic practice in Henry Grattan's Discourse on Tolerance*. Washington D.C.: University Press of America.
———. 1988. *Phenomenology of communication: Merleau-Ponty's thematics in communicology and semiology*. Pittsburgh: Duquesne University Press.
———. 1992. *The human science of communicology: A phenomenology of discourse in Foucault and Merleau-Ponty*. Pittsburgh: Duquesne University Press.
Lanigan, Richard L., Maureen Connolly, and Thomas D. Craig. 2005. What is communicology? Who is a communicologist? International Communicology Institute. http://www.communicology.org/content/definition-communicology.
Martinez, Jacqueline. 2011. *Communicative sexualities: A communicology of sexual experience*. Lanham, MD: Lexington.
Mayer, Ruth. 2000. "Africa as an Alien Future": The Middle Passage, Afrofuturism, and postcolonial waterworlds. *American Studies* 45, no. 4: 555–66.
Nelson, Alondra. 2002. Introduction: *Future Text* 20, no. 2: 1–15.
Rollefson, J. Griffith. 2008. "The Robot Voodoo Power" Thesis: Afrofuturism and Anti-Anti-Essentialism from Sun Ra to Kool Keith. *Black Music Research Journal* 28, no. 1: 83–109.
Rushkoff, Douglas. 2013. *Present shock: When everything happens now*. New York: Current.
Szwed, John. 1998. *Space is the place: The lives and times of Sun Ra*. Da Capo Press.
Thomas, Sheree Renée. 2000. *Dark matter: A century of speculative fiction from the African diaspora*. New York, NY: Warner Aspect.
Womack, Ytasha, 2013. *Afrofuturism: The world of black sci-fi and fantasy culture*. Chicago, IL: Chicago Review Press.
Woodyard, Jeffrey Lynn. 2003. Africological theory and criticism: Reconceptualizing communication constructs. In *Understanding African American rhetoric: Classical origins to contemporary innovations,* eds. Ronald. L. Jackson and E.B. Richardson, 133–54. New York, NY: Routledge.
Yancy, George. 2008. *Black bodies, white gazes: The continuing significance of race*. Lanham: Rowman and Littlefield.
Yaszek, Lisa. 2005. Afrofuturist reading of Ralph Ellison's Invisible Man. *Rethinking History* 9, no. 2-3: 297–313.
Youngquist, Paul. The Afrofuturism of DJ Vassa. *European Romantic Review* 16, no. 2 (2005): 181–92.

## Chapter Ten

# Africana Women's Science Fiction and Narrative Medicine

*Difference, Ethics, and Empathy*

### Esther Jones

Medicine—whether as a system, institution, or discourse—wields, quite arguably, the most power in our contemporary era to identify, name, and categorize difference. In spite of its humanistic and altruistic underpinnings, those who embody difference are treated differentially within the medical establishment. Notwithstanding all the ethical principles of autonomy, beneficence, non-maleficence, and justice undergirding medical ethics, many physicians have noted a decline in the capacity of doctors to practice empathy toward their patients since the rise of science in medicine. Interestingly, the rise of science in medicine was accompanied by a rise in the codification of racist and racial discourse about the difference of non-European others. At the bottom of this scientific, biological hierarchy resided African people, and the long history of medical abuses against black bodies that continues even today suggests that the early stereotyping of Africans lingers, pervasive within the cultural and scientific medical imaginary, casting blacks outside of the purview of medical ethics. While there has been a growing movement to recapture the humanism of medicine through the cultivation of empathy by studying and analyzing literature, the continued mistreatment of black bodies, collectively and individually, begs the question of how precisely narrative ethics—the study of literature and medicine—might engage with the problem of racial difference in their methods.

The relationship between literature and medicine and its capacity to increase empathy has received increasing attention over the past 25–30 years (Holmgren et al. 2011, 46) in what is now referred to as narrative ethics.

Doctors reflect on stories about patient experience that reminds them to consider the whole patient—their unique experiences, their backgrounds, the fullness of their lives—in a manner similar to how we come to understand the fullness of a well-developed character in a novel or speaker in a poem (Holmgren et al. 2011, 249). Some of the most well-respected medical schools offer courses in literature and medicine as part of their ethics training (Charon 2005, 599). And the benefits of reading literature to increase empathy are praised by those practitioners who routinely engage literature as clinical practitioners (Jones 1997, 246). As Karla Holloway argues, "what one discovers in stories are the thick public matters of culture and community—histories of families and social and political national stories that have their own meanings in the expansive sense of a speaker's meaning" (Holloway 2011, 149–50). There is evidence to suggest that medical schools that offer narrative medicine as part of the curriculum produce a superiorly equipped physician who engages with their patients with increased empathy and compassion (Holmgren et al. 2011, 251).

However, people of African descent continue to suffer from the failure of physicians to extend empathy to them and their families. In this essay, I explore the connection between the history of scientific racism, racial/sexual pathologizing of black people, and the disjuncture between the rising trend of returning the humanistic elements of empathy and compassion to the practice of medicine through narrative ethics and the continued maltreatment of blacks within the medical system. I argue that narrative medicine may not adequately deal with issues of racial and gendered difference in their development and application of methods for increasing empathy. Moreover, as Priscilla Wald points out, while "the field of medical humanities has long turned to realist fiction to help address such ethical questions . . . few commentators have explored the perspective on those questions offered by the (often debased) genre of science fiction" (Wald 2008, 1908) and I would also add the exponentially disregarded subfield of Afrofuturist fiction.

I suggest that narrative medicine may be well-served to turn to science fiction writings by black women writers to begin to engage the cultural and ideological complexities of what it means to relate to "distant others." In the examination of three black women science fiction writers and their novels— Nalo Hopkinson's *Brown Girl in the Ring* (1998), Nnedi Okorafor's *Who Fears Death* (2010), and Octavia Butler's *Parable of the Sower* (1993) and *Parable of the Talents* (1998)—I demonstrate the ways in which black women use their presumably subjugated statuses to challenge narratives of authority, recoup denigrated African spiritual and non-mainstream ideologies as sources of legitimate knowledge and authority, and develop ethical codes that result in patterns of relating more humanely across difference.

As near-futuristic novels, these three texts conduct the important work of using science fiction to "explore the necessary relations of science, society, and race, and to stake claim for themselves and for their communities in the global future imaginary."[1] Writing against the "blackness as catastrophe" trope,[2] the near future worlds depicted by Hopkinson, Okorafor, and Butler are deeply rooted in the historical realities and contemporary concerns that particularly affect black well-being at the same time that they defamiliarize, or estrange readers from the empirical details of social realities. Speculative literatures and Afrofuturist forms, as Wald argues, depict

> the fantastic, futuristic, and often alien settings that are conventions of the genre [which] lend themselves to broad speculation about the boundaries between what is and what is not human. Furthermore, the strangeness of these settings enfranchises speculation since it does not reproduce readers' preconceived ideas about present-day social issues with which they believe they identify. (Wald 2008, 1908)

The Afrofuturist form enables their engagement with the specificity of historical black relationships to social health institutions and systems of medicalized oppression to envision, instead, alternative modes of ethics and justice that have been denied women, minorities, and the poor in historical and contemporary reality. As English has pointed out, throughout the history of African American literary production, blacks have had to turn to speculative fiction—an imagining of blacks in other times and other places—in order to "imagine full black subjectivity" and the justice that has been withheld historically (English 2013, 77). In particular, "Afro-futurism considers issues of time, technology, culture and race . . . foregrounding Black agency and creativity" (Jackson and Moody-Freeman 2011, 3). The novels analyzed in this chapter feature worlds populated with images of black bodies in times and spaces that fundamentally challenge our habituated patterns of thinking—our social and cultural scripts—about race, gender, sex, and health. Through this form, these novelists write a future of health justice by rewriting old yet persistent cultural and social scripts that undercut the authority of black women as healing agents in their personal lives as well as that of their communities.

## MEDICINE, AUTHORITY, AND THE HEALTH HUMANITIES

In his *Mystery, Magic and Medicine: The Rise of Medicine from Superstition to Science* (1933), Harvard physician Howard Haggard, sang the praises of the rise of science in medicine and extolled the primacy of the role of medicine in every aspect of modern civilization: "In the past medicine had its place only at the bedside of the individual patient. Today medical science has transcended these narrow limits and has become a guiding force in modern civilization . . . [it] has enlisted to its aid every agency of our society, even to the participation of the individual citizen" (Haggard 1933, 5). As recently as 2007, Frank González-Crussi acknowledges the far-reaching influence and authority of the medical profession and its practitioners, arguing that "The spectacular progress in their field reinforces physicians' authority, even that of those who had no part in producing the advances" (Gonzalex-Crussi 2007, x). He goes on to acknowledge the troubled history of how scientific medical knowledge has been acquired while ultimately diminishing it: "for all the bunglings and failings—sometimes even crimes—of its practitioners, [medicine] remains an essentially altruistic endeavor. And in a world that often seems bent on using science and technology to create better means of mass extermination, one can only think well of a discipline whose goal is to devise better ways to alleviate the suffering and to cure the ills of our fellow man"(González-Crussi 2007, xi). He further notes that, "[Physicians] must find ways of reinforcing the skills and attitudes that make a doctor caring and understanding of the needs of the whole human being. Whether this can be taught . . . in addition to the heavy load of facts required to practice medicine, is not the least of the problems that the profession faces, especially in a system of medical care that seems adverse to the fostering of these very qualities" (Gonzalez-Crussi 2007, x).

But as the work of Harriet Washington (2006), Karla Holloway (2011), and Dorothy Roberts (2011) has revealed, African-descended people have for too long been denied the altruistic efforts of medical science. Instead, medical science has been "the most effective tool for giving claims about human difference the stamp of legitimacy" (Roberts 2011, 27), and black women, in particular, have been singled out as the literal embodiment of disease and difference. According to Roberts, Carl Linnaeus, a Swedish botanist and physician born in 1707, developed twelve editions of his catalogue of living things, *Systema Naturae*, published between 1735 and 1778. Linnaeus divided Homo sapiens into four natural varieties (americanus, europaeus, asiaticus, and afer) linked to the four known regions of the world, color-coded the subspecies red, white, yellow, and black, and assigned each a set of physical, personality, cultural, and social traits, borrowing from the classical concept of the Great Chain of Being described by Saint Thomas Aquinas (Roberts 2011, 29). Of the four descriptions of the so-called varieties of races, only the description for H. sapiens afer singles out the female for special differentiation, focusing on sex organs: "females with genital flap and elongated breasts. Crafty, slow, careless. Covered by grease. Ruled by caprice" (Roberts 2011, 29–30). A bevy of European scientists and philosophers—among them Georges Cuvier, Johann Blumenbach, and Immanuel Kant—would follow suit with their own versions of racial classification schema, their own race always at the top of the hierarchy (Roberts 2011, 27).

Early scientific taxonomy, with its methods of observation and generalization, was founded upon supremely unscientific extrapolation corrupted by

European ethnocentrism and cultural bias. The physical difference reflective of the customs of a particular tribe in one region of a vast and diverse continent became the basis for sweeping generalizations and devaluation of an entire group of people who likely would not have categorized themselves accordingly. Thus, what we now know to be the stereotyping of Africans reveals an obsession with classification and categorization that inextricably links difference with pathology and maps that pathological difference onto the observable racial, sexual, and gender characteristics of the Other (Gilman 1985, 11–12).

I focus on black women's science fiction, then, because of these historic linkages between black women's sexualized pathology and the scientific legitimation of racial and gender hierarchies. To date, the historical research on the medical establishment's relationship to African-descended communities has focused upon the problems of historical and contemporary experimental medical abuses, continued unethical research practices conducted in black communities across the globe, and equity and access issues to the basic standard of care, especially in poorer communities. Scholars such as James H. Jones (1981), Dorothy Roberts (1997; 2011), Harriet Washington (2006), Rebecca Skloot (2011), and Karla Holloway (2011), have amply documented the uneven (if we are generous) and at times outright abusive research and care practices of health professionals against blacks. This is not relegated to the era of slavery as with J. Marion Sims' anesthesia-free gynecological experimentations on black women, (Washington 2006, 2, 61), nor the Jim Crow / Pre-civil rights era of the government-sponsored Tuskegee syphilis experiments on black men. Medical ethics and the law continue to refuse to recognize blacks and poor people as humans worthy of ethical treatment and provision of the basic standard of care as early as the eighteenth century (Washington 2006, 7), and as recently as during the aftermath of Hurricane Katrina, when Anna Pou, the attending physician at New Orleans' Memorial Medical Center, euthanized non-terminal black patients under her care (Fink 2009). It is time that those invested in narrative medicine consider in more concrete terms the ways in which pathological stereotyping and unconscious bias undermine ethical practice.

Since the rise of science in medicine, then, the essential beneficence of which González-Crussi speaks has been obfuscated by pernicious racial stereotyping, which for centuries held the stamp of scientific legitimacy. In the past thirty years or so, however, a growing cadre of physicians has sought to restore the humanistic values that have traditionally resided at the core of medicine. The meta-discourse now taking shape as narrative medicine has sought to transform the primarily positivist approach of medical science by bringing to bear the constructivist epistemological approach that characterizes humanistic inquiry (Jones 1997, 1243). Rita Charon, one of the leading proponents and theorists of narrative medicine and the scholar responsible for the coinage of the name of the field has defined narrative medicine as a set of competencies practiced by the physician that includes empathy, reflection, professionalism, and trustworthiness. Mastery of these competencies would help to achieve the skills of "attentiveness, representation, and affiliation" which literary analysis is uniquely suited to develop (Holmgren et al. 2011, 251). Narrative theorists argue that "analysis of fictional representations of illness can enhance a medical practitioner's treatment of patients" and "strengthen the human competencies of doctoring," because of the "ethical reward and insight into human behavior enhanced by literary analysis, which is thought to improve one's capacity for empathy" (Holmgren et al. 2011, 249).

The goals of narrative medicine are noble. Yet, examples of medical injustice for people of color persist. Such injustices are racialized, classed, and gendered. These identity markers represent some of the main operatives of difference upon which medical ethical decisions are based. In other parts of the world, these vectors of difference may operate along other social or physical markers. Nonetheless, the fundamental issue of developing patterns of relating more ethically across difference in order to "do no harm" and maintain the dignity of human life remains a core competency yet to be achieved fully and applied broadly within healthcare practice.

Certainly, for people of African descent, any method that would result in improved relationships with the medical establishment and better health outcomes would be welcome considering the long and troubled history of medical abuses against black people. The issue I want to interrogate more specifically here, however, is whether the theories of narrative medicine adequately engage with the problem of difference and the pernicious operation of pathological stereotyping which likely accounts for the breaches in ethical behavior enacted by medical practitioners upon blacks and others who embody difference. The ongoing record would suggest that the physician's capacity to relate to distant others remains a theoretical abstraction when it comes to black people. As such, a number of questions arise: How does one develop empathy for groups and individuals representative of that group in the face of systemic racism and racial stereotyping? What kinds of literature, specifically, would increase empathy for black bodies in particular? Does reading stories about black people or narratives about blacks' encounters with medicine do enough to counter the stereotypes that may already exist in the minds of some practitioners? Will reading narratives of what may represent radically different perspectives on spirituality and its place in the medical paradigm engender any greater understanding and respect for these perspectives in the intersubjective construction of illness narratives? What additional training might be required to properly "absorb, interpret, and respond to stories" by blacks that moves beyond reinforcement of stereotypes or simplistic reductionism?

## DISCOURSES OF (IL)LEGITIMACY: NARRATIVE MEDICINE, SCIENCE FICTION, AND BLACK WOMEN WRITERS

The research on the power of narrative in medicine suggests that the interrelated experiences generated by stories—telling, reading, listening—enhance the visibility and, presumably, the relatability of seemingly "distant others," increase empathy in medical practitioners; and facilitate a more collaborative doctor-patient relationship for more effective care (Jones 1997, 1246). And beyond autobiographical narratives of illness, the reading of "good literature" has long been advocated as a means of enhancing empathy on the part of medical practitioners. In part because of ideas surrounding the "truth" value of different genres of writing (Holmgren et al. 2011, 252), the field of narrative medicine has been rather slow to embrace science fiction and other speculative/fantastic forms (Wald 2008, 1908). After all, some detractors argue, the claims that science fiction can make are limited since they often feature worlds and creatures that may not exist in empirical/ordinary reality.

However, scholars such as Priscilla Wald, Jay Clayton, and Eric Rabkin have touted the ability of science fiction to make inroads to medical ethics discourse. According to Rabkin, "Science fiction, the literature defined by its concern for the possibilities and social implications of scientific and technological change, provides a dramatic mirror for bioethics" (Rabkin 2011, 138). If scientific discourse has a tradition of characterizing blacks as non- or lesser-human beings, then it is not a stretch to consider the capacity of the conventions of the science fiction genre—particularly the tropes of alien bodies, settings, and worldviews—to allow for broad speculation about what it means to be human (and to behave humanely) in confrontation with ontological Others (Wald 2008, 1908).

I concur with Rabkin and Wald on the position that science fiction enables us to interrogate our naturalized assumptions about our social patterns and behaviors, how we construct difference, and the development of ethical codes to deal with those differences. Science fiction, therefore, should not be regarded as an untenable, fantastical, and therefore absurd proxy for "factual" science. Rather, it must be appreciated for its capacity to approach the question of social justice (in the realms of law, medicine, and public policy) through the interrogation of our most fundamental conceptions of human identity and behavior. As Rabkin suggests, "If we cannot adjust our ethics through a change in our own customs, our behaviors, our relations with our group, our habits, we can adjust our ethics through enlarging our habits of mind. And that, of course, is the great gift of science fiction" (Rabkin 2011, 148).

To put it another way, science fiction contributes in fresh ways to medical humanities and narrative ethics discourse, particularly as it relates to the practice of empathy in medicine. I argue that black women's science fiction enables us to challenge stereotypes through analysis of the complexities of raced, gendered, and ideological difference for both individual identities and collective cultural groups. Moreover, this body of literature suggests that ethical *considerations* must extend to reflect changes in ethical *actions*. Such practices may work towards transforming our current uneven medical paradigm to establish a culture of health parity.

Among the key assumptions of those who practice narrative ethics is that literature generates increased empathy by expanding the lived context in which patients' attitudes toward the medical establishment and issues of compliance and trust are negotiated. Understanding this broader context presumably requires the doctor to devise strategies of deep listening as the patient tells the story of his illness and representing that narrative back to the listener, an act of interpretation and translation that occurs in the writing of the narrative. Telling and representing, according to Charon, spiral into the affective experience of "affiliation," the recognition that we are all connected as humans, "humble in the face of time, ready to suffer our portion, and brave enough to help one another on our shared journeys" (Charon 2005, 269). Charon's skills of "attention" to the telling and "representing" what has been told require, in practice, acts of reading the patient (deep listening) and interpreting or translating the story the patients have told about themselves (representing back to the teller/patient what has been shared).

But for what I call radical ontological others—groups like black women who have been either so severely stereotyped or whose beliefs are perceived to be so alien to the norms of the dominant culture—their encounters with the medical establishment have been fraught with misreadings and misinterpretations to the detriment of the black patient. Was the doctor who diagnosed Terry Ragland, a fifty-five-year-old middle class black woman, with "ghetto booty" imagining himself as "representing" her narrative of back pain to her in a way that was supposed to make sense to her?[3] In addition to being racist and sexist, such a diagnosis insults the intelligence of the patient and, arguably, harkens to the age of scientific medical racism when illness was thought to manifest differently in blacks (Washington 2006, 58). Ragland, offended, filed a complaint with the Tennessee state department of health, but Dr. Sweo, the offending doctor, fails to see that he did anything wrong.[4] Such routine and unapologetic indignities do little to inspire trust by blacks in a medical establishment that continuously fails to recognize its failures to treat them equitably and ethically. As such, we must interrogate more fully the ways in which stereotyping and unconscious bias function to blunt the skills that narrative medicine advocates.

Such acts of clinical violence as those enacted by Sweo highlight the degree to which acts of misreading and misinterpreting patients of presumably different cultures can erode the cultivation of doctor-patient trust that narrative medicine tries so assiduously to develop. This can extend, particularly, to the arena of spirituality and religion wherein non-mainstream religious beliefs and practices may conflict with scientific medical standards of care. When I teach Nalo Hopkinson's *Brown Girl in the Ring* (1998), for example, a text which imagines a near-futuristic Toronto based on empirical and historical realities of white flight and urban decay, students can relate to the sociological phenomena that provide the setting of the text as a fairly recognizable political context. They understand the power dynamics of a wealthy suburban politician who views and treats the largely minority population in the city's urban core as a farm for surplus organs. It is the Yoruba-based African diasporic religious system, a living religious tradition that continues today but remains denigrated and suppressed in many parts of the African diaspora, practiced by the text's heroines Ti-Jeanne and Mami Gros-Jeanne that renders the text too far-fetched, fantastic, and entirely unrelatable for students to engage. This, in spite of Hopkinson's efforts to demonstrate the marginalized status of the Yoruba belief system and to make clear the complex generational and émigré politics that inform Ti-Jeanne's own ambivalence about the belief in and public practice of traditional African religion. This, in spite of the fact that a significant percentage of the world's population believe in spiritual systems that feature the miraculous, mystical, and magical as routine occurrences. This, in spite of our ongoing theoretical class discussions about difference and empathy.

My experience teaching this text suggests a tendency to bifurcate biological difference and ideological difference, when in reality the kind of difference we attribute to biology (the physical, observable, "immutable," and public) and the kind of difference we attribute to belief (intangible, esoteric, "mutable," and private) are mutually constituted and mediated through various stereotypes. In other words, black bodies are always already representative of a worldview that is intellectually inept, spiritually backward, and ideologically bereft, and therefore in need of either reeducation or suppression. From the slave era up through the twentieth century, these were characterized as efforts to "civilize" and "modernize" black people; under these paradigms, slavery was a beneficent civilizing institution which blacks needed in order to approach the status of modern subjects through the influence of and contact with whites. As Washington argues, "Western physicians had placed African holistic plant- and spirit-centered healing systems outside the purview of medicine, relegating them to the realm of superstition, the occult, 'voodoo,' and old wives' tales" (Washington 2006, 56). Formally trained doctors denigrated black midwives and healers as uneducated even though they also had "no academic preparation beyond a few months in a proprietary medical school or a few years of apprenticeship, which many blacks also shared" (Washington 2006, 50). The well-documented history of the suppression and criminalization of granny midwives further demonstrates the aggression with which stereotypes about all blacks—even ones esteemed and revered by their own communities as competent and trustworthy heal-ers—colored the medical establishment's attitude towards and treatment of all blacks as ignorant, unclean, naturally disease-prone, and noncompliant (Washington 2006, 50).

Black healers' knowledge was discredited because the people who pro-duced it had been delegitimized, to paraphrase Toni Morrison. The suppres-sion of these systems of knowledge which credit the spiritual as integral to the healing and wellness paradigm cannot be extricated from the mainstream culture's process of Othering and pathologizing of blacks. And it has played a largely uninterrogated role in determining who is worthy of ethical treat-ment in medical discourse. The process of Othering, of defining who is human and which bodies are worthy of ethical treatment is a high-stakes game in the medical arena with all too often life and death consequences. To that end, black women's science fictions contribute to narrative ethics in three significant ways to be expanded upon in the sections that follow.

First, they engage in the project of humanizing Others who exemplify embodied difference by fleshing out the complexities of multiplicity and intersectionality in the formation of individual and collective identities, chal-lenging traditional narratives of authority. Secondly, they develop alternative ethics derived specifically from denigrated African religious traditions, al-lowing the potential for readers to enlarge their habits of mind as a means of increasing empathetic actions toward alien Others. The exploration of the role of traditional African spiritual systems and their conceptions of health and wellness is a process central to imagining a responsive holism in main-stream narrative medicine. Finally, black women science fiction writers dem-onstrate that relating to others empathetically across difference is a matter of political, moral, and ethical *action*, not simply abstract exercises of sympa-thetic thinking and feeling. In so doing, they expand the purview of narrative medicine and challenge the process of discourse legitimation.

## LIMINAL SUBJECTIVITY, SICK SOCIETIES, AND NARRATIVE AUTHORITY

The protagonists of the three main texts that I analyze here share characteris-tics that make them especially useful for demonstrating the claims of this essay. Nnedi Okorafor's Onyesonwu in *Who Fears Death* (2010), Nalo Hop-kinson's Ti-Jeanne in *Brown Girl in the Ring* (1998), and Octavia Butler's Lauren Oya Olamina in the *Parables* series (*Parable of the Sower*, 1993; *Parable of the Talents*, 1998) are all very young black women (between the ages of eleven and twenty during the bulk of the narratives) who are healers and/or spiritual leaders, proponents of belief systems that lack legitimacy at the beginning of their tales. These protagonists are culturally liminal figures who reside betwixt and between competing elements of their cultures but who manage to embrace their healer/leader statuses in spite of their subjugated positions as black girls. They each, in various ways, have been targeted as vulnerable and therefore, eligible for rapid extinction in their societies. Finally, they all must devise an ethical standard and set of concomitant practices or actions that will enable not only their individual survival, but the survival of broader social groups in which they live. These converging elements result in what I call a womanist survival ethic: the spirit-based beliefs and actions devised and implemented by black women that enables not only their individual survival in hostile cultural environments but which also ensures that those survival capacities extend to broader vulnerable groups.

For each protagonist, their minoritized, liminal status enables a critique of the dominant culture's problematic belief systems that delimit their capacity for survival. Further, their vulnerability status is intimately linked with the highly disordered societies in which they live. Oyesonwu is *Ewu*, the term for a mixed-culture child born of rape. The war-torn society that is the context of her survival efforts is characterized by tribal violence and ethnic cleansing. The rape of Okeke women by Nuru militants is used as a tool of war and genocide to decimate the Okeke at their biological core. The culture denigrates women, mixed-race people, and especially those who are products of rape. Ti-Jeanne of *Brown Girl in the Ring* is a third generation Caribbean-Canadian young single mother whose community is being exploited by Rudy, a dangerous drug lord whose reign is enabled by a negligent and absentee government. Butler's Olamina is impaired with hyperempathy syndrome, a psychological delusional disorder that causes her to feel the pain she believes others are experiencing. This impairment heightens to a disability status in the dangerous postapocalyptic environment where violence and torture, death and disease are rampant. As such, she is highly invested in the ethical thoughts, beliefs, and behaviors of the desperate masses. Each text, in turn, articulates the interplay between individual vulnerability and societal sickness to challenge the issue of narrative authority. In the case of *Who Fears Death* and the *Parables*, narrative authority is represented by controlling documents that inculcate widespread problematic beliefs and practices. How these controlling narratives operate in the world is a fundamental issue, and the protagonists engage in the re-writing of such narratives as a starting point for devising a new ethics of relationality. In *Brown Girl in the Ring*, Ti-Jeanne is engaged more so in an act of cultural translation and integration that allows the authority of competing ideological paradigms to coexist with equal power side by side.

*Who Fears Death* extrapolates the modern day issue of ethnic cleansing in recent Sudanese tribal conflicts and demonstrates the ways in which perceived differences are given value through the social meanings assigned to them. Oyesonwu is a member of a despised outcast class of "Ewu" children

196 *Esther Jones*

born to dark-skinned African-featured Okeke women who have been raped by fairer-skinned Arab-featured Nuru soldiers as a means of ethnic cleansing (Okorafor 2010, 25). Traditional beliefs surrounding the evil and violence that begets the sandy-colored freckled Ewu children as well as the lower status of women in the Okeke and Nuru cultures stress the social construction of difference institutionally supported, in this instance, by religious institutions and their texts. The Great Book, the religious tome used to justify the ethnic cleansing of the Okeke people, signifies the codification of oppressive traditions and practices, and holds clear parallels with the ways in which selected narratives from the Bible have been interpreted to justify the enslavement of Africans in the transatlantic slave trade as well as the more recent current-day realities of ethnic and inter-tribal conflict in the Sudan.

Told through the perspective of Onyesonwu, one sees the ways in which perceived biological difference, cultural beliefs and attitudes, and the human desire to belong to a community inform the decision-making processes of the protagonist. In her effort to overcome the clear physical markers that cast her outside of the community, she undergoes the adulthood initiation rite of circumcision on her eleventh birthday to stake her claim as a member of the community by demonstrating belief in a shared ideological and cultural practice. It is during this initiation ritual that her gifts as a sorceress with abilities to both heal and kill begin to emerge and she struggles for the right to be apprenticed to develop those gifts. As Ewu and woman, the resistance to teaching her is redoubled. Yet, this prejudice also works to her benefit: the sexism of the sorcerers who prophesy the coming of an Ewu child who will put an end to the violence of the ethnic cleansing causes them to alter the message to state that it will be a Nuru man. She is underestimated by General Daib, the sorcerer general at the helm of the ethnic cleansing, and goes on to rewrite The Great Book and to begin the process of healing the entire culture by rewriting its most fundamental system of belief.

This notion of rewriting The Great Book functions as an allegory for the uses of narrative and its role in healing not simply on an individual level, but on a broader cultural level. Ethical action towards groups and individuals representative of those groups cannot take place without consideration of the systems that perpetuate and reinforce bias and stereotype. Okarafor's text moves questions of illness and wellness from individual pathology (being a child of rape) to the social construction of pathology, problematizing the broader context in which narratives of individual illness are defined. Ironically, from a Western standpoint, the moments in which Onyesonwu is physically ill are understood as transitional spiritual initiations in African culture. The true illness is that of the broader culture: the ongoing ethnic cleansing of the Okeke by the Nuru based on religious/ideological intolerance that is mapped directly onto the bodies of the darker-skinned Okeke.

Butler proposes a similar rewriting of grand narratives and controlling cultural scripts in the *Parables* (1993; 1998). Like *Who Fears Death*, the *Parables* extrapolate a near future in which violence and danger are the order of the day, and survival is the protagonist's prime objective. The convergence of economic collapse, governmental decline, and multiple devastating natural disasters have so weakened the societal structures that the U.S. has devolved into a state of virtual dissolution, which creates a rapidly diminishing middle class and a burgeoning sector of desperate, dangerous, homeless street poor. As is characteristic of societies that experience rapid cultural change, a culture of normlessness and a loss of guiding moral principles abounds as the masses justify any and all actions that they feel will enable their survival. Olamina is among the most vulnerable to a quick and painful death among the street poor because she is young, black, female, and afflicted with hyperempathy syndrome.

In response to these conditions, Olamina develops a religio-ethical system named Earthseed, which seeks to distill the single consistent truth articulated in every scientific law and major religious belief system she knows of: the power, pervasiveness, and inevitability of change. Therefore, God is Change (Butler 1993, 70). Reimagining God as a force rather than a persona radically revises the Christian narrative of God as unchanging and imbued with human emotions like empathy and compassion or judgment and anger. It is in this reimagined conception of God that the exploitative and abusive misapplications of the Bible as exemplified in the Ku Klux Klan-like activities of the Christian America church of the text are thrown into bold relief. Christian Crusaders, ostensibly Christian "fundamentalists" who view ideological difference as the cause of the nation's instability, revive the worst elements in the history of the Christian tradition when they target those who believe differently for violent attacks, enslavement, rape, and reeducation (Butler 1998, 202–7).

Like Carl Linnaeus, Olamina's method of understanding and organizing the world is based on observation and taking notes. But unlike Linnaeus, her minoritized subjectivity and life experiences as a young impaired black girl determined to survive in a dangerous and hostile environment demand that her assessment of the observed world result in ethical statements that promote behaviors of beneficence and justice. She compiles the didactic *Earthseed: Books of the Living* as a means of explaining and clarifying "what God is, what God does, what we are, what we should do, what we can't help doing" (Butler 1993, 70). As a study of both human behavior and theological insight, the text of *Earthseed* articulates principles that will produce consistency in ethical thought and action. Stressing the values of interdependency (upon which any notion of autonomy must rely), an inclusivity that emphasizes the imperative of embracing diversity, and a model of community that enables resilience for all its constituents, *Earthseed* provides a newly articulated set of ethics that fosters the capacity for its adherents to relate more equitably across human difference.

While Hopkinson's *Brown Girl in the Ring* (1998) does not explicitly engage with narrativity through revision of sacred texts and their accompanying misuse as justifications of oppression, it does identify the sickness of society as the context in which survival strategies and newly conceived ethical practices are born. Hopkinson's text might be more readily interpreted as an act of cultural translation and adaptation. The authoritative, controlling narratives to which she responds have primarily to do with the subordination of her youth to the wisdom and demands of her elder, Mami Gros-Jeanne. Due in large part to her ambivalence towards Afro-Caribbean spiritual cultural practices, Ti-Jeanne initially fails to understand and acknowledge the syncretic practices of dual culture integration that Mami Gros-Jeanne has embraced to enable a highly resilient livelihood for her and her progeny, both before the riots that burned Toronto's city core and afterwards.

This dualism is represented in Gros-Jeanne's training as both a registered nurse trained in Western allopathic medicine and as a myalist, schooled in the naturopathic methods of herbalism and which integrates spirit work and ancestor veneration. She uses both as tools available to her to improvise healing technologies that respond to the shifting availability of resources. Such a strategy suggests that Western and traditional health practices are not mutually exclusive methods, but rather offer opportunities for complementarity and inventiveness that enable survival. Even though Ti-Jeanne does not even begin to learn all that her grandmother has to teach her about the spiritual side of healing work, she learns enough to improvise a strategy to fight Rudy's machinations by conceptualizing the CN Tower, where Rudy's office is located, as an oversized center pole which serves in myalist ceremonies as the bridge for the spirits to enter the world of the living (Hopkinson 1998, 221). She makes use of both modern technologies and African traditional practices to perform the unheard-of feat of calling all of the Seven African Powers down from the heavens and the souls of all those Rudy had killed up from the earth to break his power. In the end, in spite of having overcome her fear and resistance to the spiritual inheritance of Mami Gros-Jeanne and coming to peaceful terms with the use of her spiritual powers, she retains the right to her autonomy, to decide for herself how and when she will use her gifts as opposed to simply stepping into her grandmother's role as might be expected. Such assertions of autonomy resist controlling cultural scripts of what we think about when we imagine a black teenage mother surviving in the inner city.

## AFRICAN RELIGION AND ETHICAL ACTION

The previous discussion of narrative authority and the revision of controlling cultural scripts necessarily involves an examination of religion and spiritual ideologies because of the dominant culture's tendency to dismiss the relevance of spirituality to the medical paradigm. Since the rise of science in medicine, the role of spirituality in understanding health and wellness has been largely dismissed as hoodoo and quackery, but for centuries prior, medicine was intimately connected with religion (Haggard 1933, 13). Now, with the rise of scientific medicine in the nineteenth and twentieth centuries, questions relating to the spiritual aspects of health have been jettisoned for more empirically verifiable approaches (Haggard 1933, 28). Black women science fiction writers consistently recuperate denigrated African-based spiritual practices and engage with them as a holistic part of health and wellness; spirituality is understood to be intimately connected with wellness, and the healer figure is often times a spiritual leader as well. Onyesonwu is a sorceress and a healer who must overcome the sexist prejudices of her culture in order to develop her skills as a healer and warrior with repercussions for the entire culture. Mami Gros-Jeanne struggles to overcome the Canadian denigration of her Afro-Caribbean religion while her granddaughter Ti-Jeanne works to understand her spiritual gifts for their healing capacities as opposed to the solely dark powers of obeah that Rudy, who exploits the impoverished poor of the inner city of Toronto, practices. Olamina revises and adapts multiple received religious beliefs and scientific laws to develop her own religio-ethical system called Earthseed which declares as its key truth that God is Change. Earthseed is womanist in its strategic underpinnings of inclusivity, interdependency, and community-building and evocative of her African namesake the Yoruba orisha Oya—goddess of water, storms, and winds, agent of rapid change and transformation, teacher of truth, and bringer of justice.

Onyesonwu, Ti-Jeanne, and Olamina take seriously the ethical principles of autonomy, beneficence, non-maleficence, and justice which are supposed to consist in medical ethics. They are uncompromising in their struggle to realize those struggles in spite of living in social contexts that severely delimit the capacity to achieve those ideals. For Onyesonwu, the rampant sexism of the culture reveals itself most notably in the violence inflicted upon girls' and women's bodies. These acts of violence—circumcision, rape—are centered on women's sexuality and are accompanied by myths about the danger and instability of women because of their reproductive functioning. One of the first acts of medical ethical autonomy that Onyesonwu performs is the breaking of the Eleventh Rite juju (Okorafor 2010, 229) that she and her friends underwent as part of their initiation into a liminal phase that casts them as both child and woman. Not only are the girls circumcised, but the scalpel with which the circumcision is performed is fixed with juju, or sor-cery, that makes the young women feel pain whenever they are too sexually aroused. This pain is bound to occur until the next initiation into woman-hood, which is marriage, and functions as a means of controlling female sexuality (Okorafor 2010, 76).

The Eleventh Rite is performed by elder women and reveals the extent to which the culture's ethical principles require challenging and revision in order for these young women to fully access those ideals. Just as with the Eleventh Rite, women are often just as culpable as men in perpetuating the beliefs and practices that suppress women and make them responsible for the violence that is inflicted upon them. Onyesonwu's ethics demand that she hold both communities of Nuru and Okeke accountable for the beliefs that allow women to be raped and their children to bear the brunt of the hostility and responsibility for the outcomes of rape. If the Nuru were responsible for the unconscionable rape of women in order to destroy the Okeke people, the Okeke people are equally responsible for perpetuating oppressive behaviors that blame the woman for her rape. Sickness is manifest in both cultures as it pertains to the mythology surrounding victims of rape and their mixed off-spring, and Oyesonwu's response must be to rewrite the controlling narrative that governs both groups' beliefs and resulting actions.

In *Brown Girl in the Ring*, Rudy's use of obeah, the malevolent control and use of the spirits, is articulated in distinct contrast to Mami Gros-Jeanne's service to the spirits in which she works as a healer, eats a primarily vegetarian diet in gratitude to the animals she breeds for her myalist ceremo-nies, and functions as a benevolent benefactress for those who need medica-ments, spiritual guidance, or simply a decent meal (Hopkinson 1998). When the city government abandoned the city core, minoritized subjects like Mami Gros-Jeanne and Romany Jenny began to more openly practice their belief systems.

Hopkinson is careful to express the distinction between the kind of benev-olent spirit work Mami Gros-Jeanne and other practitioners of New World African religions perform and Rudy's problematic obeah work: "anybody who try to live good, who try to help people who need it, who try to have respect for life, and age, and those who gone before, them all doing the same thing: serving the spirits. . . . Now Rudy, he does try and make the spirits serve *he*" (Hopkinson 1998, 219). Rudy has twisted his knowledge of the spirits to make the spirits serve him by catching spirits of dead people, working the dead to control the living (Hopkinson 1998, 121–22). Mami Gros-Jeanne is fully aware of the maleficence of Rudy's work—he was formerly her husband—but she has ignored the instruction of her father spir-it, Osain, and done nothing to stop him; she has been content to go on practicing her own beneficent work to counterbalance his evil.

Likewise, her daughter Mi-Jeanne, Rudy's daughter, refuses to learn how to master the spiritual gifts that manifest as visions and is lost to madness during the Riots that created the Burn. When Ti-Jeanne starts to see visions, she fears them and does not understand them. She has internalized the denigration of Afro-Caribbean spirituality and resists developing these gifts because she perceives them as evil and backward. But as Mami Gros-Jeanne repeatedly points out to her granddaughter, the work she does is not obeah, it is a gift from God-Father that must be put to use for good (Hopkinson 1998, 47). In a ceremony designed to implore the spirits to help Tony, who has been conscripted into Rudy's service to procure a human heart donor, Mami Gros-Jeanne's spirit guide, the healing orisha Osain, delivers the message, "Tell Gros-Jeanne is past time for she to do my work. Is too late for she and the middle one, but maybe the end one go win through. Ti-Jeanne, she have to help you to get Rudy dead bowl and burn it" (Hopkinson 1998, 98). In other words, the forces for good cannot leave those of evil unchecked. Ti-Jeanne must confront Rudy and break the bad obeah he uses to terrorize the Burn and its inhabitants.

It is important to note that Rudy does not work his obeah, however, without broader systemic support from the distant official Toronto government. Their simultaneous negligence and opportunism enable Rudy's reign over the Burn and its residents as the government fails to acknowledge any responsibility towards the citizens it has left behind in the city core. The geographical disconnect between the suburbs and the urban city core parallels the psychological and relational distance between the people who populate each district. The city core and the suburbs are separated from each other by bridges and gates that keep the impoverished locked in the city even while suburbanites continue to have access to the Burn's night life and red light districts via rooftop helicopters that allow private entry into and out of the spaces without ever needing to venture into the streets of the neighborhoods in which they reside. And while the Burn is depicted as having developed a thriving communal barter culture, the power dynamics between the two areas of the city continue to intrude upon the well-being of the Burn's inhabitants. When Premier Uttley, an ailing politician in the suburbs in need of a heart, decides to buck the medical system and demand a human donor for her heart transplant when porcine organs have been the established standard of care for years, the political spin of "humans helping humans" rings false. Unsurprisingly, no human donor is available in the suburbs, so they turn to the Burn and the presiding drug lord, Rudy, to "find" a heart, refusing to concern themselves with the unethical methods he will use to procure it.

This kind of unidirectional access with no genuine contact with the people of the Burn creates a people-as-commodity culture in which the practices of sex tourism, cultural voyeurism, and organ harvesting reduce the most vulnerable members of society to their use-value and treat them as economic surplus: inconsequential, interchangeable, expendable. Such attitudes severely constrain the capacity to view such people as in any way relatable and therefore worthy of the same ethical considerations they extend to those with whom they readily identify—other wealthy suburbanites. Moreover, the residents of the Burn must remain in constant vigilance against the exploitative and inherently unethical practices of Rudy.

Clearly, the inhabitants of the Burn have their own sense of ethics, and that sense of ethics is certainly not monolithic. Rudy has no empathy or feeling for anyone; driven by bitterness and revenge, no relationship is sacred. He has captured his daughter's spirit in his duppy bowl and commands it to go hither and thither doing his evil works, killing, and providing visual access to places where he should not be able to see. He is willing to kill Mami Gros-Jeanne, his ex-wife, for her heart, and to kill Ti-Jeanne for interfering with his business. Mami Gros-Jeanne, on the other hand, thinks it is sufficient to keep out of Rudy's way and continue her rootwork, nursing, and ministering to her small congregation. However, the text suggests even Mami Gros-Jeanne's overall beneficence is insufficient to protect her or her loved ones from the reach of Rudy's malevolence and the government's negligence. Evil must be rooted out at its core and actively struggled against. In the end, Ti-Jeanne is able to triumph with the help of the Seven African Powers and the limited spiritual training Mami Gros-Jeanne was able to impart before she was killed.

While the evil Ti-Jeanne confronts is consolidated in the figure of a single nemesis whose unethical behaviors are institutionally supported by the politics of the Toronto suburbs, the danger that confronts Butler's Olamina is diffuse, ubiquitous, indiscriminate, and largely impersonal. It is the conditions of society as a whole that give rise to widespread desperation and normlessness, turning those who under better social conditions would submit to the Hobbesian social contract of security and safety into survival-oriented, ruthless, and dangerous opportunists. In Butler's near-futuristic fiction, there is no single problem, no clear-cut enemy. Rather, the problems that individuals face and which the society faces are a result of our collective failure to deal with problems of our own creation. Taylor Bankole, Olamina's husband who characterizes the period known as "The Pox" as an installment-plan World War III, argues,

> I have . . . read that the Pox was caused by accidentally coinciding climatic, economic, and sociological crises. It would be more honest to say that the Pox was caused by our own refusal to deal with obvious problems in those areas. We caused the problems: then we sat back and watched as they grew into crises . . . I have watched education become more a privilege of the rich than the basic necessity that it must be if civilized society is to survive. I have watched as convenience, profit, and inertia excused greater and more danger-

ous environmental degradation. I have watched poverty, hunger, and disease
become inevitable for more and more people. (Butler 1998, 8)

Bankole's analysis shifts focus from an individual act of malintent to the
systemic culture of abuse and negligence that, as a collective, U.S. society
failed to acknowledge until the situation was beyond remedying. With the
majority of the nation's citizens reduced to a daily struggle for survival,
Olamina recognizes that in order to address the broad-ranging sickness of the
culture, an equally expansive ethical system is required.

While Earthseed cannot be reduced to a single belief system, African or
otherwise—for, as *Who Fears Death* demonstrates, not all African beliefs
and practices should be replicated—the methods of cultural adaptation and
improvisation that Olamina uses to realize Earthseed have been key to
African spiritual survivals in the African diaspora. Just as Mami Gros-Jeanne
and Ti-Jeanne learn to combine the elements of Western technology with the
traditional knowledge and spiritual practices of their Afro-Caribbean culture,
so Olamina makes use of what tools are available to her to improvise an
ethical system that enables not only her survival, but that of the broader
community. Like her namesake, Oya, she becomes an agent of rapid change
and transformation, a teacher of truth, and a bringer of justice. Those who
adopt the Earthseed system enter into a gender egalitarian, communal social
structure where individuality is respected but interdependency is understood
to be paramount as in the old African adage, "I am because we are." These
foundational philosophies and strategies engender a survival ethic that fully
enables the principles of autonomy, beneficence, non-maleficence, and justice.

TOWARDS A COMPLEMENTARY ETHICAL SCHEMA:
WOMANIST SURVIVAL ETHICS AND AN ETHIC OF
RELATIONAL RESPONSIVENESS

Thus, on the whole, this study suggests the following about our understanding of narrative ethics and its application to ultimate ontological others. First,
the principles of autonomy, beneficence, non-maleficence, and justice have
always been differentially applied to minoritized subjects like black women
because they were never meant to survive. Each heroine is embattled with
direct murderous assaults on their persons and must find a way to survive in
the most literal sense of the word. In fact, the most challenging principle for
these heroines to engage is that of non-maleficence; they are often required
to engage in violent acts in order to secure their own survival. This is especially true in these science fiction novels because the broader cultures abound
in violence. Thus the reconsideration of what this term means, for these black
girls are all targets for violent death, is necessary in these highly violent

narrative settings. Second, in order to begin to achieve these ideals, black women writers have had to turn to science fiction to first elucidate their positions as not wholly subjugated and marginal, but rather as liminal—an in-between status that occupies the position of both power and powerless-ness. In the assertion of power in positions of seeming powerlessness, they critique the cultural and systemic nature of oppression and violence against them. Third, they articulate an alternate conception of these principles and revise their meanings and the practice of their revised ethics according to spiritually-based methods and values.

These elements of liminal identity, spiritual worldview, and empathetic action constitute what I call a womanist survival ethic in black women's science fiction: the idea that the health and wellness of the human commu-nity as a whole—what Octavia Butler would call species survival—is predi-cated upon understanding the interdependence of all people, regardless of our perceived differences, in order to avoid self-destruction. As these texts re-veal, the womanist survival ethic is a strategy black women develop and adopt to survive hostile social environments. For those non-black others who wonder how this black women's differential understanding of ethics and wellness might enable them to craft their own interactions with this kind of difference, I want to suggest a complementary ethical strategy: an ethic of *relational responsiveness*. The concept of relational responsiveness is what non-black others in their roles as doctors and healthcare practitioners must cultivate to mitigate the conscious and unconscious biases and stereotypes that inform their interactions with black people and the poor. I propose the concept of relational responsiveness to suggest that one need not understand nor identify with the beliefs and ideologies held by a group or individuals in order to provide compassionate care. Rather, one must first, if we are to take the goal of a "Levisianian intersubjectivity between doctor and patient, pro-ducing the trust and clinical partnership necessary to the physician's tasks" seriously (Holmgren et al. 2011, 251), *recognize* the validity of the individu-al's experience and cultural background and *resolve to respond* to the holistic needs of the patient regardless of capacity to relate to their sense of the world and the meaning made of their illness within that worldview.

If biodiversity—a scientific way of articulating difference—is essential for species survival, as current science indicates, then the means and methods of Othering constitute a set of defeating practices that surely will result in the mass extermination of the human race unless we can learn to relate more humanely across our perceived differences. This is the warning toll that black women science fiction sounds, from the individual experience of the liminal and outcast to the collective of humanity. Such narratives help us to question the assumptions that shape our narratives of human identity and belonging, to redefine who belongs within a community of care, and to develop an ethical system that makes humane, ethical action the standard for all people.

# NOTES

1. Lisa Yaszek, "Race in Science Fiction: The Case of Afro-futurism and New Holly-wood," *A Virtual Introduction to Science Fiction* (2013), http://virtual-sf.com/?page_id=372.
2. Ibid.
3. Cadance McCowan, "Mid-South Doctor Gives Ghetto Booty Diagnosis." WREG.com (July 12, 2013).
4. Ibid.

# REFERENCES

Butler, Octavia. 1993. *Parable of the sower*. New York: Warner Books.
———. 1998. *Parable of the talents*. New York: Warner Books.
Charon, Rita. 2005. Narrative medicine: Attention, representation, affiliation. *Narrative* 13, no. 3: 261–70.
English, Daylanne. 2013. *Each hour redeem: Time and justice in African American literature*. Minneapolis: University of Minnesota Press.
Fink, Sheri. 2009. The deadly choices at memorial. *The New York Times*, August 25. Retrieved December 28, 2013.
Gilman, Sander L. 1985. *Difference and pathology: Stereotypes of sexuality, race, and madness*. Ithaca: Cornell University Press.
González-Crussi, Frank. 2007. *A short history of medicine*. New York: Modern Library.
Haggard, Howard W. 1933. *Mystery, magic, and medicine: The rise of medicine from superstition to science*. New York: Doubleday, Doran & Company.
Holloway, Karla F.C. 2011. *Private bodies, public texts: Race, gender, and a cultural bioethics*. Durham: Duke University Press.
Holmgren, Lindsay, Abraham Fuks, Donald Boudreau, Tabitha Sparks and Martin Kreiswirth. Terminology and praxis: Clarifying the scope of narrative in medicine. *Literature and Medicine* 29, no. 2 (2011): 246–73.
Hopkinson, Nalo.1998. *Brown girl in the ring*. New York: Grand Central Publishing.
Jackson, Sandra and Julie E. Moody-Freeman, eds. 2011. *The black imagination: Science fiction, futurism, and the speculative*. New York: Peter Lang.
Jones, Anne H. 1997. Literature and medicine: Narrative ethics. *The Lancet* 349 (1997): 1243–46.
Jones, James H. 1981. *Bad blood: The Tuskegee syphilis experiment*. New York: Free Press.
McCowan, Candace. 2013. Mid-South doctor gives ghetto booty diagnosis. WREG.com, July 12, 2013. Accessed December 28, 2013.
Okorafor, Nnedi. 2010. *Who fears death*. New York: DAW Books.
Rabkin, Eric. 2011. Science fiction and bioethical knowledge. In *Bioethics and biolaw through literature*, eds. Daniela Carpi and Klaus Stierstorfer. Berlin and Boston: Walter de Gruyter.
Roberts, Dorothy. 2011. *Fatal invention: How science, politics, and big business re-create race in the twenty-first century*. New York: The New Press.
Skloot, Rebecca. 2011. *The immortal life of Henrietta Lacks*. New York: Pan Macmillan.
Wald, Priscilla. The art of medicine: Cognitive estrangement, science fiction, and medical ethics. *The Lancet* 371 (2008): 1908–9.
Washington, Harriet A. 2006. *Medical Apartheid: The dark history of medical experimentation on black Americans from colonial times to the present*. New York: Anchor Books.
Yaszek, Lisa. 2013. Race in science fiction: The case of afro-futurism and new Hollywood. In *A virtual introduction to science fiction*, ed. Lars Schmeink, 1–11. http://virtual-sf.com/?page_id=372.

*Chapter Eleven*

# "To Be African Is to Merge Technology and Magic"

*An Interview with Nnedi Okorafor*

## Qiana Whitted

Afrofuturist writer Nnedi Okorafor is the author of four novels, two children's books, and numerous short stories and essays. Her approach to speculative fiction resists easy categorization, drawing upon elements of fantasy, magic realism, hard science fiction, and dystopian horror for a wide and diverse readership. While Okorafor has said that "labels can be very confining" when it comes to her writing (Womack 2010), she values the notion of Afrofuturism as a way of being for the indomitable female protagonists that so often populate the magical Nigerian landscapes of her stories. Born in Cincinnati, Ohio, to immigrant Igbo parents, she is the first African American to win the World Fantasy Award for her critically-acclaimed novel, *Who Fears Death* (2010). She has also received the Wole Soyinka Prize for Literature in Africa for the young adult novel, *Zahrah the Windseeker* (2005) and the Carl Brandon Society Parallax Award for best speculative fiction by a person of color for *The Shadow Speaker* (2007). In this interview, the writer and Chicago State University professor talks about the role of Afrofuturism in her work, including the cultural merging of technology and magic, on being compared to J. K. Rowling, and her enthusiasm for bringing black speculative fiction to the comics medium.

## AFROFUTURISM IN FICTION

**QW: On the matter of fantasy fiction, Samuel Delany once wrote that, "what it presents us, even as it seems to lure us away to another age and clime, is our own home reviewed through the distorting (or, better, organizing) lens of a set of paraliterary conventions" (Delany 1993, 20). Delany was referring to the imagined historical past of his Nevèrÿon series, but the same might also be said of the future realms in which many of your stories take place. Do you feel that the lens of Afrofuturism encourages you and your readers to see the present-day concerns of home in new ways?**

NO: I don't see speculative fiction or Afrofuturism as "tool" when I'm writing. As I said, I'm not very interested in labels. I'm a subconscious writer. I write what comes to me, and often what comes to me comes from some unknown place or voice. So the fact that I'm writing what is considered speculative fiction isn't really intentional. I see the world as a magical place and therefore that's how it comes out in my work. I am interested in looking into the future, usually that of Africa and that's why what I write is considered Afrofuturism.

**QW: How do the conventions of speculative fiction shape your willingness and ability to tackle more controversial issues, for instance, such as female circumcision, dangerous mining for oil and other natural resources, and political and military corruption in West Africa?**

NO: All these issues that I address, they are issues that have been around me nearly all my life. They are real to me. They are not an academic discussion. They are not distant. I know people who have been circumcised; it is even something that used to be done in Traditional Igbo culture. I know about genocide, too, because of the Biafran Civil War. I know about the Niger Delta conflict. I've had personal experience with military corruption in Nigeria and corruption in general there. These are what I write about.

## JUJU AS TECHNOCULTURE

**QW: One of the mystical Leopard People in your novel, *Akata Witch* (2011a), describes the main character's initiation through the metaphor of a computer, already installed with programs and applications that need only to be activated through a series of ritual lessons. And later, on a humorous note, the story identifies disreputable Leopard People as some of the culprits behind the Nigerian 419 scam emails. What do you hope to accomplish in works like *Akata Witch* and others with this merging of technoculture and ancient magical practice?**

NO: Technology is just another form of juju in *Akata Witch*. And it's not the most powerful or useful. But really I don't feel I NEED to merge them. I feel they are naturally merged. Especially in African culture. To be African is to merge technology and magic. That's a bold statement to make and I can imagine certain groups of African people rising up like angry snakes against such a blanketing statement but so be it. In my experience as an African, the mystical and the mundane have always coexisted. It's expressed within the explanation of things, in ways of doing things, the reasons for doing things. That's just life. So add the fact that technology is a part of African life, too, and you get a natural merging. I'm not doing anything in my fiction that doesn't exist already. I got the idea FROM my experiences of being an African, from being amongst Africans, and being IN Africa.

## WRITING RACE, GENDER, AND NATURE

**QW: I'm also curious about the relationship between race and the animal kingdom in your fiction. You have noted elsewhere that a childhood interest in entomology informs your depiction of fantastical insects. You've praised animal books like the Tove Jansson's *Moomin* series that you discovered as a young girl during a time when you were growing frustrated by the lack of black characters in fantasy and science fiction. You explained: "So I started migrating to books that featured animals . . . where the main characters were not even human so they didn't have to deal with that whole racial thing" ("Geeks Guide" Podcast). How do you approach the animals in your own writing? Do the animals and insects that you invent offer a kind of reprieve from those burdens of social identity or are they integral to the constructions of race and culture?**

NO: I don't write "constructions." I'm literal. I see animals as people, literally. It's not about metaphors or ideas; this is what I believe. When I look at pigeons in the streets of Chicago, I see communities. When I find an ant in my home, I take it outside and hope it rejoins its family. There are many types of people on this earth and most of them are not human. I've always been this way. When I was a kid, I migrated to reading books about non-humans because the ones about humans didn't include me and I could relate more to the other types of people, real or mythical. These days, I've since learned that even when humans write about animals, however, they are often equally as racist and sexist, for their animals are indeed just representations of human beings.

# FAMILY AND COMMUNITY IN AFRICAN-CENTERED FANTASY

**QW: Many of your stories, including *Who Fears Death*, *Akata Witch*, "The Go-Slow" (2010b), and "Spider the Artist" (2011b), emphasize the power of *awakenings* as the protagonists come to the realization that there is wisdom and strength through difference. Yet these awakenings often materialize in spite of (or perhaps, due to) the painful family relationships and antagonistic communities that surround them. Can you comment on the role of family and community in your fiction, and the significance of the surrogate parents, siblings, and mentors that emerge to take the place of traditional family units in times of trouble?**

NO: I was raised within a close knit traditional nuclear family because my parents were immigrants and the rest of the family was still in Nigeria. Yet, we remained deeply connected to extended family back in Nigeria. My father, my mother, two older sisters, and one younger brother—we used to all eat dinner together at the table every day. Uncles and aunties visited and we visited Nigeria often and my parents called Nigeria even more often. My father talks about spending as much time living and being raised by his uncle as by his father and mother. My mother speaks fondly about being raised by her aunts as much as by her parents. I was taught early on the African form of family. In the African form of family, aunts and uncles aren't always blood. It's not taboo or shameful to spend more time with your aunt than your mother. And it's normal and beneficial for one to be raised by many. So for example, if your father is a jerk, you just look to that good uncle. Or if your mother dies, you were close to grandma anyway, so there is someone to catch you. When there is trouble, there are options in order to deal with the trouble. This naturally comes out in my work.

## HARRY POTTER IN NIGERIA

**QW: Lewis Carroll's *Alice in Wonderland* has been used to describe your approach to fantasy in your first novel, *Zahrah the Windseeker* (2005), while reviews of *Akata Witch* (2011a) often praise the novel by comparing it to J. K. Rowling's work as a "female Harry Potter" or "Harry Potter in Nigeria." What is your response to these comparisons? What do you think these kinds of assessments suggest about the way your works are read and interpreted by American audiences?**

NO: The comparisons are understandable. However, I think these comparisons are often a reaction reviewers have to dealing with cultures they find are unfamiliar. By boiling my work down to what is familiar to them, they therefore don't have to discuss those many things that are not familiar to them. It's a cop out. And they also miss a huge part of the story. I think

American audiences could benefit from stepping out of themselves more often, out of what is familiar. Right now, I think too many Americans are very insular and when they do peek out at the rest of the world, they get overwhelmed. And because they are overwhelmed, they stamp all those things outside of their narrow window of familiar as "foreign," "bad," "not fun," "wrong," and "difficult." Then they go retreat back into their little cave where they can look at and play with those things that make them feel comfortable and secure. That's not the way to live.

## CONFRONTING THE LEGACY OF RACISM IN FANTASY

**QW: Among your literary ancestors, you have cited the influence of writers like Octavia Butler, Ngũgĩ wa Thiong'o, Roald Dahl, and Isaac Asimov. But you've also written at length about Stephen King, an author that you admire deeply, but whose representations of race and blackness are sometimes problematic ("Stephen King's Super-Duper Magical Negroes" [2004]). And after becoming the first black person to win the World Fantasy Award for *Who Fears Death* in 2011, you wrote quite powerfully on your blog about the tensions between that honor and the racism of well-known fantasy author, H. P. Lovecraft—the figure whose head is featured on the award statuette: "This is something people of color, women, minorities must deal with more than most when striving to be the greatest that they can be in the arts: *The fact that many of The Elders we honor and need to learn from hate or hated us.*" How have your thoughts on the Elders progressed since you've written those words? What has been the response of fellow writers and fan communities to your challenge to think critically about the legacy of racism in science fiction and fantasy?**

NO: My thoughts on the issue remain the same. I was just glad I had a platform to voice them. The response was great because apparently I'd spoken what was on the minds of many people. Of course there were those who were shocked and angry that I'd taken a shot at one of their sacred icons but I don't think even they will be able to look at Lovecraft in the same way again. Success!

## BUILDING AFROFUTURIST WORLDS IN COMICS AND FILM

**QW: In the last couple of years, you have also begun to write for comics; could you share some information about your interest in graphic narratives? How has the experience of writing for a different medium, particularly one with a visual component, affected your storytelling strategies, if at all?**

NO: I've always been interested in comics, though not in the most traditional way. I grew up addicted to the Sunday comics in the newspaper and I've always loved cartoons. However, when it came to traditional comic books, they never pulled me in. I didn't feel that I existed in their worlds. I didn't even feel welcome in comic book shops! I'd take one look at the covers of the comic books, the shop owners and the customers and then just walk right back out. Everyone was always white and male (or in the case of the comic book covers, targeted toward white males). However, about eight years ago I discovered comics that were beyond those traditional superhero white male narratives. These were realistic comics, comics that told deep stories similar to novels, comics that were about characters other than superheroes. I grew excited and I read voraciously. Reading these graphic novels opened me up to reading some of the traditional superhero comics. I went on to read *Watchman* [by Alan Moore and Dave Gibbons], *The Dark Knight Rises* [by Frank Miller], *Wonder Woman,* etc.

I began to see that my own stories could become something else within this genre. I've always been a very visual writer. And I'm a world builder, too. I started to dream about people actually literally SEEING my characters. I write about Africa in the future, strong African characters who are not royalty, who look African. I realized that comics could open things up on a whole new level. Especially in the highly visual society we live in today. I also suspect that I can reach a new audience to gather into the one I currently have. Has my experience with comics affected the way I tell stories? Not at all. I think the way I tell stories already naturally lends itself to graphic narrative, so it's a smooth transition.

## REFERENCES

Adams, John Joseph, and David Barr Kirtley. 2010. "Geek's Guide to the Galaxy #021: African SF & Fantasy! Nollywood! Entomology! (Guest: Nnedi Okorafor)," *Tor.com Podcast*, May 24. http://www.tor.com/blogs/2010/05/geeks-guide-to-the-galaxy-021-african-sf-a-fantasy-nollywood-entomology-guest-nnedi-okorafor.

Delany, Samuel. 1993. "Return . . . a Preface," *Tales of Nevèrÿon*. Hanover, NH: Wesleyan University Press.

Okorafor, Nnedi. 2004. "Stephen King's Super-Duper Magical Negroes." 2004. *Strange Horizons*, October 24. http://www.strangehorizons.com/2004/20041025/kinga.shtml.

———. 2010a. *Who Fears Death.* New York: DAW Books.

———. 2010b. "The Go-Slow," *The Way of the Wizard,* ed. John Joseph Adams. Gaithersburg, MD: Prime Books.

———. 2011a. *Akata Witch.* New York: Viking.

———. 2011b. "Spider the Artist." *Lightspeed Magazine,* March.

———. 2011c. "Lovecraft's Racism and The World Fantasy Award Statuette, with Comments from China Miéville," *Nnedi's Wahala Zone Blog,* Dec. 14. http://nnedi.blogspot.com/2011/12/lovecrafts-racism-world-fantasy-award

———. 2012. "African Sunrise," *Subterranean Magazine Online*: http://subterranean-press.com/magazine/fall_2012/african_sunrise_by_nnedi_okorafor.

Okorafor-Mbachu, Nnedi. 2005. *Zahrah the Windseeker.* New York: Houghton Mifflin.

———. 2007. *The Shadow Speaker*. New York: Hyperion Books.
Womack, Ytasha L. 2010. "Sci Fi Author Nnedi Okorafor Talks Literature and Afrofuturism," *Post-Black: How a New Generation Is Redefining African American Identity,* Aug. 9, 2010, http://postblackthebook.blogspot.com/2010/08/sci-fi-author-nnedi-okorafor-talks.html.

# Index

aesthetic praxis: African-American signification, 45; ancient magical practice, merger with, 209; conceptual grammar, 64; design, transgression of, 31. *See also* Afrofuturism; technoculture

African American youth, existential reorientation of, 130

Africana Studies: Afrofuturism within, xi; presuppositions, liberation from, 175; science and technology within, xiii

Africology, 127

Afrika Bambaataa. *See* Sun Ra

Afriscape, definition, discussion of, 37

Afro Punk, 31. *See also* semantic, cultural arts network

Afrocentric: normative assumptions, development of, xiii; quantum computing, multiverse identities of, 150

Afrodisaporic: cultural production, 66; projection, hostility to, viii

Afrofuturism: definition of, 30, 63; dialectic and methodology of, 169; evolution, methods and theories of, 177; subject areas, ix; theoretical approach, 129

Afrofuturist: cosmology, analysis of, 97; ethics, alternative modes of, 187; history, representation of, 178; inquiry, dominant theme of, 177; practice, 179; writers, critics, 47

Afro-pessimism: blacks and gratuitous violence, constrained by, 50; non-revolutionary emancipation, 51

Akata Witch, discussion of, 208

Alien Nation, 73–76

Armageddon, 66

Astro-Blackness, vii

Badu, Erykah. *See* Sun Ra

Bailey, Xenobia. *See* Afro Punk

Baraka, Amiri: Technology and Ethos, essay, 31, 63

The Black Church: Afrofuturism, intersection with, xvii; Post-Modernity, relevance to, 127

black experience: metaphysical manifestations of, 176; slavery, phenomenological ambiguity of, 179

black science fiction, concepts of, 65

black women : black female subjectivity, xv; black girl protagonists as targets, 203; black women science fiction writers, spiritual ideologies of, 199. *See also* empathic medicine

Brown, James: Say It Loud, I'm Black and I'm Proud, 31

Cassirer, Ernst (1874–1945). *See* communicology

chronopolitics: definition of, 80; in Afrofuturism, Afrocentrism, 83

# About the Editors and Contributors

**Reynaldo Anderson** currently serves as a member of the executive board for the Missouri Arts Council and as an associate professor of communications at Harris-Stowe State University. Reynaldo was recognized by Gov. Jay Nixon in 2010 for his leadership in the community and serves on various non-profit boards. Finally, Anderson publishes research in regard to several dimensions of the African American experience and the African diaspora including Afrofuturism, rhetoric, communications, Africana womanism, globalization, and world systems theory, and recently taught as visiting lecturer in Accra, Ghana.

**Tiffany E. Barber** is a scholar, curator, and writer of twentieth and twenty-first century visual art and performance with a focus on artists of the black diaspora living and working in the United States.

**Lonny Avi Brooks** is interested in how strategic narratives about the future of new media, human-computer interaction, futurists think tanks, and ubiquitous computing gain currency between policy-makers, professional futurists, modelers, and the media, and gain interpretive flexibility, utility, and status. Finally Brooks is interested in how new media technologies shape interpersonal communication and racial identity online and offline.

**David DeIuliis** is a PhD candidate and visiting instructor in the Department of Communication and Rhetorical Studies at Duquesne University. His research interests include communication theory and philosophy of communication, particularly the philosophy and aesthetics of Marcel Proust. DeIuliis has guest edited the *Pennsylvania Communication Annual* and published chapters in edited volumes in the area of communication theory and cultural studies, as well as articles and reviews in *Communication Research Trends* and *Empedocles: European Journal for the Philosophy of Communication*, among others.

**Nettrice R. Gaskins**, PhD, was born in Baltimore, MD. She majored in visual art at DuPont Manual High School in Louisville, KY. She earned a BFA in Computer Graphics with Honors from Pratt Institute in 1992 and an MFA in Art and Technology from the School of the Art Institute of Chicago in 1994. She worked for several years in K–12 and post-secondary education, community media, and technology before enrolling at Georgia Tech where she received a doctorate in digital media in 2014. Her model for "techno-vernacular creativity" is an area of practice that investigates the characteristics of this production and its application in STEAM (science, technology, engineering, art, and mathematics). When she is not advancing interdisciplinary education, Ms. Gaskins blogged for Art21, the producer of the Peabody award-winning PBS series, *Art in the Twenty-First Century*, and publishes articles and essays about topics such as Afrofuturism and ghost nature. Her essay was included in *Meet Me at the Fair: A World's Fair Reader* published by ETC Press.

**Grace Gipson** is a doctoral student in African American studies at the University of California Berkeley. Her research interests are black popular culture studies, film/media studies, (mis)representations of race/gender in African American film and comic books, black gender and sexuality studies, and performance of blackness.

**Ricardo Guthrie** is associate professor of ethnic studies at Northern Arizona University. He examines political narratives of the black press and writes about cinema as cultural political artifacts. His publications include book chapters: "Reading Radmilla: The Semiotics of Self (Black and Navajo)," in *The Politics of Identity: Emerging Indigeneity* (UT-Sydney Press, 2013); "Oprah Winfrey and the Trauma Drama," in *Presenting Oprah Winfrey, Her Films, and African American Literature* (Palgrave, 2013); and "Minstrelsy and Mythic Appetites: The Last King of Scotland's Heart of Darkness in the Jubilee Year of African Independence," in *Hollywood's Africa After 1994* (Ohio University Press, 2012). He is currently researching the life and influence of Dr. Carlton B. Goodlett and the San Francisco *Sun-Reporter* (1945–1966).

**Charles E. Jones** is an architect in the field of African-American studies. At Old Dominion in Norfolk, VA, Jones's first job, he built a minor program in black studies and headed the Institute for the Study of Minority Issues. Then he went on to Georgia State where he built an undergraduate program and then a master's program. Dr. Jones is a board member of the National Council of Black Studies (NCBS), the leading professional organization for those in the field of African American studies. Jones has spent a career grooming the future of Africana studies—from building programs to doing original research to encouraging students in the classroom. Now he is looking forward to completing his "marathon," as he refers to his career, at University of Cincinnati. He is currently teaching Black Politics and Intro to Africana Studies.

**Esther Jones** specializes in the study of black women writers in the Americas, with a focus on the intersections of race, gender, class, and nationality, and theorizations of difference. She has a particular interest in speculative literatures and science fiction by feminists and writers of color, and how such texts attempt to theorize and/or critique how difference operates within contemporary culture. Her current book project, *Traveling Discourses: Subjectivity, Space, and Spirituality in Black Women's Speculative Fictions* proposes a theory and method for reading experimental, or "problematic texts," generally, and black speculative fiction, specifically, as a discourse that operates within the liminal spaces between genres, or within the "slipstream." Professor Jones's research and teaching interests also include historical fiction and autobiographical/life writing. Professor Jones teaches both general and special topics courses in African American literature, theory, and culture.

**Jeff Lohr** is a PhD candidate in the Department of Communication and Rhetorical Studies at Duquesne University. He has published entries in several encyclopedias in the areas of critical theory and philosophy of communication, as well as critical and communication theory.

**Ken McLeod** is an associate professor of music history and culture at the University of Toronto. He has published on identity politics in popular music, popular music appropriations of art music, and the intersections between technology, science fiction, and rock music. His book *We Are the Champions: The Politics of Sports and Popular Music* (Ashgate, 2011) examines the interconnection of sports and popular music in constructing racial, gender, ethnic, socio-economic, and national identities. He is currently researching issues surrounding technology and identity politics in Japanese popular music and hip hop as well as the relationship of popular music to automotive culture. His work is supported by the Social Sciences and Humanities Research Council of Canada.

**Andrew Rollins** has done extensive study and research on metaphysics, the occult, and post-modernism. In March 2013 he spoke on "Transhumanism and the Prophetic Voice of the Black Church" at The Speculative Visions of

Race, Technology, Science and Survival Conference sponsored by the Race and Gender Center and Multicultural Center at the University of California, Berkeley. In February 2014 he spoke at the Astro-Blackness Colloquium at Loyola Marymount University in Los Angeles on "Racial Ethics and Afrofuturism." Currently he is the pastor of St. James A.M.E. Church in San Jose, California.

**Tobias C. van Veen** is SSHRC Postdoctoral Fellow in the Department of Communications at the Université de Montréal. Writing in both popular and academic publications, Tobias's work explores questions of race, becoming, and technology in culture, music, and philosophy. Tobias is editor of the Afrofuturism special issue of *Dancecult: Journal of Electronic Dance Music Culture* (2013) and co-editor with Hillegonda Rietveld of the special issue "Echoes from the Dub Diaspora" (2015). A techno-turntablist and practitioner of interventionist media arts since 1993, Tobias is also creative director of the IOSOUND.ca music label and resident DJ of Ion Storm podcast at djtobias.com. Tobias has collaborated with festivals and media arts centers worldwide as founding director of UpgradeMTL.org and concept engineer at the Society for Art and Technology (SAT) in Montréal.

**Qiana Whitted** is associate professor of English and African American studies at the University of South Carolina. Her primary research and teaching interests focus on African American literature and American comics. Her work frequently examines representations of race, history, and popular culture, and lately she has become more interested in questions about genre in mass culture. She also enjoys studying post-modern narrative and metafiction. The subjects that she explores often intersect with southern studies and the philosophy of religion as well. She's currently working on two projects: one on EC Comics, and another that looks at race and social justice in late 1940s and 1950s comic books.